'ROUND and ABOUT the DUNES

By *NORMA SCHAEFFER* and *KAY FRANKLIN*

DUNES ENTERPRISES
BEVERLY SHORES, INDIANA

Other Dunes Writings By Norma Schaeffer and Kay Franklin:
> *Duel for the Dunes* (Champaign. University of Illinois Press, 1983).
>
> *Industry versus Preservation,* in The Indiana Dunes Story (Beverly Shores. Shirley Heinz Environmental Fund, 1984).
>
> *The Indiana Dunes* A Selected Bibliography (Hammond. Regional Studies Institute, Purdue University Calumet, 1980).

Front Cover Photo: Skip Hector
Maps: Alexander Reichl
Photos: Indiana Dunes National Lakeshore

Design by Vladimir Reichl & Associates

ISBN 0–9613419–0–4

Contents

Illustrations

Dune Terms

Dune. A sand hill formed through the steady accumulation of sand granules brought by the prevailing wind.

Foredune. A dune located closest to the water, usually a young and not too well developed dune, low and bare. The first stage in dune succession.

Permanent Dune. A stabilized dune covered with vegetation and trees.

Bare Dune. (Also called a dead or bald dune.) A dune on which no vegetation grows. The wind has blown away all its cover and steady erosion of the dune continues.

Moving Dune. (Also called a horseshoe dune.) An unstabilized dune fed on the leeward side by blowing sand. Such a dune can travel 60 feet a year engulfing anything in its path.

Blowout. A sauce or bowl shaped excavation in a dune occurring wherever the protective covering of vegetation breaks allowing sand to blow rapidly. In the Indiana dunes, blowouts occur on the northeasterly side of a dune.

Tree Graveyard. Dead tree trunks and branches originally covered by a moving dune and later uncovered by the wind when the dune has moved further on.

Singing Sands. (Also called whispering sands.) Beach sands that when walked upon emit sounds. Some people believe that the contact of a top thin layer of dry sand with a layer of moist sand causes the sound.

Storm Beach. The area closest to the water upon which the waves cast up such debris as dead insects, fish and driftwood.

Climax Forest. The final stage in the evolution of a forest. In the Indiana dunes, a woods where beech and maple trees predominate.

Marsh. An area of low lying wetlands where grasses, sedges, cattails or rushes form the dominant vegetation. Usually treeless.

Swamp. An area of low lying wetlands covered with dense vegetation including trees.

Slough. A stagnant swamp, marsh or bog.

Swale. Marshy ground.

Swell. A rounded elevation. Usually occurring close to swales.

Bog. A marsh or swamp which characteristically has open water and whose vegetation consists of sedges, shrubs and moss.

Acid sphagnum bog. A type of bog found in the Indiana dunes in which sphagnum moss grows on a sedge mat. The moss, the cold temperature of the water and the lack of water circulation contribute to the acidity of the bog. Though physically wet, this kind of bog constitutes a desert-like environment for the plants that live in it because the acid waters make moisture navailable to the flora.

Quaking Bog. A bog in which the surface vegetational mat, often of sedge, anchors at its sides but not in the middle. The bog thus tends to quiver under foot.

Moraine. An accumulation of rock materials deposited by a glacier.

Virgin Prairie. Grasslands untouched by plow or overgrazing.

Succession. The progression from simple to complex in vegetation and animal life.

Habitat. A specific locale for birds, animals or insects.

System. The pattern of relationships between vegetation and animal life and their environment.

Environment. The combination of physical and social factors affecting the growth and development of vegetation and animal life.

Introduction

Eighteen years after the Indiana Dunes National Lakeshore became a reality, the park and its environs remain an unknown pleasure world to many thousands of people. Even those who live close by have often missed the countless delights of the dunes region. As residents of the area for 15 years, we prepared *'Round and About the Dunes* to help wanderers from near and far sample the varied attractions of this bypassed haven. We hope our guidebook will entice visitors to taste the ambience of an unspoiled natural world that still exists on the populated shores of Lake Michigan, an environment that offers welcome respite from its urban, industrialized surroundings.

Our first section, an introduction to the natural features of the dunes, its history, geology and plant and animal life, invites the reader to appreciate the fragile nature and small scale of Indiana's unique wonderland. We include a complete description of both the Indiana Dunes State Park and the Indiana Dunes National Lakeshore, two oases of green preserved for the enjoyment of all citizens. Here the reader will find information about the facilities and programs of both parks. Armed with our guide and the resolve to leave cars behind, the visitor can stroll, meander, bike or poke his way to private discovery or restful enjoyment of nature.

A Community Guide that lists what to do and see within an hour of the Lakeshore's Visitor Center follows next. It starts with Porter County, fans out to Lake, LaPorte, St. Joseph and Berrien Counties and ends with the Kankakee, a river valley which cuts across the five. We then discuss each town giving a short history and listing its major attractions.

Finally the Categorical Guide provides a quick reference to all the shops, parks or public fishing spots included in the book. By using it as a ready resource, readers with special interests can quickly find the perfect place to pursue their favorite pastime.

We have made no attempt to put together an encylopedic compendium. The listings reflect our judgements, tastes and personal preferences as well as our biases and prejudices. We have, for the most part, refused to list franchises or chains and have eliminated categories our intelligent readers can easily find by looking in the yellow pages. We have checked each place without the knowledge of owners or managers and here offer our honest evaluation.

And now, some ground rules to help the reader get the most from this guide. We have starred all attractions that charge admission. Unless indicated, artists, craftsmen, private gardens and the like require appointments; inhabited homes must be viewed from the road. Remember this book covers a bi-state region so the areas code differ: 219 for Indiana and 616 for Michigan. To add to the confusion, so do the time zones. Michigan sets its clock on Eastern Time, one hour ahead of Indiana. In the summer, because they do not observe Daylight Saving Time, New Carlisle and the South Bend area show the same time as our other Indiana counties while in the winter they are one hour ahead.

It's a good idea to phone before setting out to visit a particular place. While we guarantee each listing's correctness at the date of publication, change occurs rapidly. Dates, times and locations for special events, especially, often change without advance warning. Check carefully before getting on your way.

To cope with the Indiana county road system, bear in mind that each county uses the same numbering. Imaginary lines bisect each one dividing it into north, south, east and west quadrants so be sure you are in the right county before attempting to find a rural location.

For assistance in planning a trip or for further travel aid we include the following potpourri of facts:

Both Indiana and Michigan have toll free tourist information numbers. For Hoosier advice, phone 800-622-4464 within Indiana; if out of state, call 317-232-8860. From inside Michigan call 800-292-2500; if out-of state, 800-248-5700. To get additional help in Indiana write to Wander Indiana, 1 North Capitol, Suite 700, Indianapolis, IN 46204-2243. For collecting maps and answers to questions in Michigan, contact the Travel Information Center located on I-94 at the Indiana-Michigan State line (469-0011) or the Michigan Travel Bureau, Box 30026, Lansing, MI 48909 (800-248-5700).

The following will provide help with transportation: for those traveling by car the Indiana State Police (800-552-8917) will give up to date information on road conditions. In Michigan call the State Police at (429-1111) for the Benton Harbor area, (469-1111) for the New Buffalo Area and (683-4411) for the Niles area, or tune in your car radio to 940 or 1260 am or 96.1 fm for highway conditions. Rail buffs can use several train routes. Amtrak (800-872-7245) operates a number of runs through the area including a Chicago to Detroit and Chicago to South Bend schedule with intermediate stops at Hammond, Gary, Michigan City and Niles. Conrail (800-621-7201) provides a commuter train from Chicago to Valparaiso with a stop in Hobart. To get schedules, routes, fares and information about special excursions via public transportation, including the South Shore Railroad, throughout northwest Indiana, call the Trans-Info Center (838-4636) within Indiana or (800-552-7433) if out of state, weekdays from 8 a.m. to 7 p.m. In addition, maps detailing public transportation routes in the Dunes region are available from the Northwestern Indiana Regional Planning Commission, 8149 Kennedy Avenue, Highland, IN 46321 (923-1060 or 312-731-2646).

Most area newspapers have weekend sections with a calendar of happenings for the immediate vicinity. Three additional publications will assist our guidebook in keeping you up to date: *Dunebeat*, a weekly freebee out of Michiana Shores; *Dunes Country Magazine*, currently a quarterly published in Porter and *Today in Michiana*, a monthly magazine published in South Bend.

Finally, we want to thank our many friends, neighbors and acquaintances for their help. Without the assistance of the following we could not have produced this book: Carol Beal, Helen Bieker, Phyllis Brandy, Ann Budich, George Bunce, Dale Engquist, Myrtle Greiger, Hazel Hannell, Irene

3

Herlocker, Donna Hoffman, Bob Koch, Wendy Lindquist, Dick Morrisroe, John Nelson, Bob Nikovitch, Georgette Oberle, Elizabeth Peralta, Susan and Charlie Schwartz, Sam Vaughan, Larry Waldron, Dave Williams and Lanell Wolf. Our special gratitude to Emma Pitcher who did a painstaking job of proofing the material, to Peter Schaeffer who patiently helped us unravel the intricacies of using our computers both for writing and typesetting and to John Cifonelli for use of transmission facilities.

We wish you a fond bon voyage as you set out to discover the Dunes. You will find almost everyone you meet willing to help you find your destination. And now our last suggestion. Set some time aside to just wander along a county road. Over the next rise, you may find a beautiful vista or a brand new, interesting shop. Take your time and discover your own favorite haunt. Go forth and enjoy!

Footprints in time.

Indiana Dunes Recreation Areas

HISTORY

Most people today know the Indiana Dunes for its unique beauty and superb recreational opportunities. However, the area also has a fascinating history, both human and natural. Understanding the background of the dunes adds to the richness of any visit and will tempt travelers to return again and again.

Although "civilized" man has only short acquaintance with the dunes, human association goes back 2,000 years. Scientists believe that mounds scattered throughout the region represent the burial sites of Indian tribes which then inhabited the Lake Michigan wilderness.

Centuries later, the great Algonquin nation, primarily centered in the eastern United States, had tribes living along the Great Lakes. First the Miami and then the Potawatomi inhabited the southern and southwestern shores of Lake Michigan and the interior valleys. These nomadic Indians lived off the bounty of the land, gathering its fruits, and hunting its animals, and fish. The Potawatomi had moved from the forests of northern Wisconsin to northern Indiana which became their great hunting and camping grounds. By 1800, they had established 50 villages throughout the area.

They also developed a major interstate system 250 years ago that modern man uses today as the route for his roads and railroads. The Great Sauk Trail connected Detroit with the West and passed through the dunes. The Trail began at Rock River, Illinois, on the Mississippi River, crossed Illinois and entered Indiana at Dyer, on the present Rt. 30. It passed

Patterns in the sand.

Lake and foredune on a windy day.

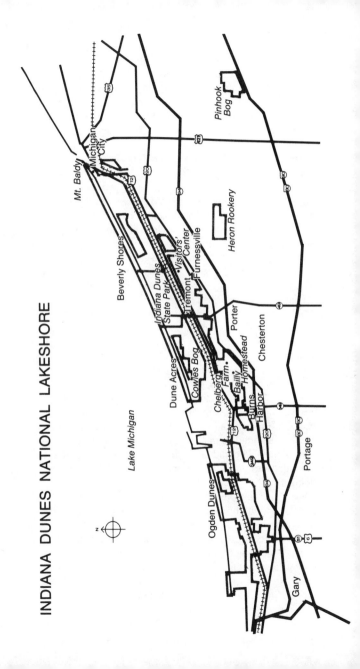

INDIANA DUNES NATIONAL LAKESHORE

Lake Michigan

Mt. Baldy
Michigan City
Beverly Shores
Dune Acres
Ogden Dunes
Indiana Dunes State Park
Visitors' Center
Tremont
Furnessville
Cowles Bog
Chelberg Farm
Bailly Homestead
Burns Harbor
Porter
Chesterton
Portage
Gary
Pinhook Bog
Heron Rookery

through the communities of Merrillville and Valparaiso, ran north and east along the current Rt. 2 to Westville and then to LaPorte and New Carlisle. Crossing the St. Joseph River it continued northeast across southern Michigan from Bertrand and Niles following what is now Rt. 12 through White Pigeon, Sturgis, Coldwater, Jonesville, Clinton and Ypsilanti to Detroit.

A northern branch of the Sauk Trail split off at Merrillville. This trail passed through Chesterton, Porter, Baillytown to Lake Michigan and along the beach to Chicago. Indians coming from Chicago often used the old Potawatomi Trail which converged with the Great Sauk Trail at New Carlisle.

The French explored the dunes first, beginning in the early 18th century. Motivated by commercial interests, primarily fur trading with the Indians, they nevertheless built forts, including one in the Indiana Dunes State Park now indicated by an historical marker, and took along missionaries.

Defeated by the British in the French and Indian Wars in 1763, France lost all rights to its dune lands. The British assumed control and won the allegiance of the Indians. The dunes, however, remained Indian territory until almost 40 years after the Revolutionary War had ended the British rule. The United States signed repeated treaties with the Potawatomi, recognizing their ownership of the dunes. However President Andrew Jackson's determination to force all Indians west of the Mississippi meant the end of Potawatomi control. On a march called the Trail of Death, Federal troops forcibly deported them to a Kansas reservation in 1838. Pioneer farmers who had begun homesteading during the previous decade then officially opened dunelands to Yankee settlement.

Most of the farmers, however, by-passed the dunes. Marshy and full of mosquitoes, the area lay far from established transportation routes. Little would grow, while to the south, pioneers found good, accessible and cheap farm land. Instead, speculators purchased the unwanted dunelands, securing large holdings. Even with the advent of the South Shore Railroad in 1908, the dunes remained uninhabited: too far, too wet and too useless for development.

About the turn of the century, nature lovers and scientists

began to explore the dunes on a systematic basis. Led by the Prairie Club of Chicago, they organized a citizens' movement, to work for preservation of this wilderness. Stephen Mather, the first director of the National Park Service, endorsed a plan, that failed, for a national park in the dunes.

However this first dunes conservation movement did bear fruit in 1923, when the State of Indiana established the present Indiana Dunes State Park. Contributions from Judge Elbert Gary, president of the United States Steel Company, Samuel Insull, president of the South Shore Railroad and Julius Rosenwald, a Chicago philanthropist, spurred the effort. The dunes in Porter County remained largely unspoiled throughout the '20's and '30's.

By the late l940's, rumors circulated among conservationists that industrial interests had bought the best dune formations for the construction of new steel mills. In 1952, a group of Ogden Dunes housewives, under the leadership of Dorothy Buell, initiated a new campaign for a national park. At the same time, political leaders in Indiana, industrialists and others began a parallel push to create an Indiana deep water port on Lake Michigan. The conservationists formed the Save the Dunes Council and, unable to persuade Indiana representatives or senators to espouse their cause, enlisted Senator Paul Douglas of Illinois, a long time dune lover, as their spokesman. After years of consideration Congress approved both projects, the Indiana Dunes National Lakeshore and the Port of Indiana, as a package in 1966. The legislation provided for the establishment of the Lakeshore and authorized the National Park Service to purchase all land within its boundaries, except for that owned by state or municipal bodies, which requires donation, and to demolish all unneeded structures.

GEOLOGY OF THE DUNES

Scientists estimate the age of the earth at 4.5 billion years. Put in this perspective, the Indiana Dunes represents a modern story which began about 15,000 years ago when the great sand dunes first started to take shape. Their beginnings go back to a time when northern Indiana had a hilly, undulating

Pinhook Bog, where Lakeshore visitors can observe

carnivorous plants.

terrain like that of southern Indiana today. The climate, though, emulated that of northern Canada and forests of spruce and fir covered the hills. Neither Lake Michigan nor any of the other Great Lakes existed.

During a preceding ice age, more than a million years ago, four glaciers moved south from Canada, advanced across the upper Midwest, melted and receded northward as the temperature climbed. These glaciers, a mile or so thick, resembled the glacier that exists in Greenland today. (Regardless of the area covered, a glacier takes shape from the compression of snow under the weight of its own great thickness. Its strength depends on how much precipitation becomes snow and on the compaction that results from the pressure of layer upon layer of snow. Under the force of gravity, the glacier begins to move. Whenever a glacier pauses in its retreat, it forms a hill of deposited earth materials, sands, gravels, and boulders called a moraine).

The last major ice advance, called the Wisconsonian, began 75,000 years ago; the recession of this glacier played a critical role in the evolution of the Indiana Dunes. In its waning phase, it stopped not very far south of the southern shores of present day Lake Michigan and formed a curved belt of hilly land known as the Valparaiso Moraine.

As the Wisconsonian glacier retreated over many millenia, its melting waters got trapped between the high lands of the Valparaiso Moraine to the south, east, and west and an ice barrier formed by the receding glacier itself to the north. These waters formed ancient Lake Chicago, precursor of modern day Lake Michigan. By 10,000 B.C. the water level of Lake Chicago stood 60 feet higher than Lake Michigan's today and its shoreline followed the eastern slope of the Valparaiso Moraine covering present day Chicago, Gary and Chesterton and went northward into what are now the shoreland areas of southern Michigan and Wisconsin.

During the next 9,000 years the water level of Lake Chicago dropped several times before establishing the modern level of the lake. Geologists studying the history of Lake Chicago have identified several of its old shorelines. The Glenwood Stage Shoreline, which existed at Lake Chicago's highest level, runs just north of Rt.20. At the Calumet Stage, Lake

Chicago's level had declined 20 feet; Rt. 12 follows its shore-line through much of the Lakeshore. About 1,000 B.C. the water reached its present level creating Lake Michigan as we know it today. Large configurations of sand dunes formed as each of these shorelines evolved.

DUNE FORMATION AND SUCCESSION

Wind and wave combine to form the Indiana Dunes. For thousands of years storm winds across Lake Michigan have whipped up the waves which eat away at the bluffs north of Evanston, Illinois and the cliffs along the Wisconsin shore-line. These storm waves act as giant grinders disintegrating and rounding the quartz stone. Lake Michigan's dominant northwesterly winds control the lake currents and the charac-ter of the waves with resulting along shore drift which carries the quartz particles (sand) to the south and east shores of the lake. Day in and day out the waves bring this sand onto the beaches to form new sand bars.

Next the wind takes over to screen the sand. Heavier parti-cles remain on the beach; the lighter granules swirl inland. Whenever flying sand meets an obstruction, a tiny dune forms. If some vegetation does not hold the low pile of sand together, the wind will surely come along and blow it away. With wind spray providing the moisture, the seed of a sand binder, typically marram grass or sand cherry, takes root. This process creates the foredune which grows at right angles to the predominant wind direction. Cottonwood, the major tree of the foredune, withstands constant blowing sand by shooting out new root systems as more and more of its trunk gets covered.

Foredunes provide protection from the wind for older dunes growing behind them. Such protection allows plant decay to occur and soil to accumulate. Seedlings of the jack pine, which, along with the white pine and juniper of the northern woods reaches its southern limit in the dunes, grow here. In time pine dunes form with their characteristic cool and scented air.

In turn these dunes protect still older oak dunes behind

A tree graveyard exposing ancient trunks.

Maple sugar at the Chellberg Farm.

The West Beach Visitor Center.

Summer fun at West Beach.

them. Here black oaks, white oaks, basswoods, elms and sassafras flourish in the richer soil and dense vegetation.

Still further inland, about a mile and a half from the beach, the end of the succession occurs. Here stands the mixed oak climax forest of the Indiana Dunes, which has taken 10,000 years to form. It creates such dense shade that oaks and pines cannot survive. Instead, tulip trees and ferns abound.

Between the dune ridges, trapped water has fashioned small lakes, ponds and bogs. The dunes landscape constantly moves under the pressure of the winds blowing down the lake. From one decade to another, it never looks the quite the same.

PLANT LIFE IN THE DUNES

Any visitor to the Indiana Dunes will likely find at least one old friend among its flora regardless of the part of the country from which he comes. Even people from foreign lands may find close relatives of plants they have known at home.

In May a southerner will find flowering dogwood in bloom in some of the forested areas. In late June and early July a Mexican will spot familiar prickly pear cactus, a plant normally associated with southwestern deserts. Plant lovers will find mosses, lichens and bearberry of the tundra; jack pine, white cedar and paper birch of the not-so-far north; and the beech, maple and white pine of the east. A visitor who has hiked in Vermont's Green Mountains will recognize the common trailing arbutus while a visitor from the Alps coming upon the extremely rare downy gentian in a dry dune prairie in late September will probably notice it faster than would a native Hoosier.

Desert, bog, hill and dale; dry prairie and wet; mesophytic forest, river flood plain and other habitats all exist in Dune Country. This rich variety of habitats so close to metropolitan Chicago and its centers of learning has stimulated extensive study of the natural history of the dunes.

Ecology in North America originated in the Indiana Dunes. Here Dr. Henry Cowles and his students developed the concept of ecological plant succession at the turn of the century (1896-1901). The story goes that Cowles, traveling from the east to Chicago looked out of his train window while passing through the dunes. He noticed the unusual mixture of plants growing together. Excited, he got off the train in Miller, hired a horse and buggy and returned to study the area. Cowles became so interested in the variety of plant life that he devoted much of his career as a University of Chicago botanist to studying the dunes.

The concept of ecological succession (an orderly, progressive sequence of replacement of biotic communities over a given area) has enormous historic and scientific importance. Here's how it works in the dunes.

Simply stated, succession describes the adaptation of plants and animals, over the course of time, to changing conditions of light, water, temperature, air movement, soil texture and nutrients. In part, succession explains why the hot, dry, loose soil of the dunes supports such a large variety of plants. Biotic populations tend to modify the physical environment, creating conditions favorable to other plants and animals until a balance between the living organisms and their physical surroundings occurs. In the process, plants may change their surroundings to such an extent that they can no longer survive.

Starting at the beach and hiking inland toward the oak forest the visitor will encounter, sooner or later, many plants characteristic of the various dune habitats.

A still little known microscopic world of plants and animals lives beneath the surface of the sand at the water's edge. Storm waves have littered the dry loose sand of the beach with driftwood and other debris. Here rotting fish and other dead animals and plants fertilize the quartz sand; this flotsam protects the germinating seeds of the searocket plant, a pioneer annual. The thick fleshy leaves and stems of the searocket, its waxy covering, long roots and shape demonstrate how it has adapted to the dry, hot, windy habitat in which it lives. The stunted Kansas sunflower or cocklebur may also grow here. All these plants begin to hold the sand, add organic material to the soil, reduce wind speed, increase humidity, provide shade and reduce soil temperature. In so doing they change the environment slightly. However this temporary zone usually does not survive the winter storms which wipe it out allowing the cycle to start anew the next season. The first perennial plants appear in the next zone, the foredune.

The visitor's view of the foredune covered with marram grass depends on whether the level of Lake Michigan has risen or dropped. With a low lake level, the beach rises gradually away from the lake displaying a low ridge or two covered with yellow-green grasses. If the water has risen, the foredune may appear cliffed up to ten feet high, with many roots exposed due to erosion caused by storm waves. The cliffed dune shows how the marram grass survives burial each winter and pushes through its sand covering each new growing season. The stolons, roots and shoots of the marram grass reinforce the sand of the foredune as concrete reinforces steel. Anyone who has gone barefooted in the foredune early in the season when the shoots emerge from the packed sand knows how well the plant has adapted to this environment.

Once at the top of a foredune, the visitor may see a row of cottonwoods growing in marram grass in a straight line that marks a previous high water mark when waves washed a former dune away. He will also see a prominent woody shrub in this habitat, the sand cherry whose branches look slender and dark against the snow in the winter, whose flowers mass white in the spring, and whose leaves flash green with purple-grey undersides in the summer sun. In autumn this tree wears black fruits and striking red leaves.

Sand stabilized by marram grass provides a medium suitable for the germination of the sand cherry seeds. Studies show that the roots of sand cherry seedlings tend to follow organic matter left by the burial of the dune building grasses.

Behind the foredune a blue-green grass, the little bluestem, replaces the marram grass. Since little bluestem does not have to contend with extensive burial by sand, it lacks the creeping stolons of the marram grass. The new grass reproduces chiefly by seed.

Marram grass has created the conditions—stabilized sand, reduced wind velocity and shade—suitable for the little bluestem seeds to germinate and the plants to grow. The little bluestem grassland in turn will give way to the jack pine forest, and it in turn to the oak forest now seen in much of Dune Country. Classically, the beech-maple forest eventually succeeds the oak forest, but the age of the dunes and local conditions have not yet allowed that climax forest stage to take place.

From atop a foredune, a visitor can probably also see a pond at the base of a blowout, and the front of a moving dune burying a pine forest. He can note the vigor of the partially buried cottonwoods compared with those growing in the bluestem grassland. He can also note that marram grass grows on the moving dune where the conditions resemble those of a foredune. The cottonwood can send out adventitious roots from its trunk and branches and thereby survive partial burial; the pine cannot. Finally, he can see seedling pines near the edge of the pond in the bluestem grassland indicating the beginning of a pine forest.

Around some of the cottonwood trees that grow at the back of the foredunes live a variety of plants. These represent islands of vegetation seeded chiefly by birds roosting in the trees. They include wild grape, bittersweet, poison ivy, false Solomon's seal and a variety of other plants depending on location and the degree to which humus has built up beneath the trees. Wind blown leaves and stems caught first by the trunk of the cottonwood tree and then by the plants growing at its base make up the humus.

Near the pines the visitor will find rather dense mats of bearberry creeping between bunches of bluegrass, shading the soil to prevent germination of many seeds, but creating conditions that seem to favor germination of the pine seeds. Bearberry produces little pink flowers in the spring followed by berries, green at first, changing to orange, and later, red as the season progresses. Old berries may appear almost black. Sometimes, cactus grows in the bearberry mats.

The organically rich pine forest begins with an accumulation of pine needles; the older the trees, the greater the accumulation. Soon the oaks will invade replacing the pine forest with one of oak.

The visitor who inspects the interdunal ponds will observe a rapidly changing and disappearing habitat. Some of these ponds resulted from the lake receding but others formed at the base of blowouts from wind excavation. (During dry spells, the wind can move the dry sand all the way down to the water table. With the return of a higher table, the depression fills and new ponds form). Succession also occurs with ponds. As they fill with decaying vegetation they become wet meadows and eventually, forests, if suitable conditions prevail.

Each interdunal pond seems to have its own characteristics. One young pond may contain Chara, a green algae that requires pure water containing calcium, and not much else. Fringed gentian may grow at the edge of another pond. Slightly less fussy, the rose gentian may choose another. Kalm's lobelia grows near any of the ponds. Other flowering plants commonly grow along the edges of dune ponds: the yellow flowered shrubby St. Johnswort and the foxglove-like purple gerardia. The yellow, horned bladderwort blooms in or near the water's edge from June through summer. Ladies tresses orchids, a plant of special interest, flourish in the grassy meadow portion of dune ponds during September.

Grasses, sedges, rushes, willows and many other plants grow near the dune ponds and in the rest of the dunes. Hoary or hairy puccoon, with its yellow flowers, seems to flourish everywhere. Dune visitors will likely see blue spiderwort, orange milkweed, lavender lupines, red columbines, tulip trees and sassafras that exists only on the south and east shores of Lake Michigan.

Rare plants also live in the dunes—white, yellow and pink ladyslipper orchids and the carnivorous sundew and pitcher plants. These must remain undisturbed so that future generations can enjoy their beauty.

BIRDS OF THE DUNES

The dunes resemble a bird paradise. Protected from hunters, relatively undisturbed by human contact and amply supplied with wild fruits, berries and nuts as well as insects and fish, birds rest, nest or winter here. Some birds such as plovers and warblers fly up from as far away as South America and others like the snow goose fly down from as far north as the Arctic Circle. Because the dunes stand in the path of the great Mississippi Flyway, thousands of migrants appear overhead in the spring and fall. Bird lovers have counted well over 200 varieties in the dunes recreation areas.

However the dunes constitutes more than a bird refuge. A number of birds here reach either the northern or southern limits of their range. Northern birds which frequently migrate south as far as the dunes include scoters, oldsquaws, northern shrikes, crossbills, redpolls, evening grosbeaks and snow buntings. The southern birds which come as far north as the dunes include: the great blue heron (which breeds along the Little Calumet River in a rookery protected by the Lakeshore) yellow crowned night herons, Acadian flycatchers, Carolina wrens, mockingbirds, white eyed vireos, blue winged warblers, prairie warblers, Louisiana waterthrushes, Kentucky warblers, hooded warblers and yellow breasted chats.

Five distinct habitats exist within the recreation areas:

1. Lake Michigan. Its waters and beaches attract such birds as loons, grebes, bay ducks, sea ducks, mergansers, gulls, terns and numerous shore birds. Visitors can see terns swooping down to catch fish or sandpipers combing the sand in search of tiny morsels of food. In the spring and fall flocks of herring gulls and sea ducks fill the skies. The Indiana Dunes State Park beach, West Beach and the parking lot at the foot of Lake Street near the Miller Woods provide good vantage points for viewing these migrants.

The great horned owl makes a rare sight on a cold day. Beach walkers early in the morning can sometimes spot this nearly two foot tall, white throated bird with his conspicuous ear tufts. From far away he resembles a clump of ice.

2. Foredunes. Prairie warblers and chipping and field sparrows nest in the sand reeds and marram grass on the low dunes just behind the beach. Beverly Shores and Dune Acres make good viewing spots for nests of bank swallows which burrow into the steep banks above the beach. It takes a high lake to create the proper conditions for these erosion dwellers. If a stranger approaches a killdeer's nest, he'll sound his distress cry and perform his broken wing act. During the winter tree sparrows, redpolls and once in a while snowy owls appear in these dunes.

3. The Permanent Dunes. A more abundant bird life ex-

ists here than in any other area of the Lakeshore. Where the red and black oaks and the red cedar have taken root and woods have covered the sand base, warblers, thrushes, vireos, kinglets, titmice, flycatchers, woodpeckers, cuckoos, wrens, orioles, grosbeaks, nuthatches and owls abound.

Along the edges of these woods, the most common of all dunes birds, the chickadee, resides during the entire year. His companions include rufous sided towhees, Indiana's state bird, the brilliant red cardinal (who especially loves sunflower seeds), lovely blue indigo buntings, brown thrashers, catbirds and house wrens. In the spring visitors may recognize the noisy oven bird calling "teacher, teacher, teacher," but finding his dome shaped nest is another matter. Trail 9 and the south side of the Trail 10 loop in the Indiana Dunes State Park cross wooded dunes and make good sighting locations as do the woods west of the Visitor Center and those north of Cowles Bog.

4. Wetlands. South of the permanent dunes in the bogs, marshes and ponds, herons, dabbling ducks, rails, shorebirds, marsh wrens, kingfishers, swallows and swamp and song sparrows nest. Here the common yellowthroat calls "witchety, witchety, witchety" in the spring and summer. To observe these birds, visit Cowles Bog, the marsh and pond in the West Beach area or Trail 2 which traverses a wooded swamp in the Indiana Dunes State Park.

5. Fields. Bobolinks, pheasants, sparrows, kingbirds, bluebirds, barn swallows and phoebes commonly frequent this habitat. Watch for the meadowlark, whose yellow breast trimmed with a black V makes him easy to recognize, sitting on a fence. These birds cluster at the Chellberg Farm and power line rights of way bordering Rt. 12 from Beverly Shores to Dune Acres.

Small stands of conifers scattered throughout the Lakeshore attract red breasted nuthatches, long eared owls and winter finches.

Dunes dwellers especially enjoy the ruby throated hummingbirds that visit their feeders. These smallest of all birds dart with amazing speed to suck colored sugar water. From spring to fall, at dusk, they sip nectar from flowers with their long needle-like beaks. They love the columbine that blooms on sandy banks in Inland Marsh and along Ly-co-ki-we Trail.

Watch the most majestic of all large dunes birds in flight, the great blue heron. This shy blue-gray, four foot tall bird ranks second in size only to the bald eagle, the largest bird in North America. The heron sometimes emerges from the very secluded marsh areas near the lake. His folded neck, seven foot wingspan, slow wing beat and long trailing legs make him easy to identify. Turkey vultures present another sight to see. Look for them aloft from the foredunes south to the fields. They soar, riding the currents atop the dunes with their five foot wingspread. Though charming and graceful in flight, their bare red heads make them downright ugly on the ground.

Other familiar guests in the dunes during the spring, summer and fall enchant the birder: grackles, song sparrows, American redstarts, starlings, wood thrushes, marsh wrens. Downy woodpeckers and blue jays stay year round. Easy to spot with their bright blue coats, the greedy jays can gulp down 15 or 16 seeds at a time and come back for more within a second.

The cacophony of the birds carries everywhere in the dunes. Bird buffs get up before dawn in the late winter and early spring to catch the hootings of the great horned and barred owl. For sheer noise volume, its hard to beat the ceaseless racket of the wrens. Lucky birders sometimes hear the marvelous laugh of the loons down on the beach. Easier to recognize are the white breasted nuthatches who dash back and forth crying "ma-ma, ma-ma, ma-ma" or the seemingly compulsive chant of the whip-poor-wills very early in the morning or at dusk in the late spring or early summer.

Try Not To Miss:

• The semi-annual visit of the blackbirds to the marsh at the corner of Beverly Drive and State Park Road in Beverly Shores. Rusty (only in fall) blackbirds, red winged blackbirds with shiny epaulets and grackles cover the reeds and cattails in this swamp. Their din carries for miles.

• The goldfinches that nest along the South Shore right of way. These brightly colored birds show up easily against new soft green foliage.

- Two dunes game birds, quail and the almost tame strutting pheasants that sometimes dart across roads.
- The kestrels sitting on telephone wires waiting to attack some small animal. Other predators in the dunes include shrikes, scavenger crows and some owls.

And, most spectacular, the twice yearly flight of Canadian geese in formation along the horizon where the lake meets the sky.

The Chicagoland list of the birds of the Indiana Dunes is carried at the Save the Dunes Council shop. If you want to know more about bird life in the dunes either attend one of the illustrated bird programs sponsored by the Lakeshore or take part in an Audubon bird count. For information call the Visitor Center (926-7561).

ANIMALS OF THE DUNES

Visitors stretched out on a sandy dune may find to their surprise that they have company. The area abounds in insect and animal life and each dune zone supports its own species. The storm beach, formed and reformed by wind and wave action, provides a feast of drowned insects for birds and predator insects like the fiery searcher. The foredune's furnace-like heat in midsummer cannot sustain life for most creatures. The digger wasp and burrowing spider, however, cope by tunneling down to the core of cool sand below. So does the night prowling wolf spider.

Behind the foredune the pine dune houses an abundance of wood and tiger beetles, ants and termites; back of it comes the oak dune with far richer soil and more varied life, including the doodle bug. The climax forest supports the greatest assortment of insect and animal life.

Only one poisonous snake, the increasingly rare Massasauga rattler, inhabits dunes swamps. Always sluggish and slow to rattle, he produces a serious but hardly ever deadly bite. In maturity he stretches about 32 inches and has a rounded snout, small eyes and a chunky body. His color ranges from gray to black, always with white markings. Most dunes snakes do not cause harm or offense and often cause benefit. A hognose snake may hiss and flatten its head like a rattlesnake, but it's all bluff. Hikers should observe snakes from a distance and let them live their lives.

Two hundred years ago visitors might have seen black bears, timber wolves or martins. Lynx, cougars, bobcats, elk and bison all inhabited the dunes. All those mammals have long since disappeared, hunted out by pioneers and fur speculators. Today, with luck, watchers may spot a mink, a coyote or a fox though their populations too have diminished. White tailed deer on the other hand have flourished in recent years. Sightings take place frequently on Beverly Shores roads or on the beaches. Drivers should look out for them. They almost always travel in groups.

Many animal species reach their geographic limits in the dunes making the area zoologically important. For instance, the Bonaparte weasel, grey squirrel, white tailed deer and rufescent woodchuck travel no farther south than the dunes. The opossum, pipistrelle bat and southern woodchuck go no farther north. The dunes country makes up the eastern boundary for the western raccoon, Illinois skunk, Misissippi Valley mink and the Franklin ground squirrel. The chipmunk, Bachman's shrew and pocket gopher go no farther north or west.

Try Not To Miss:

• Opossum. Two or three feet long, four to 12 pounds, the opossum has a silly grin, a pointed chin and a ratlike tail which he uses as a hand. He also hangs by the tail and plays dead to avoid a fight. The female opossum, like the kangaroo, carries her young in a pouch. Called marsupials, the species has survived since the time of the dinosaurs.

• Eastern chipmunk. This tiny animal with big cheeks sometimes gathers four quarts of hickory nuts and corn in a day. Chipmunks feast on berries, seeds, nuts, fruit and, of course, garden bulbs. They hate heat and tend to hibernate in summer. Community minded, they live in groups rather than jealously guarding private territory.

• Red squirrel. This fellow with the rusty coat sometimes goes by the name of pine or red robber or red jig or woodland squirrel. He alternately chatters, barks, sputters and stamps. Smallest of the tree squirrels, he plays the clown of the pine woods. He flips from branch to branch, and tree to tree and also can retreat through a labyrinth under and through the pine woods. A born conservationist, he can bury hundreds of seeds and cones, many of which he never recovers. These sprout and in time become aerial highways for his descendants. The red squirrel also serves as one of the true sentinels of the forest. When he calls an alarm, the woodlands listen.

• Fox squirrel. This, the largest of North American squirrels has a bushy tail and reddish, gray or black coloring. This diminishing breed has already disappeared from New England. The fox squirrel often takes over a tree cavity left by a red headed woodpecker and enlarges it with his teeth. In hot weather he may build a dozen leaf nests, ranging over a territory of 40 acres. When chased, the fox squirrel prefers a ground escape route, because of his clumsiness. He frequently falls when attempting an aerial leap. He likes midday activity, enjoys the sun and hoards a large store of nuts, corn, mushrooms and insects.

• Thirteen lined ground squirrel. Some people call him the Federation Squirrel because he sports thirteen whitish stripes, interrupted by rows of spots or stars. He measures better than a foot, has a long head, a bushy tail and big eyes. He chatters "seek-seek" as he guards his 20 foot long prairie burrow. He loves the sun and prefers to stay home, and inside, in gray weather.

• Woodchuck. Largest of the squirrel family, the woodchuck also goes by the names of ground hog, marmot or monax (Indian for digger). The size of a cat, the chunky woodchuck has a dark brown coat and a bushy tail. He lumbers along on short legs, and has buck teeth which give him a foolish look but help him greatly in gnawing. The latter he does in burrowing and eating.

The woodchuck aerates the soil digging down as much as five feet a day as he burrows and turns over the subsoil. He spends much time hibernating. Late in October he curls up in the woods for the cold weather after having prepared for this time by fattening up all summer on clover and alfalfa, buttercup and daisies. Unlike the nocturnal raccoon and opossum, the woodchuck loves light and works and travels by day.

• White tailed deer. The only deer found in the dunes, the

white tail has keen eyesght, hearing and sense of smell. He eats no meat and enjoys ice cream and oranges when offered. In times of danger, he raises his white tail as a warning flag. He also has glands in his feet that leave a scent so other animals know when he's running from danger. His fallen antlers provide a source of calcium for many forest animals. This deer has a repertoire of sounds: shrieks, bugles (for battle), bleats (for pain), snorts (for rage). During winter the gregarious white tail prefer to stay in herds.

• Raccoon. The dunes area abounds in raccoons, their fanciers and feeders. Some families have played host to raccoons for decades, entertaining several generations of the same animal families. As a result, when the feeding merits, the usually nocturnal raccoon's internal clock gets turned around.

One of nature's most adaptable creatures, the furry raccoon can climb, swim, fish and use his ''hands'' with unbelievable skill. He washes his food before eating, not to clean it, but because he lacks salivary glands. These highly intelligent creatures have a great capacity for concentration. People have spotted them at living room windows busily watching the movement on the TV screen.

• Red fox. This hard to spot beauty does indeed live in the dunes. The red fox has a bright, rust colored coat, black legs, black ears, black nose and a white tip on his tail.

DUNE POISONS AND DUNE EDIBLES

Though grasses, seeds, nuts and weeds may appear like a five course dinner, don't partake until you can separate what's edible from a tummyache or worse. A wise parent keeps his children from nibbling anything out in the wild. In the dunes avoid the following in particular:

Jack-in-the-pulpit. All parts of this plant cause intense irritation of the tongue and mouth.

May Apple contains more than a dozen toxic substances.

Water Hemlock. All parts of this swamp plant cause violent convulsions, often death.

Buttercups can seriously damage the digestive system.

An advancing dune burying a pine forest.

Nightshade with its purple flowers and red berries is usually fatal.

Mushrooms. Avoid them unless you are sure. Dunes natives adore morels in early spring. They are harmless and delicious if you're sure you can identify them.

Unfortunately, poison ivy grows abundantly in the dunes. The three leafed, shiny plant nestles amongst the tempting blackberries, blueberries and raspberries that grow wild.

The following edible plants do grow in the dunes and with positive identification provide a lucious treat: Wild asparagus, wild blackberry, wild blueberry, choke cherry, chicory, yellow clover, wild grape, day lily (seed pods and flowers), water lily seeds, wild mustard, wild onion, sassafras, wood sorrel, wild strawberry and sunflower seeds.

The omnipresent cattail wins the prize as the most versatile of all dunes flora. It has edible roots, shoots, stems and pollen. The cotton from its head can stuff a cushion; its leaves can "rush" a chair. The whole plant or any of its parts make attractive dried floral arrangements.

INDIANA DUNES STATE PARK*

Establishment of a state park system in Indiana began in 1916 as part of the Indiana's centennial celebration. However authorization of the Indiana Dunes State Park did not occur until 1923 and then only after a struggle between those who favored preservation of this duneland and those who wanted the land used for industrial development. Originally conservationists had hoped to see the entire shoreline in Porter County set aside for park purposes, but the State Legislature opted for a three mile stretch between what is now the communities of Porter Beach and Beverly Shores. Unlike other units in the state park system which came about because of public subscriptions or donations,Indiana Dunes took a state tax levy of two mills per $100 of assessment to provide the funds for the purchase of the land from private owners. Completion of these real estate transfers occurred by 1931.

With the acquisition of 2,182 acres including the three high dunes, Mount Tom, Mount Jackson and Mount Holden, Indiana undertook an extensive building program, constructing a pavillion, a hotel designed by Frank Lloyd Wright's son, John, which came down in the late 60's, as well as parking lots, trails, campgrounds and other facilities. A residence on the property became the Governor's Cottage and served as a vacation retreat for successive governors until it too fell to the wrecking ball in the late '60's.

In 1976 two-thirds of the land became a state nature preserve thereby guaranteeing that it would remain unimpaired. From its inception the Indiana Dunes State Park has proved a popular attraction for Hoosiers and visitors from the Chicago metropolitan area. It now attracts more than a million patrons each year and ranks as the busiest park in the state system during the summer months.

Visitors primarily use the park in the summer time for swimming and camping. However it has year round attractions. In fact, visitors interested in hiking or nature will find much to enjoy from fall through spring unhampered by the crowds. In recent years, the park has added cross country skiing to its list of activities. To contact the park, write Indiana Dunes State Park, 1600N and 25E, Chesterton, IN 46304 or call 926-4520.

CAVEATS.

Fences surround the State Park to discourage entrance without payment of the required fee; prosecution of trespassers has occurred. Visitors can also purchase an annual state park system pass. Indiana residents over 60 can get a golden age pass.

Cars must enter at the main gate located at the northern terminus of Rt. 49, two miles north of Exit 26B on I-94. Starting in 1984 from Memorial Day to Labor Day, pedestrians, bikers and South Shore riders may use the gate at the northern terminus of Tremont Road by paying an entrance fee. It takes five minutes to walk from the train stop to the gate and from there, go a third of a mile to the nature preserve, a half mile to the campground and a mile to the beach.

Boaters should not land their craft on the park beach. Park officials consider it an illegal entry.

No dogs allowed on the beach. Keep dogs and cats on a leash at all times elsewhere in the park.

No loaded firearms of any kind permitted in the park.

Do not pick twigs, branches or limbs for firewood. They must remain on the ground to provide replenishment for the soil.

To See and Do

NATURE PRESERVE.

The easterly two-thirds of the park, 1,530 permanently protected acres, comprises the Dunes Nature Preserve. No development, fires or organized activities. Listed on the National Register of Natural Landmarks.

Two and a half miles wide and a mile long, the largest of Indiana's state nature preserves, extends from the beach on the north to the South Shore Railroad tracks on the south. Natural features include isolated stands of jack pines on the foredune and Mt. Tom, 192 feet tall, highest remaining Indiana dune. Other important natural landmarks include three of the largest blowouts in the park and habitats varying from dry foredunes to interior marshlands.

Only hiking permitted in the preserve. Enter by walking east from the Nature Center on Trail 9.

NATURE STUDY.

The park's Nature Center, located at the eastern edge of the campgrounds (926-1390), serves as the focal point for a wide-ranging environmental education program. Open Memorial Day to November 1, 8:30-4, the Center contains displays as well as a library of reference material. Two park naturalists help to educate the public about the natural world. Two adult and one children's program available. Successful completion of these programs results in earning a shoulder patch.

Self-guiding nature trail guide tracing the stages of succession from a mature oak forest back to its origin on the beachfront available at the Nature Center.

PROGRAMS.

The park offers a number of special activities for its patrons. Regular campfires, singalongs, and night prowls. Occasional performances by professional groups ranging from jazz bands to story tellers. Schedule available at the Nature Center, Park Office or the Main Gate.

RECREATION.

Camping*. 309 sites, 124 with electricity. Some reservations available from Memorial Day to Labor Day. Stay limited to two weeks. Also tent camping* for organized youth groups under adult supervision. No heated showers provided for wintertime camping but water, pit toilets and electricity available and the fee drops 50%. The campgrounds fill up quickly. Write or call after March 1 for summer use.

From May 15 to Labor Day a campground grocery operates which sells wood, ice, picnic supplies and foodstuffs.

Cross Country Skiing. Trail 2 and parts of Trails 8 and 9 convert to cross country skiing in the winter months. Equipment rental available, December, 9-2; January-March, 9-3. The crush gets greatest on Sunday afternoons, so get there early.

Hiking. Eight marked and easy to follow trails include: trail 1—A short walk which provides a good exposure to dune formation; trail 2—An easy three mile tramp which wends through great expanses of early spring flowers and ferns. Use only in dry weather. Trail 3—View the prickly pear cactus growing in the dunes. Trail 4—A short hike of moderate difficulty which climbs through dunes covered with black oak trees. Trail 7—Similar to trail 4, only slightly longer. A good way to see late spring flowers in bloom. Trail 8—The most difficult of the trails. Climbs over the tops of Mount Tom, Mount Jackson and Mount Holden. Trail 9—A moderate three mile hike which follows dune ridges and gives a good view of the lake and the Furnessville blowout. Trail 10—five-and-a-half-miles; passes by stands of white pine and the tree graveyard in the big blowout. A good morning walk. Also scheduled hikes in the summer months led by Park Naturalists. Inquire at the Nature Center for schedule.

Picnicking. Individual and group picnics permitted on the beach and in a 125 acre designated area. Tables, grills, toilet facilities, playground equipment and playfields available. Six picnic shelters for rent*. Reservations taken up to a year in advance.

Swimming. Lifeguards on duty, Memorial Day-late August, 10-7; late August to Labor Day, 10-6. Swimming permitted in designated sections only during these hours. Lockers, fast foods, snacks and souvenirs.

INDIANA DUNES NATIONAL LAKESHORE

The Indiana Dunes National Lakeshore offers a remarkable opportunity to examine man and his environment. Unlike the nation's famous western parks that stretch for hundreds of miles in the wilderness, the Lakeshore resembles a patchwork quilt. Giant industries, residential communities and a web of railroad tracks, highways and power lines intersperse with areas of great natural beauty, some substantially untouched by man. Though not contiguous, the Lakeshore's holdings include the recreational, aesthetic and historical elements that typify all of our country's great parks. In addition, because the national park system contains only a few midwestern units, the Lakeshore lies within easy driving distance of millions of Americans who live far from most national parks.

Because of the small scale, this park represents a sheltered refuge for man as well as for plant and animal life. Here, the visitor must forsake modern transportation and go afoot to experience its delights. By tramping the dunes, walking the beaches, feeling the north wind, blowing sand, moist heat and biting cold, by smelling the faint marsh sour and the perfume of the fields, and by quietly examining the vast profusion of flowers, trees, insects and birds, the visitor can participate in a world that existed before man intruded.

The Lakeshore's present 12,000 acres including almost ten miles of Lake Michigan shoreline—a quarter of Indiana's entire lakefront—stand as a testament to man's need to escape his technological advances and return to the natural environment. The Lakeshore presents vivid contrasts that capture the whole panorama of the area's history: surroundings that predated man's arrival, the life of the first white settler, the farm life that existed for almost a century, and the twentieth century industrialization, as typified by the nearby steel mills. Ancient natural history together with examples of modern economic development give visitors to this park a unique experience.

The location of the Lakeshore at the extreme southern shore of Lake Michigan, the effects of glaciers thousands of years ago, and the dominant northwesterly winds combine to make the Lakeshore an ecological wonder. Henry Chandler Cowles, the father of North American plant ecology, undertook some of his pioneering studies in the Lakeshore's Cowles Bog. He first proclaimed to the world that here in the Indiana Dunes man can witness the succession of plant life which elsewhere might take centuries to occur. Cowles pointed out that in these changing dunes man can observe how plant and animal life adapts to a changing environment. Because the climate zones for birds, animals and plants mix and mingle here, the visitor can observe flora and fauna native to the tundra, the plains and the desert.

LOCATION.

By car, travellers from the west should take the Indiana Toll Road (Rt. 80-90) to Exit 21 (Burns Harbor). Turn left (north) on Rt. 249 to Rt. 12. Continue east on Rt. 12 about ten miles to Kemil Road to the Visitor Center.

Travellers from the east should take I-94 to exit 26B (Indiana Dunes Recreation Areas). Turn north on Rt. 49 to Rt. 12. Continue east on Rt. 12 about three miles to the Visitor Center.

From the south, drivers may take either Rt. 421 or Rt. 49 north to Rt. 12 and respectively turn west or east to the Visitor Center.

By train, the nearest year round stop to the Lakeshore on the South Shore Railroad is Beverly Shores, located about two miles from the Visitor Center. Other South Shore Railroad stops within the Lakeshore include: Miller, Ogden Dunes, Dune Acres, Tremont and Kemil Road on weekends. Some park excursions and hikes incorporate arrivals by train. Call for schedule. Ace Taxi and Limousine Service, 110 East 11th, Michigan City (874-6244) will provide service if called from the Beverly Shores station or if notified to meet a train.

Visitors without a car should plan for a considerable hike from the Beverly Shores station to the Visitor Center, however, by continuing for one more stop beyond Beverly Shores, on the train, visitors can rent a car in Michigan City if they make advance arrangements.

By plane, the nearest scheduled service to the Lakeshore is the Michigan City-Chicago route via Joe Phillips Airlines. From O'Hare Airport in Chicago, take the Tri-State Bus to Portage and rent a car.

BOUNDARIES.

At the present time, the boundaries of this long, narrow park extend from the Lake Michigan shoreline on the north, to the Miller Woods in Gary on the west, almost to the Michigan City limits on the east, to a jagged line that runs between Rt. 12 and Rt. 20, depending on the specific location, on the south. (See Lakeshore map.) The Park Service provides a small map at the Visitor Center. Since some of the acreage included within the Lakeshore's boundaries does not belong to the government, because no purchase has yet taken place or because the former owners have a lease on their home, visitors should check with the Visitor Center to make sure their activity will take place on Lakeshore land.

GENERAL INFORMATION.

The National Park Service operates the Indiana Dunes National Lakeshore. Address all mail to 1100 North Mineral Springs Road, Porter IN 46304. For information call 926-7561. The Lakeshore has its main Visitor Center (referred to here as the Visitor Center) at the corner of Rt. 12 and Kemil Road. This center stays open year round daily, 8-5. Visitor Centers at Bailly-Chellberg and West Beach (referred to here by their individual names) are open summer, daily, 10-4:30; weekends the rest of the year. Guided tours explore most of the park; evening programs take place at the Visitor Center. Park rangers staff this facility to provide information and answer questions. All Visitor Centers, major beaches and trailheads provide bus and car parking.

A day use facility, the Lakeshore permits no camping within its boundaries. Campers can use the nearby Indiana Dunes State Park or commercial facilities.

The Lakeshore has exceptionally good facilities and programs for the handicapped. Call for details.

CAVEATS.

Visitors can picnic on some Lakeshore beaches but may not build open fires. They may use charcoal, gas or manufactured fuel stoves or grills at these beaches. No fires of any kind permitted at West Beach. Picnickers must remove charcoal and not bury it in the sand.

Visitors may not take pets on the beaches and must keep them on leash in all other parts of the Lakeshore. The Park Service does not permit any hunting within the Lakeshore but does allow fishing in accordance with federal, state and local laws. All fishermen must display an Indiana fishing license and a trout-salmon stamp obtainable from most sporting equipment stores.

Picking flowers or digging them for transplanting anywhere in the Lakeshore absolutely violates Park Service regulations. Visitors may pick the Lakeshore's nuts, berries without a permit for personal consumption only. They should respect the fragile vegetation and walk only on established trails or boardwalks.

When climbing dunes visitors should take care in grassy areas. because roots and runners just below the surface damage easily. Climbers should try to stay on open sand, or on the main trails and not try to make new paths through the grasses. Too many of these already spoil the dunes.

Visitors should avoid the deceptively solid looking shelf ice along the lake, it can be dangerous.

To See and Do

ARCHITECTURE.

Bailly Homestead. Between Rts. 12 and 20 from Babcock to Wagner Roads. The home and grounds of the Joseph Bailly family as well as their family cemetery. Born of French Canadian parents, Bailly chose this site for a fur trading post in 1822 because of the confluence of two major Indian trails and a canoe route. With his half Indian wife, Marie, Bailly stressed a civilized life though he exploited the wilderness for his living. The devoutly Catholic Baillys educated their four daughters in Fort Wayne and Detroit; travelling priests performed Mass at the homestead.

When the fur trade declined due to increased settlement and overhunting, Bailly built a tavern on what is now Rt. 12. He also planned a community, Baillytown, near his home. His death in 1835 ended the plans for the town. Bethlehem Steel now occupies the Baillytown site.

The Park Service continues its restoration of the Bailly complex, home of the area's first white settler. The homestead includes:

Coachman's House. Employee quarters built about 1900 from what remained of a dairy and tool shed.

Kitchen/Chapel. This building started life as a kitchen and apartment in the 1820's. The Bailly's daughter Rose Howe converted it to a chapel in 1869.

Main House. The Bailly family lived here from 1835 to 1917. This, the third house replaced two previous log cabins. The building looks as it did in 1917, the first year for which restorers could find accurate documentation of its appearance.

Brick House. Moved in 1904 to its present location, this house originated in the 1880's as a studio and retreat.

Storehouse. Where the family stacked the belongings of Bailly's Indian friends while they traveled.

Cemetery. Bailly used the site of an earlier cemetery to bury his ten-year old-son, Robert in 1827. Joseph, Marie and many other members of the Bailly family have their final resting place here. Once badly vandalized, the graveyard has undergone complete restoration by the Park Service.

The Park Service offers tours from the Bailly/Chellberg Visitor Center to the Homestead site. Schedules available at the Visitor Center.

Chellberg Farm. Mineral Springs Road north of Rt. 20. Enter from the Bailly-Chellberg Visitor Center. This farm property, tilled for three quarters of a century includes fallow and planted fields, a forested section which shows the beginnings of a beech-maple climax forest, and eight historic buildings.

Barn. (c. 1880). This structure exemplifies the Swedish

style brought by the immigrants who built it. Wooden pegs hold the beam frame together.

Chicken House. A board and batten construction built in the late 1890's. Plastered inside for warmth.

Corn Crib.

Windmill. Originally wooden, the structure was reconstructed using concrete blocks about 1930.

Granary. With its narrow stairs and square nails, this building, the oldest on the farm, held grain and other supplies.

House. Dates from 1885 and replaced a still earlier house that burned. Bricks came from the Porter brickyard. In 1910, the family put on a frame addition for a kitchen.

Tenant House. Built in 1930 for farm employees.

Maple Sugar House. Used for boiling sugar maple sap into syrup. Built in 1930.

BOGS.

Cowles Bog. Situated between the Northern Indiana Public Service Company's property on the west and Mineral Springs Road in Dune Acres on the east. This 120 acre marsh and spring mire, with an extensive variety of flora and fauna became a National Natural Landmark in 1966. This status protects the fragile terrain from the roads, ditches and cropped fields that threatened its existence early in this century. Only accessible by Ranger-led tours. Check the Visitor Center for dates and times.

Pinhook Bog. Located five miles south of Michigan City on Wozniak Road near the Indiana Toll Road. Because of its easily damaged nature, this section of the park is accessible only by Ranger-led tours; call the Visitor Center for information and reservations. This bog, a National Natural Landmark, contains many varieties of wetland plants and insects. In addition, flowers, trees and insects usually found in the northern lake states and in Canada flourish here. Considered one of the finest quaking bogs in the Great Lakes area.

ENVIRONMENTAL EDUCATION.

The Lakeshore provides special trips and programs for children throughout the year both in the park and in community schools. Call (926-7561) for further details.

COURSES*.

The Lakeshore offers a variety of non-credit field study courses for adults on topics related to the park. Experts teach classes in trees, flowers and birds. The offerings vary with the seasons so call for a schedule. Rangers also conduct workshops for teachers and other professionals which may offer credit.

INTERPRETIVE PROGRAMS.

Throughout the four seasons, the park's Rangers try to have something for everyone. In the fall, for example, children might enjoy the after school special, Indian Trails and Tales or Spine Tinglers, an evening of storytelling and legends of Halloween at Chellberg Farm. Adults can participate in a variety of programs, both indoors and out, joining a Ranger for Birds of Darkness: The Owl, a slide program or Christmas Crafts, making ornaments from natural materials. Winter programs, January through March, might include, National Park Travel Series, Pioneers and Homesteaders, Animals of the Woods. Stop at the Visitor Center for the current Activity Schedule.

NATURE PRESERVE.

Hoosier Prairie State Nature Preserve. From the Visitor Center take Rt. 80-94 west to Rt. 41 south. Turn east on Main toward Griffith. Allow 30 minutes driving time. The parking lot is on your right after crossing Kennedy. A trail leads from the lot to the prairie. 304 acres. The biggest piece of virgin prairie left in Indiana, Hoosier Prairie shelters more than 300 native plants, many now rare in this state. They thrive here because of a range of moisture conditions. A good place to see many now rare native birds and animals in their natural habitats.

RECREATION.

Beaches. The Lakeshore maintains four bathing beaches. All have parking facilities. From west to east they are:

West Beach. Lake-Porter County Line Road. This almost 600 acre section has a bathhouse with showers and bathrooms, concession stands, a parking lot (*summer) and lifeguards. The area also includes a heavily sand-mined section as well as a number of open and vegetated dunes and interdunal ponds, such as Long Lake. West Beach offers excellent hiking, with the best trail in the Lakeshore for seeing succession, bird watching and wild flower viewing.

State Park Road. Beverly Shores. Life guards. The parking lot on the eastern side of State Park Road about 500 feet from the beach, fills up by noon on any sunny summer day. Portable toilets.

Central Avenue. Beverly Shores. Life Guards. The parking lot, close to the beach, fills up by noon on any sunny summer day. Portable toilets. Unfortunately, this beach offers graphic evidence of the effects of erosion on the high dunes. From here one can walk to Mount Baldy along the beach, about 1 1/2 miles.

Mount Baldy Beach. At the foot of the Lakeshore's highest dune. A substantial climb from the parking lot on Rice Avenue just west of Michigan City. No lifeguards. Here the visitor can see one of the Lakeshore's best examples of a moving or living dune, one in the process of killing all vegetation in its path.

Visitors may use the beaches anywhere along Beverly Shores but must park in either of the two Lakeshore lots. The town strictly bans parking on its streets. Violators may have their cars towed.

Biking. Calumet Trail. A flat nine mile bicycle trail paralleling Rt. 12 from the Dune Acres railroad station to Mount Baldy. This trail has some rare wildflowers growing along its edges. A good place to hear the peepers in the spring. Visitors may also use the trail for jogging, hiking or, in the winter, snowshoeing or cross country skiing.

Beverly Shores roads also make for good biking. There are hills for the 10-speeders and flats for those who like to take it easier. Be sure to park cars in designated lots.

Boating. Visitors with boats can sail, fish, waterski, row and paddle a canoe in Lake Michigan waters abutting the Lakeshore beaches. The rules require all boats to stay 500 feet away from all marked swimming areas, even when beaching. Those with canoes can go up the Little Calumet River.

Cross Country Skiing. One of the most popular winter

activities in the Lakeshore. The Park Service maintains four trails:

Calumet Trail. Mineral Springs Road and Rt. 12 to Michigan City. Ideal for beginners.

Inland Marsh trail. On the south side of Rt. 12 across from Ogden Dunes. A three mile trail for advanced skiers traverses rolling terrain. Parking lot.

Ly-co-ki-we Trail. Rt.20 and 275E. This trail has four loops of increasing difficulty, one to five miles long. The well marked route shows blue, green and red trails for beginners; yellow for more advanced. The yellow trail also takes off from behind the Visitor Center.

Marquette Trail. Lake-Porter County Line Road to the Lake. This trail runs from West Beach to Grand Avenue. It follows the Long Lake wetland.

Visitors can rent cross country ski equipment at the Ly-co-ki-we trailhead. The concession trailer also has ski accessories for sale.

Fishing. The Park Service allows shore fishing outside all of its bathing beach areas and bank fishing along the Little Calumet River. It also permits fishing at the Heron Rookery, a restricted natural area located along the Little Calumet River. The rookery has only limited parking and special regulations apply. Visitors must register at the Visitor Center to fish there.

Hang Gliding. This sport which looks so beautiful from the ground makes use of the wind currents atop Mount Baldy. The colorful contraptions often glide for miles above the beach. Park Service permit required.

Hiking. The Lakeshore offers good hiking on trails, Ranger-led or on your own, on town roads in Beverly Shores, along the beaches and on the grounds of historical sites. Here is a partial list of hiking trails and what they offer:

Bailly/Chellberg. Between Rts. 12 and 20 from Babcock to Wagner. 2 trails. The 1 1/2 mile round trip includes the historical structures and grounds. The 2 1/2 mile trip includes the cemetery.

Calumet Dune. A 1/2 mile trail shows woods and older dune vegetation.

Cowles Bog. Trails 2-5 miles round trip. A variety of environments: bog, marsh, wooded dunes and beach. All trips

Ranger-led showing the bog itself from the vantage point of nearby interdunal ponds and woods. Call for schedule of hikes.

Mount Baldy. Rice Street just east of Beverly Shores. One of the Lakeshore's few remaining high moving dunes. Mount Baldy offers the visitor an opportunity to see trees buried in the sand and trees almost buried. Guided hikes begin from the parking lot. Check for dates and times.

Miller Woods trail. Trails 1-3 miles round trip. Open oak savannah and interdunal ponds together with pines and cottonwoods exemplify various stages in dunes succession. Call for schedule.

For an introduction to dunes hiking try the short paved trail behind the Visitor Center. This circles over forested dunes and is accessible to visitors in wheelchairs with assistance. The trail guide offers self-guided interpretation.

Horseback Riding. Ly-co-ki-we Trail. Rt.20. Bring your own horse.

Snowshoeing. One of the best ways to observe marshy areas too wet to traverse in warm weather.

SPECIAL EVENTS.

Duneland Dimensions. Visitor Center. Kemil Road (926-7561). Occasional Friday evenings. A series of programs featuring writers, artists, photographers and performers knowledgeable about the dunes and related subjects. Call for program schedule.

Duneland Folk Festival. Bailly Homestead grounds (926-7561). Parking on the Bailly grounds*. July. Music performances, craft demonstrations and pioneer foods for sale on the final Saturday and Sunday of this weeklong festival that on the other days takes place at the Westchester Public Libraries. Everything from how to make a dulcimer or shoe a horse, to sheepshearing and spinning. Many well known folk artists perform to the delight of the huge, enthusiastic crowds. Always a good time.

Maple Sugar Time. Chellberg Farm (926-7561). March. A program that recreates the maple sugar tradition begun by the Indians of the area. The whole process from tapping for sap to using the sugar shack and evaporator. Call for dates and times.

DUNE BIRD AND FLORA CALENDAR

BIRDS

FLORA

January

Ducks and gulls winter on Lake Michigan. Purple finches, redpolls, evening grosbeaks and pine siskins frequent evergreen woods.

This is an ideal time to identify trees by their individual shape, bark, leaf scars and buds.

February

Early courting of titmice and chickadees occurs all through the dunes. Owls mate.

Skunk cabbage matures throughout the swampy areas late in the month.

March

The early migrants arrive: robins, grackles, kinglets, geese and ducks.

Pussy willows blossom. A few early blooming hepaticas push up through the fallen leaves in all the oak woods, at Bailly and the Blue Heron rookery.

April

Sandhill cranes pass through early to mid-month. The last of the wintering birds, juncos and tree sparrows, head north while the early warblers arrive. Other sparrows begin to nest. The mating call and spiralling flight of the woodcock over a swale is an unforgettable experience.

Marsh marigolds bloom in swamps. Lyre leaf rock cress grows in open sandy locations. Trailing arbutus blossoms on northern dune slopes.

May

Peak warbler migration occurs early this month. Black bellied plovers and other shorebirds frequent the beaches. Ducks, and coots alight on small ponds. Marsh wrens and rails call. The cry of whippoorwills fills the evenings.

Trail 2 in the State Park has a splendid array of spring flowers: red and yellow columbine flower among the black oaks; masses of white trillium, spring beauty, bellwort, toothwort, douglas cress, red trillium, yellow violets, blue cohosh.

BIRDS   FLORA

June

The great blue herons, mallards, turkey vultures and teal nest. Male birds sing in their territories. Most migrants have gone on to their breeding grounds. The evening air fills with newly arrived nighthawks feeding on insects.

Throughout the dunes the lovely birdsfoot violet seems everywhere. In open areas late in the month thousands and thousands of lupine bloom at Inland Marsh. Blue phlox abounds in damp areas around the State Park.

July

The chirping of baby birds fills the woods. Mourning doves, ruby-throated hummingbirds, red-headed woodpeckers and house wrens tend their second brood. Male ducks molt their flight feathers to get new ones for their long journey south in the fall.

Puccoon blooms profusely. Many consider the prickly pear cactus the loveliest of the June flowers. The Philadelphia or wood lily blooms during the last two weeks of the month.

August

Sanderlings, yellowlegs and pectoral sandpipers are among the shorebirds southward bound. Goldfinches and warblers begin to change to winter plumage while ducks regain their bright colors.

In damp soil, find the Turk's cap lily. Arrowhead appears in ditches, prairie coreopsis on low open dunes and showy false indigo in meadows. See the greatest variety of ferns on Trail 2 in the State Park.

September

The peak migration of land birds now takes place. Ducks, geese, and other water birds begin moving south. On a clear day with a north wind, watch the hawks start southward from atop Mt. Baldy.

Blazing star covers many of the swales and meadows. Clumps of cardinal flower color wet areas; goldenrod, Joe Pye weed, false foxglove, ironweed, sunflower and boneset blossom everywhere.

45

BIRDS   FLORA

October

Lake Michigan and dune ponds provide stopping points for waterfowl migrants. Winter residents, the roughlegged hawks, redbreasted nuthatches, tree sparrows, purple finches and juncos, arrive in woods and fields.

Asters abound. In damp places fringed and soapwort gentians flower. The sour gum tree's leaves have turned a shiny, brilliant red.

November and December

The last of the migrants, red shouldered hawks, red winged blackbirds and grackles depart. Blue jays, cardinals, tufted titmice, chickadees, nuthatches, goldfinches, juncos and woodpeckers remain in woods and fields. A few mallards stay on the ponds. Mergansers, herring, and ring bill gulls frequent the beaches, harbors and lake. Often old squaws and buffleheads fly off the shore. In 1980, Indiana Dunes had 243 redheaded woodpeckers in the annual Christmas birdcount, more than in any count in the United States. In 1983, the number rose to 337.

The leaves of the sumacs, white oaks, sassafras, white ash and red maples set the dunes afire. When the leaves have gone, the witch hazel flowers.

Striking red clusters of berries may still persist on winterberry bushes in wet areas.

Immature Great Blue Heron.

Ferns and bearberry.

A demonstration of spinning at the Duneland Folk Festival.

Community Guide

PORTER COUNTY
(119,816 population)

Porter County's 419 square miles extend from the shores of Lake Michigan south to the Kankakee River and from LaPorte County on the east to Lake County on the west. Farming predominated during the county's first century. Gradually, however, scientists and conservationists recognized the value of its wild, sparsely populated dunelands. With its high sand hills, beautiful beaches, and unique flora, this northern section of Porter County has attracted artists and nature lovers for generations.

Corn, soybeans, and dairy herds occupy the rich farmland in the county's southern half. In the late 1950's, with the construction of new steel mills along the lake's edge, Porter became the fastest growing county in Indiana. Now for the first time, it has a predominantly urban population. The Bethlehem plant, which opened its doors in 1964, sprawls through several municipalities and parts of unincorporated Westchester Township. It still ranks as one of the newest and most modern steel making facilities in the country. The mill carries on every step in the manufacture of steel within its confines. Though the steel industry has suffered in recent years, Bethlehem has recently invested $120 million in the Burns Harbor plant to rebuild the coke ovens, open a new continuous heat treatment for sheet steel, and construct a new continuous slab caster.

Some believe that the nickname Hoosier originated in Por-

49

PORTER COUNTY

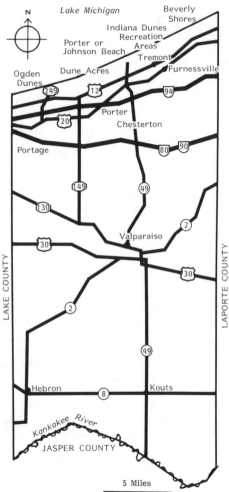

ter County. An old stagecoach stop called the Hoosier Inn, three miles west of Valparaiso, supposedly got its name from the contraction of "who's there" called out by an inarticulate or inebriated innkeeper.

BEVERLY SHORES
(864 population)

In the late 1920's a giant land speculation took place on the site of Beverly Shores. A well-known Chicago real estate developer, Frederick Bartlett, acquired the acreage and built eighty five miles of winding roads along Lake Michigan, around dunes, and through marsh lands. Special South Shore excursion trains brought thousands of Chicagoans to the area where fast-talking salesmen met, wined, dined and gave these eager investors the grand tour. Many turned over their savings, sure that they could make fortunes through this real estate gamble, only to lose everything in the Great Depression. Today, two thirds of the town has become part of the National Lakeshore and although park boosters have often included the remainder in park expansion proposals, it remains a private enclave.

Prior to the Bartlett era, large scale cranberry and blueberry farming took place in Beverly Shores. After World War II Chicagoans created a summer colony retreat so that today summer residents greatly outnumber full timers.

The town's meandering back roads give a good feel for dune country. They offer lovely views of the woods, dunes and marshland covered with wild vegetation, particularly beautiful in spring and fall. Bird and flower lovers can hike for miles in solitude, and in wintertime, see spectacular ice formations along the shore.

To See and Do

ARCHITECTURE.

Bartlett Houses. Spanish style white stucco with red tile roofs. Perched on Beverly Shores' highest dunes and the railroad station, Broadway and Rt. 12.

Lustron Houses. First prefabricated houses manufactured in the United States.

South side of Lake Front Drive west of Dunbar.

First house south of Lake Front Drive on State Park Road.

World's Fair Houses. Mr. Bartlett brought ten buildings from the 1933 World's Fair across Lake Michigan by barge as part of his promotional campaign. Six still stand and are worth seeing:

House of Tomorrow. Lake Front Drive west of Broadway.

Old North Church (minus its steeple). Beverly Drive west of Broadway.

Rostone House. North side of Lake Front Drive near Dunbar.

Armco-Ferrara House. Lake Front Drive one house west of the House of Tomorrow.

Florida Cypress House. Lake Front Drive one house east of the House of Tomorrow.

House of Seven Gables. Pearson.

ART AND ARTISTS.

Kevin Firme (874-4038). Sculptor.

David Tutwiler (879-5611). Gone in the summer. Paintings and lithographs. Uses local subjects with great skill; The Indiana Dunes National Lakeshore Visitor Center and the Save the Dunes Council Shop carry his work.

ENVIRONMENTAL CENTER.

Save the Dunes Council. Rt. 12 just west of Broadway (879-3937). Open daily, 10-4. Environmental center provides information about the Indiana Dunes National Lakeshore and environs. Volunteer run shop sells books, paintings, photos, pottery, and dunes related odds and ends.

RESTAURANT.

Red Lantern Inn. Lake Front Drive (874-6201).Winter, Tuesday-Saturday, 4-10; Sunday, noon-6:30. In summer, open Mondays as well. Bar. Beautiful lake view.

SPECIAL EVENT.

Fireman's Ball. Fire station, Broadway. On the Saturday night closest to the 4th of July. Dancing to every kind of music as long as it's loud. Food courtesy of the ladies' auxiliary. Cash bar. Raffle.

BURNS HARBOR
(920 population)

The newest community in Porter County, Burns Harbor, dates from 1967. It has a new town government complex. Local social events take place at the Westport Community Club. Part of Bethlehem Steel's Burns Harbor Plant is in the town.

To See and Do

Tour.

Bethlehem Steel Company, Rt. 12 (787-2120). Only specialized large group tours. Must provide own bus. Write well in advance to make arrangements.

CHESTERTON
(8,531 population)

In the beginning, Chesterton, alias Calumet, alias Coffee Creek, tried to rival Chicago. One hundred thirty years later, this "Gateway to the Dunes" still has the charm of another century.

Because some original settlers had the good sense to plant hundreds of maple trees, the Chesterton autumn blazes with New England color.

During the Civil War, the underground railroad had a stop in Chesterton. The town also hosted several shoot-outs when Chicago gangsters made it a favored haven.

For years Chesterton's big industry, the Hillstrom Organ Company, shipped instruments great distances, some as far as Africa. There little girls in an embroidery class run by missionaries, copied the designs painted on the organ and stitched them on their skirts. More than one little Nigerian flounced about with "Hillstrom Organ, Chesterton, Indiana" stitched on her bottom. The Bethlehem Lutheran Church,

135 Lincoln, still has a Hillstrom organ, now electrified, in its archives.

Railroad Park, now Thomas Centennial Park, celebrates Chesterton's early heyday as a rail center. The Michigan Central alone ran 24 trains through town each day. Farmers in the area, eager to have transportation for their crops, trundled cords of wood into town and loaded the park with four foot high piles in oder to stoke the engines. Chesterton's rail supremacy lasted long enough to snuff out rival settlements in the area. Today, freights, which tie up traffic at frequent and unpredictable hours, comprise the only trains that come trough.

Chesterton has a mixed population: old Scandinavian and German farm families, Irishmen who came to work the rails, steel workers employed in the nearby mills, and an increasing smattering of artists and professionals who just like the place.

To See and Do

AMUSEMENT PARK.

Enchanted Forest. Rt. 20 west of Rt. 49 (926-2161). Memorial Day-Labor Day, daily, noon-9:30. Rides, small zoo, picnic area.

ANTIQUES.

Carol's. 214 South Calumet (926-4757). Open daily, 10-4. Specializes in Orientals.

Five Gables Antiques. 500 South Calumet (926-7411). Freda and Bud Rice feature American country furniture and accoutrements. Tuesday-Sunday, 1-4:30.

Kathy's. 530 Indian Oaks Mall (926-1400). Monday-Saturday, 10-5; Sunday, 12-5.

Russ and Barb's Antiques. 222 Lincoln (926-4937). Sundays 12-5, Tuesday, Thursday, Saturday 10-5.

Second Hand Rose. 402 Grant (926-3894). Tuesday-Saturday, 11-4:30. Country furniture, glassware, and collectibles.

ARCHITECTURE.

Holmes-Brown Mansion. 700 West Porter. Now the administration center for the Duneland School Corporation, this red brick Victorian mansion was once owned by farmer Brown who supplied most of the wood for the Porter brick factory kilns. His home reflected his affluence with its high peaked roofs, stained glass fan light over the front door and a ballroom on the third floor.

Friday Farm. Friday Road. A beautiful old red brick farm house with handsome barn.

Mansion at Sand Creek Camp Ground. 1050N and 350W. This typical Hoosier dwelling of the Civil War era has a gabled rood, two stories with wings and a bull's eye window under its roof peak.

St. Patrick's Church. 312 West Indiana (1876). Graceful period building.

Weller House. 1200 North Road. Listed on the National Register of Historic Places.

ART AND ARTISTS.

Chesterton Art Gallery. 115 South 4th (926-4711). Tuesday-Sunday 1-4. Run by the Association of Artists and Craftsmen of Porter County (who also sponsor the Chesterton Art Fair) to exhibit members' work. New exhibits monthly. Demonstrations, programs, and classes.

Loretta Cohn (926-5813). Hand crafted wheel and coil pottery.

Evelyn Finnstrom (926-1343). Painter.

Judith Gregurich (926-5645). Works in stained glass.

Hannell Pottery. Furnessville Road (926-4568). A long drive through lovely woods leads to Hazel Hannell's good-sized pottery studio. Open daily except for winter months and supplied with a blackboard for messages when the owner is out.

Skip Hector (926-6030). Dunes photographer.

John Mullin (926-8937). Sculptor.

AUCTION.

Frye Auction Barn. Old Porter Road (926-2501 or 926-3500). Monday and Wednesday nights at 7:00.

GARDENS.

Mr. and Mrs. Sylvan Cook (926-4029). Call for appointment. A small but choice rose garden with many prize varieties. The Cooks are consulting rosarians of the American Rose Society.

Herbs and Wildflowers. 301 Indian Boundary (926-2218). Whether you're into pesto or poultices, Josephine Janowski has the right herb for you. She sells over 200 varieties of culinary, medicinal and aromatic herb plants from her extensive garden. Wildflower plantings for cultivation.

HISTORICAL COLLECTION.

Westchester Public Library, Chesterton Branch. 200 West Indiana (926-7696). Mini-archives of local treasures that will likely increase in size and importance.

RECREATION.

Boats-Charter. Jack's Gun Shop. Rt. 20 (787-8311).

Camping. Sand Creek Campground. 1000N, 350E (926-7482). Open all year. Picnicking, swimming, grocery store, playground, club house.

Sleigh Rides. Jeff Christiansen. 1081 North 400E (926-6918). Rides are given on his own property. Provides hot cocoa to group after ride. Has insurance.

RESTAURANT.

Wingfield's. 526 Indian Oak Mall (926-5152). Monday-Saturday, 11-10, Sunday 11-8. Decorated with unusual old photos of the dunes area. Casual dining, moderate prices. Bar. Occasional live music and fashion shows at lunch.

SHOPS.

Chesterton Feed and Garden Center. 400 Locust (926-2790). Items ranging from hamsters to horse feed to finest Holland bulbs.

Mrs. Walter Erickson. 450 Burdick (926-6866). Sells plants from a home filled with antiques.

Freight Station. 123 North 4th (926-6030). Tuesday-Saturday 10-5, Sunday, noon-5. Second hand books, art, pottery, a little of this and a little of that. Features work of local artists and artisans in refurbished N.Y. Central Railroad station. Picture framing.

Jeweled Gazebo. 132 South Calumet (926-2555). Tuesday-Friday, 9-5:30; Saturday, 9-5; Sunday, noon to 5. Fine jewelry with custom designed pieces available. Gifts.

Second Time Around Shop. One Block north of Rt. 20 on 200E (926-5555). Daily 10-4. Used clothing, glassware, and furniture.

Sleepy Hollow Leather. 145 Indian Boundary (926-1071). Ken Timm makes and repairs a variety of leather goods from hats to boots and slippers and much in between. Custom orders.

Yellow Brick Road. 762 Calumet (926-7048). Daily 9:30-5. Dolls, dolls, and more dolls.

SPECIAL EVENTS.

*Chesterton Art Fair.** St. Patrick's School grounds. 640 North Calumet. First weekend in August, 10-5. Now more than 25 years old, this gala, juried show displays every art and craft imaginable. Supervised painting for the kids. Hot meals and snacks available in the school. Call the Chamber of Commerce (926-5513) for dates.

Duneland Folk Festival. July. In conjunction with the Indiana Dunes National Lakeshore, the Westchester Public Lbrary, 200 West Indiana (926-7696) sponsors slide lecture programs on subjects of local historical interest.

Festival of the Dunes. Downtown. Last week in July. A potpourri of events—225 booths featuring art, crafts and food also bluegrass and jazz music—culminating in the crowning of Diana of the Dunes, the annual winner in a much trumpeted contest. Call Chamber of Commerce (926-5513) for information.

SPECIAL FACILITY.

Westchester Chamber of Commerce. 123 South Calumet (926-5513).

DUNE ACRES
(291 population)

Squeezed between the steel mills and Porter Beach stands the select little community of Dune Acres with its elegant homes nestled on and around high dunes. A private guard keeps the general public out. A mixture of commuters and weekenders, the community has its own club house, water system and fire department—the first in the area to get special training to fight brush fires. This town has a high regard for aesthetics and planning. Although Cowles Bog (see Indiana Dunes National Lakeshore section) is located adjacent to Dune Acres, the community has chosen to remain outside of the National Park.

FURNESSVILLE
(part of Chesterton)

Sandwiched between Tremont and Beverly Shores lies the tiny community settled by the Furness family in 1840. The family influence continues in local designations: Furnessville Road; the Furnessville blowout (a magnificent dune formation in the Indiana Dunes State Park); the charming little Furnessville Cemetery (where one can visit earlier generations of Furnesses as well as the Ways and the Teales of Edwin Way Teale literary fame); and the ramling white Furness mansion or Rt. 20 just west of Kemil Road.

To See and Do

SHOP.
   The Schoolhouse Shop. Furnessville Road (926-1875). Tuesday-Saturday, 9-5; Sunday, noon-5. A gift shop par excellence, started in an old red brick schoolhouse by two self-exiled Chicagoans, and now managed by their son. Over the years it has remained extensive and tasteful. The marvelous aroma comes from a mixture of sachets, candy sticks, elegant soaps, dried herbs, and absence of cigarette smoke. The store carries a line ranging from lemon drops to evening skirts, from butter molds to wrapping papers. Men's and women's clothing and much kitchen equipment.

JOHNSON'S BEACH or PORTER BEACH or WAVERLY BEACH
(part of Porter)

Johnson's Beach, north of Rt. 12 off Waverly Road has splendid high dunes, blowouts and clusters of houses, some year round, some very simple and summery. In 1917, dunes preservationists sponsored a gigantic outdoor pageant which attracted 50,000 spectators to this site. The eastern part of the area now belongs to the National Lakeshore while the western section, like Dune Acres which it abuts, remains out of the park.

Johnson's Beach got its name from a commercial fishing family who once had a thriving fishery where the Indiana Dunes State Park now stands. When the park officially opened in 1927, the Johnson brothers moved westward on the beach and opened an inn, a restaurant, and a fishery. Johnson boats went out daily and brought back perch, herring, and sturgeon. In the late 1950's the Johnsons sold out their interests and the fishery has now closed. Little remains save a town beach.

OGDEN DUNES
(1,489 population)

Since its founding in 1925, this strictly residential community has prohibited all commercial enterprises. Gary realtors developed the town and named it for Francis Ogden, original owner of the property. They rightly predicted the attraction of a suburban community in the dunes. Visitors can travel the Stagecoach Road, which begins on the south side of Rt. 12, just east of the town's entrance and meanders to Gary following the stagecoach route used more than a century ago.

Before the establishment of Ogden Dunes, Diana of the Dunes, a famous female hermit also known as Dune Hilda, made her home on the site. Diana, reputedly the daughter of a physician, came back to civilization only occasionally to peddle a wine she had brewed from the berries that covered the Dunes.

Built in 1927, an olympic-size ski jump once stood atop a high dune in town. Ogden Dunes boasts a Frank Lloyd Wright house, the first home on Cedar Trail north of Ogden Road. Later owners added the garage.

To See and Do

ART AND ARTISTS.

Charles Chesnul (762-5740). Pottery.

Lee Hibbs. Box 378, Ogden Dunes. Photography, water-color. Write for appointment.

Karyn Johnsen. Box 903, Ogden Dunes. Weaver. Write for appointment.

James Maples. (762-4397). Wood sculptor. Specializes in birds of the shore and estuary.

THE PINES
(962 population)

A forest of white pines once covered the land where the town of The Pines stands today, hence its name. Now a residential suburb of Michigan City, with businesses along Rts. 12 and 20, The Pines began as a subdivision platted in 1922. It incorporated as a town in the late 1940's. A stagecoach inn on the Chicago-Detroit run once stood at the bend in Rt. 12 where it intersects Woodlawn Avenue. At the turn of the century, Michigan City banker Chauncy Blair built a country mansion there. No trace of either building remains.

To See and Do

FLEA MARKET.

The Junk Shop. 3026 2nd Place (872-7485). Monday-Saturday. Extensive collection of treasures and trash for hard corps junkers.

SHOP.

Vernier China Co. 3986 West Rt. 20 (872-6605). Open daily. Large assortment of domestic and imported china, glassware and clocks.

PORTAGE
(27,409 population)

The three miles of Lake Michigan shoreline between Dune

Acres and Ogden Dunes house a large industrial and shipping complex which includes Bethlehem Steel's Burns Harbor plant, the Port of Indiana, the Midwest Steel plant, and Burns Ditch.

For years controversy raged over whether this portion of the Indiana Dunes should become a national park or a manufacturing complex. In 1966 passage of the bill authorizing the Indiana Dunes National Lakeshore resolved the issue. Congress simultaneously approved legislation providing federal funding for the construction of the Port of Indiana, a docking facility needed by the steel plants for their iron ore ships. This port gave Indiana its only public deep water harbor on Lake Michigan. It connects the state to world shipping via the Great Lakes-St. Lawrence Seaway route and to the inland water barge routes via the Grand Calumet River.

Portage incorporated as a town in 1958 and became a city in 1969. It includes within its boundaries the Port of Indiana, Midwest Steel and Burns Ditch, as well as a little of Bethlehem Steel's Burns Harbor plant. Previously, only farms and a few subdivisions dotted the area. Since Midwest began operations in 1957, Portage has continued to grow as a residential and commercial center. It boasts a number of boat launching facilities where the Little Calumet River empties into te lake.

To See and Do

ANTIQUES.
Portage Antiques. 2532 Portage Mall (763-4154). Monday-Friday, 10-5:30; Saturday, 10-4. Antique bisque dolls, handmade clothing imported from Europe.

Squirrel's Nest. Ingrid and Charles Curtiss, proprietors. 5674 Sand (762-7441). Call for appointment. Antiques and collectibles.

ARCHITECTURE.
Wolf Homestead. 450N and East Cleveland. A big red brick farmhouse built in 1885 by Josephus Wolf, then owner of the largest farm in Porter County.

ART AND ARTISTS.
Creek Bend Artworks. 5484 Central (762-7925). Monday-Saturday. Pottery.

RECREATION.

Boats-Marinas. Burns Harbor Marine. 1700 Marine (762-2304).

Lefty's Coho Landing. Rt. 12 (762-7761).

Dancing-Square. Square Jammers. YMCA Annex Garyton, 5341 Central (759-3118). First and third Saturdays, 7:30-10:30 p.m.

Woodland Park Promenaders. Woodland Park Pavillion, 2100 Willowcreek (762-5236 or 926-2778). Second and fourth Sundays, 7-10 p.m. through May.

Fishing. Public fishing permitted at the Port of Indiana docks. Call Indiana Dunes State Park (926-1390) for information.

Golf. Robbinhurst Golf Course. 1 mile west of Rt. 149, 1/2 mile north of Rt. 6 off McCool (762-9711). 18 holes and driving range.

Park. Woodland Park. 2100 Willow Creek (762-1675). Sixty acres, picnic facilities, swimming, ice skating, tennis, and nature area. Portage has five additional parks with varied programs and facilities. For program information call (763-play); for information about renting equipment call (762-1675).

SPECIAL EVENTS.

Annual $10,000 Big Fish Contest. July. Contact Chamber of Commerce (762-3300) for details.

Annual Grand Prix Jamboree. June. Portage's attempt to rival the Indianapolis 500. A 3/4 mile course which attracts upwards of 200 racing cars from the U.S. and Canada. Contact Chamber of Commerce (762-3300) for details.

SPECIAL FACILITY.

Chamber of Commerce. Portage Mall (762-3300) Monday-Friday, 9-5; Saturday 9-noon.

PORTER
(2,988 population)

Porter, a quiet little town, once had eight thriving brick yards, a booming rail traffic, and big dreams for its future. The brick-yards have gone; the trains have all but disappeared. However some fine old brick houses, all made from Porter brick, and a feudin' spirit with neighboring Chesterton still remain as remnants of better days.

To See and Do

ARCHITECTURE.

Augsburg Svenska Skola (1880). North side of Oakhill two miles west of Mineral Springs Road. This charming white shingled church seats only 30. The cemetery behind the building is believed to cover an Indian mound. View from road only. Private property.

Joseph Bailly Homestead. For description, see Indiana Dunes National Lakeshore section.

Beam House. 116 Wagner (1883.) Lovely Victorian house made of brick from the Porter yards.

Chellberg Farm. For description see Indiana Dunes National Lakeshore section.

The Porter House. 204 Lincoln (1875). This building housed the Columbia Lunch room, a restaurant and saloon popular with the Chicago racing crowd that came by train to play the ponies at the Mineral Springs Race Track, now long disappeared.

ART AND ARTISTS.

Ruth Bremner (926-6471). Watercolors.

Kate Brooks (926-6361). Acrylic paintings.

ARTISAN.

Lapidarist Jean Segal (926-1919) specializes in collecting, cutting and polishing rocks of all descriptions. Makes jewelry from local fossils. Call for appointment.

HISTORICAL SITE.

Porter Train Tower and Wreck (1894). From this tower railroaders control the switches and signals for the place where three railroads cross. On this site, in 1921, two passenger trains collided killing 37. Fifty one people escaped unharmed.

RECREATION.

Fishing. Access to the Little Calumet River for fishing and canoeing is available at Hawthorne Park and nearby Pratt Lake. Waverly Road south of Rt. 20 at Franklin. Call the Porter Town Hall (926-2771) for information.

RESTAURANT.

The Spa. Mineral Springs Road south of Rt. 20 (926-1654 or 762-8765). Monday-Thursday, lunch 11-3, dinner 5-10; Friday lunch 11-3, dinner 5-11; Saturday, dinner 5-11; Sunday, brunch 11-3, dinner 5-9. Bar. Jazz on Friday nights. This restaurant sits on the site of mineral springs that fleetingly held promise as a posh resort, race track, and baths. Now it offers good food in a beautiful setting overlooking the Little Calumet River. Diners can have fun watching birds and raccoons at feeders.

SHOP.

Saylor's Basket Place. 1300 West Rt. 20 (926-6740). Baskets of all descriptions, terra cotta pots and planters, birdbaths, and garden statuary.

TREMONT
(part of Chesterton)

Today this tiny settlement fronting on the Indiana Dunes State Park exists mainly as a flag stop on the South Shore Railroad. It has had more illustrious days. Father Marquette slept here on a sandy beach on his last trip. From 1845-1875 the region's social life centered in Tremont, then called New City West. Pioneers on their way to the Gold Rush and Pikes Peak stopped at its hostelries. The underground railroad made Tremont a leading station during the Civil War. The name comes from the three high dunes, Mt. Tom, Mt. Holden and Mt. Jackson, to the north in the State Park.

VALPARAISO
(22,247 population)

Briefly called Portersville, Valparaiso became the Porter

County seat in 1836, the same year the Indiana Legislature established the county. The town perches on the Valparaiso Moraine, a rolling land studded with glacial lakes and deep ravines, which an ancient glacier dumped as it began to melt and retreat north. Valpo, as everyone calls it, boasts fine white houses some more than a century old.

German Lutherans settled Valparaiso first and still predominate. However, the Spanish name, meaning Vale of Paradise, honors a local hero, Commodore David Porter, who did battle in Valparaiso, Chile during the War of 1812.

Rich farmlands surround the city, some of which produces the nation's largest crop of hybrid popcorn. Hi-tech industries contribute to Valparaiso's vitality and an industrial development commission monitors the town's industrial base. Once, the only School of Piano Tuning in America operated out of Valparaiso; it now boasts Valparaiso University and the Valparaiso Technical Institute.

To See and Do

ANTIQUES.

Marc T. Nielson Country Shop. Old Suman Road (462-9812). Monday-Friday. The route to the shop winds through the beautiful Suman Valley, named for Civil War General Isaac Suman. The facility simulates a medieval village including craft shops for upholstery work, cabinet-making and furniture building in the Tudor-style farm. Call for appointment to tour the craft enterprises. Virginia Phillips travels the world to buy the shop's stunning collection of English, continental and Oriental antiques.

Moulin Rouge Antiques. 39E-600N (462-0035). One mile west of Rt. 49 on Rt. 6. Two miles south on Campbell (Meridian Road). One fourth mile east on 600 North.

Potpourri. 302 East Jefferson (462-9920). Monday and Wednesday, 10-4; Friday, 10-4, 7-9 p.m.; Saturday, 11-3. As the name implies, everything from antiques and collectibles to just plain junk.

Uphaus Antique Shop. 349W-100S (462-2810). A choice line of antiques, furniture and dishes.

Architectural Tours.

Contact *Marcella Borcherding,* 502 Garfield (462-3474) or Dorcas Luecke, 603 Institute (464-1387). They have organized and conduct walking tours of historic Valparaiso homes.

Architecture.

Immanuel Lutheran Church. 308 North Washington. Listed on the National Register of Historic Places.

Heritage Hall. Campus Mall, South College Avenue. Listed on the National Register of Historic Places.

Porter County Jail and Sheriff's House. 153 Franklin. Now houses the Porter County Historical Museum. Listed on the National Register of Historic Places.

Joseph Robbins Home (1897). 800N and 800W. Built of Joliet stone and designed by a Tennesee architect thus accounting for its southern style.

Rose-Kuehl Home. 156 South Garfield (c. 1860). An octagonal white frame house with interesting gingerbread woodwork. Each of the eight sides has its own gabled roof.

Tratebas Mill (1856). Tratebas Road, east of Rt. 49. Restored by the Hopkins family as a home, this former grist mill, with its pond and dam, has retained much of its 19th century feeling.

Art and Artists.

Art Barn. 695N, 400E (462-9009). A center of creative living on 70 acres of beautiful rolling countryside. One hundred year old barn with five levels. Spacious rooms for art classes, parties, seminars. Art gallery selling work of local artists. Frame shop, photography studio. Overnight accommodations for up to ten students and seminar participants. Bring your own sleeping bag and towel.

Marjory Crawford (962-6224). Sculptor.

Marlies Glickauf (462-6657). Painter, sculptor.

Cheri Hill (464-1159). Potter.

Konrad Juestel Studio (462-2348). Call for appointment. This talented artist and print-maker restores antiques and fashions new furniture as well.

Deb Macke (464-2729). Weaver.

Russell Nelson (462-5854). Acrylic and watercolor paintings.

Kathy O'Neal (938-2936). Weaver.

Porter County Arts Commission. 74 Lincolnway (464-4080). Art Gallery. Exhibits, classes, studios, lectures, and demonstrations by, for and about local talent.

Sculpture. Courthouse Square, Titled "Caritas," the huge work by Valparaiso University Professor, Frederick Frey, resembles a metalic butterfly at rest. Although its name stands for charity and love, the work stimulated heated public controversy in the late 1970s.

Nancy Searles (462-7405). Weaver, dyer, spinner.

Harriet Rex Smith (462-4567). Painter, gives lessons and classes.

Bob Springsteen (462-8561). Weaver specializing in tapestries.

CEMETERY.

Quakerdom Cemetery. North side of Rt. 6, east of Jackson Center. Quaint old cemetery marking movement of the Quakers from Richmond, Indiana, into Illinois. Arriving here and learning of a battle between Indians and soldiers near Chicago, the Quakers settled down, built a school, a church, and eventually, this graveyard. Abolitionist Charles Osbourne's last remains rest here.

FARMS AND FARM PRODUCE.

Anderson Orchards. Rt. 6, east of Rt. 49 (464-4936). U-pick apples, pears, grapes. Also a lovely produce stand.

Farmers Markets. During summer and fall months farm markets take place on the courthouse square. Lincolnway.

GARDENS.

Ogden Gardens. Corner of Campbell and Harrison. An open garden which includes the Memorial Rose Garden completed in 1983. Future plans include establishment of perennial gardens and the planting of bulbs and wildflowers on various hillsides.

Mrs. Edith Podresky (462-3531). Call for an appointment. If Mrs. Podresky's garden is not in proper bloom, she will steer visitors to current bloomers. She is a consulting rosarian of the American Rose Society.

MOVIES.

County Seat Cinema I-VI. Rt. 49 north of town (462-1999).

MUSEUMS.

Porter County Historical Museum. 153 Franklin (464-8661). Located in the old jail building. Limited hours, call for times. An eclectic collection: mastodon bones excavated in the county in 1949, dresses from the Lincoln inaugural ball, guns, and many items from the Bailly Homestead.

Wilbur H. Cummings Museum of Electronics. Hershman Hall, Valparaiso Technical Institute, West Chestnut (462-2191). Electrical artifacts from early radios and telephones to those of today. Call for hours. Tours by appointment.

NATURE PRESERVE.

Moraine Nature Preserve. 750N one half mile east of Rt. 49. Owned by the Indiana Department of Natural Resources, open by permission only. Contact John Wolmer (464-4941). A fine example of the land forms associated with the Valparaiso Moraine, the result of ancient glaciation. This 263 acre tract contains rolling ridges, steep sidehills, muck pockets, pot holes and a shallow pond. Grassy fields or woodlands cover the uplands.

RECREATION.

Golf. Forest Park Golf Course*. West Harrison at Yellowstone (462-4411).

Mink Lake. Rt. 49 south of Rt. 6.(462-2585). 9 holes.

Horseback Riding. Timberlake Farm. 3354 South Rt. 2 (464-7796).

Lakes. Lake Eliza.* Five miles west and three miles south of Valparaiso on Rt. 30 (462-1935). April-December. Camping, swimming with large water slide, fishing, boat rental.

*Loomis Lake.** Two and a half miles north on Burlington Beach Road off Rt. 49 in Rogers-Lakewood Park (462-5144). Swimming, fishing, picnicking, boat rental, launching ramp.

Parks. Sunset Hill Farm. Corner of Meridian and Rt. 6. The

Murray family donated its old farm to create Porter County's first county park. Will open fall, 1985.

Rogers-Lakewood Park (*weekends). One mile north of Valparaiso on Campbell east of Rt. 49(462-5144). A variety of summer activities and facilities: picnic shelters, swimming, boating, hiking. Boat Rental, paddle boat, fishing supplies and bait, food stand. Swim lessons also available. Campgrounds with full facilities two week maximum stay. Call for full program details.

Skiing. The Pines. 674 North Meridian (462-4179). Monday-Friday, noon to 10; Saturday, 10-10; Sunday, 10-5. Seven slopes—two beginner, four intermediate, and one advanced. Chair lift, five rope tows, and three borer lifts to get to the top of the hills. The chalet has two ski shops, a snack bar and the Midwest's largest artificial ski ramp. Snow making machines for mild winters.

RELIGIOUS SITE.

Seven Dolors Shrine (Our Lady of the Seven Sorrows). South on 700N from Rt. 149 (759-2521). Daily until Dusk. 100 acre site includes rock formations, gardens, outdoor grotto, stations of the cross, three story monastery. Established in 1931 under the auspices of an American-Czech branch of Orders of Friars Minor and now operated by the Franciscans. Gift shop, picnic facilities.

RESTAURANTS.

China House. 120 East Lincolnway (462-5788). Tuesday-Sunday, 11:30. A wide variety of Chinese cooking styles and dishes in modest surroundings.

Court. 69 Franklin (462-2141). Monday-Saturday, 11-10. Bar. In old courthouse complete with jail cell booth. Live entertainment.

Golden Dragon. 1706 LaPorte (462-3003). Closed Monday. Sunday buffet, 11:30-2. Take out. Chinese owned and managed, this newcomer specializes in Szechwan and Mandarin delicacies. Modestly priced.

Old Style Inn. 5 Lincolnway (462-5600). Daily, 11-11. Across from Courthouse. Busy at lunch. Salad bar. Prime rib special Wednesday and Saturday nights makes reservations useful.

Strongbow Turkey Inn. Rt. 30 east of town (462-3311). Daily, except Tuesday from 11:00. Any part of the gobbler cooked in every fashion: soup, salad, pies, sandwiches and roasted, as well as other items. Practically an institution which once raised its own birds but, more's the pity, no longer does so.

Vale of Paradise Delicatessen. 64 West Lincolnway (462-7242). Daily, 10-10; Sunday, noon-10. Cafeteria style soups, salads, and made to order deli sandwiches. Paper plates and student ambience.

The White House. 303 Jefferson (464-9515). Weekdays, lunch 11-2; dinner 5-10; Sunday buffet, 11-2 and 5-8. The Pappas family has turned a 19th century mansion, originally built by Henry B. Brown, founder of Valparaiso University, into an elegant, though sometimes pretentious, restaurant. The grounds include a formal garden complete with reflecting pool and statuary. The dining rooms feature tasteful antiques. Eclectic cuisine combines continental, Greek and Valparaiso food. Good wine list. Rathskeller below offers informal atmosphere, casual dress, and lower prices. Excellent Sunday brunch buffet.

SHOPS.

The Artist's Den. 203 Jefferson (462-3883). Art supplies, gallery, framing.

Coffee and Tea Market. 108 East Lincolnway (462-7265). Largest selection of loose teas and coffee beans in northwest Indiana together with an assortment of equipment for preparing any favorite brew. Also bulk herbs and spices plus gourmet sweets. Try a cup of something special and a slice of rich dessert at a couple of tables tucked in the back.

Fetla's. 1475 South Rt.2 (462-5221). Huge discount center trading in just about everything and more of it than anywhere else.

Hans and Fritz Antique Clocks. 9 North Washington (464-2010). Fine collection of antique clocks purchased in Europe. Wide price range. Arranges for repairs.

McMahan Seed Company. 6 North Michigan (462-1411). Complete line of garden supplies. Seed from drawers by ounce, pound, or envelope.

Marrell's Gift Shop. 1004 Calumet (464-3585). Art, jewelry, imported merchandise often of the one-of-a-kind variety.

SPECIAL EVENTS.

The Art Event. Courthouse Plaza. First weekend in June. Sponsored by the Porter County Arts Commission. 100 exhibitors and special attractions. Call the commission (464-4080) for details.

Popcorn Festival. September. Annual occurrence sponsored by the Valparaiso Chamber of Commerce to immortalize Orville Redenbacher's Valpo connection. A day long fest with ten days of pre and post festival events: fun run, talent show, art contest, racquetball tournament, cutest baby contest and a host of similar hoopla. Check with the Chamber (462-1105) for dates and full schedule of activities.

Porter County Fair. Old Porter County Fair Grounds, Evans and Indiana adjoining Rt. 49. for the last time in 1984. First week in August. Starting in 1985 it will move to new grounds, 215 East Division Road (464-8661) and initiate the Porter County Exposition Center, a multi purpose exhibition and entertainment facility. Rides, agricultural and livestock exhibits—prize lambs, hams and jams, as well as a taste of the old carnival midway.

THEATER.

Memorial Opera House. On Indiana at Franklin southeast of courthouse (464-1636). A century ago, this building commemorated the community's Civil War dead. It joined only 11 others like it in the country bringing renowned performers to the area. Now refurbished, the building houses the Community Theater Guild which sponsors amateur productions year round. Worth seeing for the architecture and the theatricals.

UNIVERSITY CAMPUS.

Valparaiso University, 651 College (462-5111). The University has graduate schools of nursing and law as well as an undergraduate college. Its interesting history began in 1859 under Methodist auspices. In the 1870s, non-sectarians bought the school which became known as the "Poor Man's Harvard." It almost passed into the hands of the Ku Klux Klan in 1923 but, fortunately, the Lutheran Church purchased it instead. The campus houses the world's largest college church, the Chapel of the Resurrection, a striking structure well worth a visit. Handsome, ultra-modern and enhanced by stunning mosaics and stained glass, the chapel boasts an acoustical system sensitive enough to carry whispers from the altar to the rear of the building.

The University sponsors good musical events; the Sloan Art Gallery is located in the library basement.

SPECIAL FACILITIES.

Chamber of Commerce. 601 East Lincolnway (462-1105).

Porter County Municipal Airport. East of Rt. 30 on 100N (462-6508). Three a day scheduled flights to O'Hare and Meigs Fields via Joe Phillips Air Line. Charter flights.

Porter Memorial Hospital. 814 LaPorte (464-8611).

LAKE COUNTY
(522,965 population)

In the past Lake County's northern tier, the Calumet Region, earned the title of America's Ruhr Valley. One of the world's great industrial centers, its plants produced vast amounts of steel, oil, petro-chemicals, cement, soap and thousands of related products in a narrow strip along Lake Michigan from the Illinois border east through Gary. Today that pattern is changing as the American economy shifts from an emphasis on heavy industry to service enterprises. Many of the Calumet Region's plants have shut down or moved to the Sun Belt.

While the cities of the northern Lake County have lost residents, suburban communities that ring the Calumet Region—Highland, Munster, Griffith, Merrillville, and Schererville—have grown. Both white flight and escape from the ugliness and pollution of the older industrial communities resulted in a massive shift of population during the 1960's and 1970's.

Southward of Lake County's suburbia, a rolling farm belt

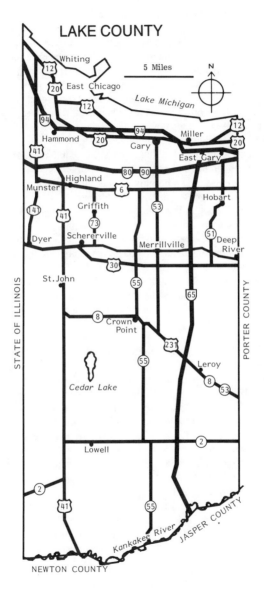

LAKE COUNTY

Whiting

12

East Chicago

20

5 Miles

N

12

Lake Michigan

94

12

Hammond

20

94

Miller

20

41

Gary

East Gary

80 90

Highland

Munster

6

Hobart

141

Griffith

53

41

73

51

Dyer

Schererville

Merrillville

Deep River

30

St.John

55

65

8

Crown Point

231

Leroy

55

8 53

Cedar Lake

STATE OF ILLINOIS

PORTER COUNTY

Lowell

2

2

41

55

Kankakee River

JASPER COUNTY

NEWTON COUNTY

73

still remains, much of its land reclaimed at the turn of the century from the Kankakee River marshland. The Kankakee River itself forms the county's southern border. Small lakes and river resorts offer traces of the days when the marshlands provided a paradise for hunters and fishermen.

Industrial growth and population expansion dominated Lake County's twentieth century history. The French voyageurs in the 1600's saw only swamps and swales. They named the two rivers flowing through the county the Little and Grand Calumet after the tiny marsh reed which the Indians used as the stems of their peace pipes. Indians roamed the entire terrain, using the Kankakee as their river highway to the Mississippi and hunting and berrying in the vicinity of what is now Dyer, Merrillville and Hobart. They built many of their villages on the high ground between the Kankakee and Calumet marshes.

The pioneer settlers, who, in 1837, founded Lake County, the last of Indiana's northern counties, discovered that they could not farm much of its 513 square miles. The dunes along Lake Michigan made travel southward difficult and the marshes proved impassable most of the year. It took travellers six days to brave the lake's icy winter blasts and the rough sand trails in order to reach Chicago from Michigan City—a distance of 60 miles.

Yet Lake County's proximity to the expanding industrialization of South Chicago made growth inevitable. The county's attractions included the potent combination of cheap, available land, excellent rail transportation, a free supply of water from Lake Michigan and a shoreline available for dredging to build harbors or for filling to create additional low cost acreage. The development of Whiting by Standard Oil in 1889, followed by Inland Steel's opening in East Chicago in the next decade, climaxed by United Steel's creation of Gary in 1905, led to Lake County's transformation by men and machines.

A melting pot of ethnic groups, with large Black and Mexican populations, Lake County seems an anamoly to most Hoosiers. Its people and lifestyles differ vastly from Indiana's norm, so much so that to this day Lake County gets short shrift in the State Legislature.

CEDAR LAKE
(8,754 population)

The glamour days of Cedar Lake, once a lively resort town, began when the Monon Railroad carried Chicagoans by the train load out there for a day in the country. Hotels began to prosper in the 1890's and became known for their chicken dinners on Sunday. Guests included honeymooners, convalescents, hunters, fishermen and even Mrs. Charles Walgreen of drug store fame and fortune (who arrived in her private plane). A thriving ice industry also existed. Day and night throughout the winer Chicago skid-rowers, their feet wrapped in gunny sacks, cut huge ice cakes from the lake to supply Windy City meat packers.

Cedar Lake's heyday ended with the 1929 depression. Today summer cottages from this era still stand, perched crazily close to one another around the two mile lake. Some motels, tenting facilities and trailer courts also operate. Thousands still flock to Cedar Lake on summer weekends to enjoy boating, swimming and fishing. On Saturday evenings during July and August, they can listen to sacred music at the Torrey Auditorium of the Cedar Lake Bible Center on 137th Street. The concerts take place on the site of the old Monon Park.

To See and Do

ANTIQUES.
   Bobin's Antiques. 10820 Wicker (365-5320). Eight rooms of stock.

ARCHITECTURE.
   Lassen Hotel. 7808 West 138th Place. Listed on the National Register of Historic Places. Now being transformed into the Lake of the Red Cedars Museum, a depository for the community's historic memorabilia.

ART AND ARTISTS.
   Sandra Kozlowski (769-1606). Acrylic painting, drawing and lithography.

CEMETERY.

Indian Mound Cemetery. Meyer Manor subdivision, Lake Shore Drive to Marquette Street, south on Marquette. Tombstones of early settlers supposedly on site of Indian burial grounds.

FLEA MARKET.

Barn & Field Flea Market. 9600 West 151st (696-7368). Friday-Sunday, 9-5. In the barn only during the winter; many additional booths outside during the rest of the year. A great place for those who like to rummage.

MUSIC.

After Four Supper Club. 13109 Wicker (374-7636). Jazz on Friday nights. Also jazz brunch on second Sunday of the month.

RECREATION.

Boats-Launching Area. Public ramp. Cline and Lake Shore Drive.

Boats-Marina. Pinecrest Marina. 14415 Lauerman (374-5771). March 1-November 15. Swimming, fishing, picnicking, boat rental, water sports.

Boats-Rentals. Chuck's Pier. 13947 Huseman (374-9832). Also fishing.

Tulip Harbor. 14611 Lauerman (374-6666).

Dancing. Midway Ballroom. 13130 Lake Shore Drive (374-9667). Nightly, country western music. A dance floor built out over Cedar Lake.

Fishing. Public fishing site. Corner of Cline and Lake Shore Drive. Perch, blue gill, crappies and bass.

Golf. Monastery Golf Club. 9728 West 129th (374-7750). April 1-October 15. 18 holes.

South Shore Country Club. 14400 Lake Shore Drive (374-6070). April 1-inclement weather. 18 holes.

Horseback Riding. Willowdale Stables. 12808 Wicker (374-9875).

PARK.

Lemon Lake County Park. 6322 West 133rd (663-

7627). Daily, Memorial Day-Labor Day, 7 a.m.-10 p.m.; rest of the year. 7 a.m.-dusk. 290 acres in lovely rolling country with picnic shelters and hiking facilities. Jogging, physical fitness and handicapped trails, lighted ice-skating rink, dawn to 9 p.m.; lighted tennis and basketball courts, 7 a.m. to dusk; arboretum, paddleboats, put and take fishing lake, cross country skiing and tubeing with equipment rental,food for sale during summer months, group hayrides, volleyball and other equipment rental, soccer and football fields. Parking.

RELIGIOUS SITE.
   Franciscan Retreat. Lake Shore Drive to Parrish, north one mile on Parrish (374-5741). Stations of the Cross. A lake with a rosary of stones and flowers built around it. Picnicking permitted.

RESTAURANTS.
   Dick's Tap. Rts. 8 & 41 (365-5041). 4-midnight. No reservations taken. Fish on Friday. Bar.
   Heritage. 13242 Wicker (374-6200). Daily, 7 a.m.-1 a.m. Bar.
   Tobe's Steak House. 7301 West 138th (374-9805). Monday-Saturday, 5-10. Bar.

SHOP.
   Artists Den. 200 Jefferson (462-3883). Gifts.

SPECIAL FACILITY.
   Chamber of Commerce. 9742 West 133rd (374-6157).

CROWN POINT
(16,455 population)

Crown Point celebrates its centennial year in 1984. The oldest settlement in Lake County, it also serves as the county seat and as a bedroom community for the industrial cities to the north.

Solon Robinson, its founder, came from New England by oxdrawn cart and pushed on to Lake County in 1837 because he found LaPorte too crowded for his taste. He wrote home urging all his friends to join him. They came in droves, and to make sure they didn't lose their way he left signs posted for them along the route. Eventually he earned the nickname of the squatter king because he led a rebellion against speculators who tried to steal the homesteaders' land.

Crown Point became the county seat despite competition from the communities of Liverpool, Deep River and Cedar Lake. Later when Hammond suggested that the courthouse at Crown Point be converted to an insane asylum, an irate Crown Pointer replied, "When that happens, its first inmate will be the Hammond crank who suggested it".

From 1916 to 1941 Crown Point enjoyed widespread notoriety as the Gretna Green of the Midwest. "Marrying justices" performed instant marriages for thousands including such celebrities as Rudolph Valentino, Colleen Moore, Red Grange and Joe DiMaggio. The community received reams of publicity when John Dillinger escaped from a Crown Point jail.

Today visitors will find a pleasant residential town ringed by rich farmland. A handsome old court house now in the the process of restoration dominates the downtown. Northward a few miles on Rt. 55 a modern county government complex rises from the flat landscape but lacks the charm of its predecessor.

To See and Do

ANTIQUES.

Court House Square Antiques. Lake County Court House basement (663-7670). English and American antiques and art.

Crowntique. 146 North Main (663-9049). Fine antiques and estate jewelry.

Dan's. 8703 East 109th (663-4571). Excellent selection of furniture and dishes.

Liberty Antiques. 2125 South Main (663-9191). Coins, pinball and slot machines.

Main Street Antiques. 930 North Main (663-6547).

Tudor House Antique and Corner Cupboard. Lake County Court House basement (663-1309).

Don't miss the annual antique show sponsored by the Eisenhower Elementary School PTA. 1450 South Main (663-

8800). On a May weekend every spring. Call the school for dates and times. One of the best in the area with a large number of dealers exhibiting superior merchandise.

ARCHITECTURE.

Old Lake County Court House (1879). Main and Joliet, at the center of downtown. Monday-Saturday, 10-5; Sunday, 1-5. Combines the Georgian and Romanesque styles of the Victorian era. Listed on the National Register of Historic Places. From its steps William Jennings Bryan spoke. The structure, preserved when a new county courthouse opened in 1979, now houses a museum on the first floor and a potpourri of shops in the basement. Restoration of the building continues.

Ye Old Homestead (1843). 227 South Court (663-0456 or 663-0590). Call for an appointment. A charming, well preserved Greek revival style house. Notice the hand wrought hinges, hardwood floors imported from Chicago, and the clapboard siding, an innovation of that period replacing the usual logs. Completely furnished with mid-nineteenth century antiques.

ART AND ARTISTS.

Weaver's Way. 306 East Goldsboro (663-1406).

Gallery Ltd. 400 North Main (663-3610). Tuesday-Saturday, 10-5. Art in all media.

CEMETERY.

Civil War burial grounds. I-65 to Rt. 8. East on Rt. 8 to Iowa, south on Iowa three miles to large grove of trees.

FARMS AND FARM PRODUCE.

Rinkenberger Farm. 5320 East 109th (663-5019). Pick your own vegetables, all varieties.

HISTORIC SITE.

Solon Robinson Memorial. Joliet and Court.

MOVIE.

Crown Theatre. 19 North Court (663-1616). Daily, 8 p.m.

RECREATION.

Bikeway. Crown Point has two signed routes: the central

bikeway passes by Thomas Street and North Street parks; the south bikeway follows tree-lined streets by Wells Street park, Sauerman's Woods and Hub Pool. Obtain a map from the Northwest Indiana Regional Planning Commission (923-1080).

Golf. Oak Knoll Golf Course. Rt. 8, west of Crown Point (663-3349). Open year round.

Pheasant Valley Golf Course. 3834 West 141st (663-5000). March 1-first snow. 18 holes.

Ringo's Golf Center. 7611 East Lincoln Highway (942-8929). 9 holes.

Summertree Golf Club. 2323 East 101st (663-0800). 18 holes.

Horseback Riding. Carriage Gate Equestrian Training Center. 14516 Reeder (663-2615).

L. Fox Saddle Horses. 4612 East 109th (663-3222). Also hayrides, sleigh rides, camp fires, English riding lessons, indoor arena.

Stock and Drag Car Racing. Illiana Speedway. 7211 West Lincoln Highway (322-5311). Friday and Saturday nights. Also midget car racing.

RELIGIOUS SITE.

Hyles-Anderson College. 8400 Burr, one-half mile south of Rt. 30 (769-4901). The chapel has beautiful stained glass windows with clear glass insets which permit sunshine to flood the church. The mosaics depict branches and leaves making one feel an integral part of the natural world.

RESTAURANTS.

Bon Appetit. 302 South Main (663-6363). Tuesday-Saturday, from 5:30 p.m. with prix fixee dinners, 5:30-7 p.m.; Sunday brunch, 11:30 a.m.-2:30 p.m. Memorial Day-Labor Day, lunch, 11:30 a.m.-1:30 p.m. in outdoor garden. Superior country French food in an elegant Victorian home. Bar. Expensive but worth it. Reservations recommended.

Lighthouse South Restaurant. 101 South Courthouse Square (663-7141). Monday-Thursday, 11-11; Friday and Saturday, 11-midnight. Bar.

S.O.B's Speakeasy. 211 South East (763-SOBS or 663-

1939). Monday-Saturday, 11 a.m.-3 a.m. Located in the old County Jail. Dine in a prison cell if you can give the password. Dancing. Bar.

SHOPS.

County Court House shops. 21 emporia of various kinds in the basement of the court house. Monday-Thursday, Saturday, 10-5; Friday, 10-8. Gifts, books, records, stationery, jig saw puzzles and other wares available.

SPECIAL EVENTS.

Lake County Fair. Fairgrounds, South Court and West Greenwood (663-0428). Third week in August. One of the oldest and best fairs in Indiana with aquatic shows, horse and dog races, farm exhibits and crafts. The fairgrounds surround Fancher Lake; the Milroy Covered Bridge also located here. Before and after the fair, this 80 acre site has fine recreational facilities with swimming, fishing, picnicking, camping and ice skating in season.

Festival Days. Downtown Crown Point. First week in July. Art and crafts displays, antique show, flea market, rib and corn roast on the square, outdoor concerts, pet and doll parades, luncheon and style show.

SPECIAL FACILITIES.

Chamber of Commerce. 154 West Joliet (663-1800).

St. Anthony's Hospital. Main and Franciscan (738-2100).

DEEP RIVER
(included in Hobart's population)

History comes alive at Deep River. Here the Lake County Park Department has restored one of the first mills in Lake County and also provided recreational facilities in a setting of great natural beauty along the banks of the Deep River. To reach the park take Rt. 51 (Grand Boulevard) north from Rt. 30 and turn east at the first stop sign, onto County Road 330 for 1.8 miles.

In 1835, John Wood came from Massachusetts and laid out this town around a typical New England common. A marker in front of the common, placed there by his descendents, proclaims his honesty, morality, temperance and liberal religion.

To See and Do

ARCHITECTURE.

A number of fine, well-kept, century old homes line County Road 330.

CEMETERY.

Woodale Cemetery. County Road 330 (738-2020). May-October. John Woods established this cemetery in l836.

MILL.

John Wood's Grist Mill*. County Road 330 (769-9030). In Deep River County Park. Daily, May-October, 9-5. Restored to its 1838 appearance with turn of the century furnishings and country store. On Sunday afternoons, local craftsmen demonstrate past life styles. Other programs include quilting workshops; maple syrup processing in March; apple butter making and apple cider pressing. Corn meal ground at site for sale. Listed on the National Register of Historic Places.

RECREATION.

Park. Deep River County Park. County Road 330 (769-9030). 200 acres. Interpretive nature center, picnic shelters, nature trails, cross country skiing trails with equipment rental available; bridle trails, food for sale on weekends in summer; canoeing with rentals available in April and May; hayrides for groups; jogging trails; softball, volleyball, frisbee, soccer and other recreation equipment available for rental.

SPECIAL EVENTS.

Wood's Mill Faire*. Deep River County Park (769-PARK). Second weekend in September. Juried arts and crafts show. Apple butter-making demonstration.

DYER-ST. JOHN AREA
(13,529 population)

The last town in Indiana before the Illinois border, Dyer 's location marks the point where the Sauk Trail crossed the state line. Nearby St. John derives its name from John Hack, the town's first German settler, who built northwest Indiana's first Catholic church there in 1843.

This is Indiana's horse country. The rolling, rustic land in the Dyer-St. John area and its proximity to Chicago has attracted horse enthusiasts, who, in turn, have established a number of stables that board, buy, rent, sell, groom or stud. Some have indoor arenas. During the summer, horse shows take place every weekend. Bridle paths abound and individual stables have their own fields and woods. Riding or driving through the countryside is especially lovely in spring and fall.

Note the marker on the south side of Rt. 30, which calls attention to the continental watershed. At this point the water on the south side of the street drains towards the Kankakee and Mississippi Rivers and then on to the Gulf of Mexico. On the north side, it drains into the Great Lakes, the St.Lawrence River and finally on to the Atlantic Ocean.

To See and Do

ARCHITECTURE.

Pioneer Church (1843). 9400 Wicker. On the grounds of St. John Church. Built of logs by German Catholic settlers and donated to the Bishop of Vincennnes. First church in Lake County.

RECREATION.

Golf. Lake Hills Golf and Country Club. 1001 West 85th, St. John (365-8601). Open year round. 27 holes.

Palmira Golf and Country Club. 12111 West 109th, St. John (365-4331). 18 holes.

Horseback Riding. Sladich Tumbleweed Ranch. 9223 Sheffield, Dyer (365-8003).

SHOPS.
Holly Wreath. 1562 Joliet, Dyer (322-2500). Nice gift shop.

SPECIAL FACILITY.
Our Lady of Mercy Hospital. Lincoln Highway (865-2141).

EAST CHICAGO
(39,786 population)

Indiana's steel industry began in East Chicago. In 1901, based upon an offer of 50 acres of free land bordering Lake Michigan, the Inland Steel Company agreed to build a plant on the site. To this day Inland remains a mainstay of East Chicago's economy. (To get a closeup view of this giant steel mill in operation, drive along the northern section of Rt. 912 (Cline Avenue), a new elevated roadway, which borders the plant.)

Pioneers avoided East Chicago's locale with its dunes and marshlands in their trek westward. However civil engineer George Clark, realized that the location had great potential and acquired a vast holding through tax sales and the purchase of land grants. His heirs operated a sawmill which provided much of the lumber used to rebuild Chicago after its disastrous fire in 1871.

In early days of the twentieth century, English bankers and American promoters, who had purchased most of the Clark estate, joined forces as the East Chicago Company to develop their holdings. They chose the name East Chicago to associate their property with then booming South Chicago. These entrepreneurs conceived and executed a grand plan. They constructed a harbor on Lake Michigan, appropriately naming it Indiana Harbor, as well as a mile long canal to connect it with the Grand Calumet River which flows through the city. The canal runs inland to the "forks" where large public wharves now stand. The Indiana Harbor Belt Railroad connects all the railroads crossing through the area with the Canal's docking facilities.

Today East Chicago's 11 square miles contain not only

scores of heavy industial sites including the Jones and Laughlin steel plant but also residential sections for a diverse ethnic and racial mix. The descendents of early mill workers, Croatians, Poles, and Turks, still live here as do newer Mexicans and Black inhabitants. A free municipal bus service link the city's two distinct sections, East Chicago and Indiana Harbor.

To See and Do

ARCHITECTURE.

Marktown Historic District. Bounded by Pine, Riley, Dickey and 129th. A model community for steel workers built in 1917. Designed by the architect Howard Van Doren Shaw. Noted for the variety of housing types within a unified architectural plan. Listed on the National Register of Historic Places.

Riley Bank. Chicago and Indianapolis. John Dillinger's robbery of this bank landed him in the Crown Point jail. Wonderful old ornate interior.

ART AND ARTISTS.

Mural in Baring Branch of East Chicago Public Library. Chicago and Baring (397-2453). Created as a WPA arts project, it was exhibited at the Chicago Century of Progress in l934.

The Gallery. 5005 Indianapolis (398-6100).

HISTORIC SITE.

3201 Watting. Site of first blast furnace in northwest Indiana.

RECREATION.

Golf. MacArthur Golf Course, Tod Park, 142 Hemlock (398-4200, ext. 264). April 15-October 15. 9 holes.

Parks. Jeorse Park. Aldis (392-8320). 35 acres. Beach on Lake Michigan has bathhouse adapted for use by handicapped. Lifeguards, city owned marina, public boat ramp, emergency overnight moorage, fishing pier, picnicking. The Inland Steel plant serves as a backdrop for this park.

Washington Park. 141st and Grand (392-8320). Conservatory with an especially nice Easter flower show. Ice-skating, tennis.

Restaurants.

Casa Blanca. 4616 Indianapolis (397-4151). Monday-Friday, 9-10; Saturday-Sunday, 11-10. Large restaurant serving Mexican food with authentic Mexican ambiance and decor. Bar.

El Tapatio. 4020 Main (398-6992). Daily, 8-10. Small replica of a meson tipico with good food. Bar.

Jockey Club. 4624 Magoun (398-2353). Located in Elks Building. Monday-Friday, 11-3; Saturday, 5-3. Bar. Weekend entertainment. A fixture of East Chicago dating back to the saloon era.

Kay and Danny's Greenhouse. 1208 Carroll (398-1010). Lunch, Monday-Friday, 1-4; dinner, Wednesday-Friday, 5-?; Saturday, 6-?. Bar.

Puntillo. 4905 Indianapolis (397-4952). Daily, 8 a.m.-2 a.m. Bar.

The Cotton Lounge. 502 West 151st (397-8411 or 397-1585). Lunch, Monday-Thursday, 11-4; Friday 11-5. Dinner, Friday only, 5-9:30. Bar. Polish dishes.

Shops.

Supermerecado del Puebla. 4610 Indianapolis. (Next door to Casa Blanca restaurant.) Monday-Saturday, 8-9. Sunday, 8-6. Full line of Mexican foods, bakery.

Supermercados Mexico. 4022 Main (398-6900 or 278-2638). (Next to El Tapatio restaurant.) Daily, 8-10. Huge selection of foods. Delicious fresh baked pastries.

Special Events.

Farmers Market. Main Street, Indiana Harbor. Fridays and Saturday mornings during July and August.

Harborfest. Downtown in East Chicago. Street festival, music, dancing, arts and crafts, food booths. Call Mayor's Office (392-8200) for exact date and times.

Mexican Independence Day. Early September. Parade, dancing, booths, food. For details call Chamber of Commerce (398-1600).

Puerto Rican Constitution Celebration Day. July 25.

Coronation, parade, festival. For details, call Mexican Chamber of Commerce, 3516 Main (397-5607).

SPECIAL FACILITIES.

Chamber of Commerce. 2001 East Columbus (398-1600).

St. Catherine Hospital. 4321 Fir (392-1700).

GARY
(151,953 population)

Long before planners promoted the concept of new towns, the city of Gary emerged from the transformation of 12,000 acres of sand hills and swamp. The United States Steel Corporation chose this location on the southern shore of Lake Michigan midway between the Minnesota ore fields and the southern coal mines to build the world's largest steel mill of that era as well as a community to house the workers and service their needs.

Construction began in 1906; 36 months and a $100,000,000 later, production of steel commenced. On the south bank of the Grand Calumet River, streets, stores and houses for mill workers combined to create the "City of the Century".

Thousands of immigrants from Poland, Roumania, Serbia, Hungary, Greece, Czechoslovakia and the Ukraine poured into Gary to become mill hands. Today Blacks, Appalachian Whites and Mexicans predominate in the labor force.

For many years Gary symbolized the company town. U.S. Steel dominated the community and steel and steel products epitomized Gary. The bitter CIO effort to organize the steel industry centered in the Gary area and union contracts signed in the late '30's began a shift towards community control. So did the changing racial complexion of the city. The 1967 election of Richard Hatcher as the first Black mayor of Gary and his subsequent successive reelections illustrate the dimensions of the change.

Today Indiana's third largest city, this 53 mile sprawling complex still has its lakefront corridor of heavy industry, a shabby, decayed downtown area in which a government building program continues and miles of residential sections ranging from middle class to poverty level. White flight hit its peak in the 1970's when many of the city's Caucasian population moved to suburbia. Glen Park and Miller remain the only sections where this groups presently resides.

Major Gary employers include Universal Atlas Cement, American Sheet and Tin Plate, and the Anderson Company which makes auto accessories. U.S. Steel's Gary Works remains the major employer and the overwhelming economic influence in the community.

The Indiana Toll Road (Rt. 80-90) traverses the southern boundary of the Gary mill section. From its elevated roadway, travellers can get a panoramic view.

To See and Do

ARCHITECTURE.

Doll House Fire Station (c. 1930). West 35th at Pierce.

Gary-Hobart Water Tower. 7th and Madison. Award winning modern design.

Gary Land Company's original office (1906). 4th and Broadway. Oldest building in Gary. Also housed first post office. Listed on National Register of Historic Places. Now restored and relocated in Gateway Park.

Prairie School houses (privately owned). West 6th and Fillmore, southwest corner; and West 7th and Van Buren, northeast corner. Notice the characteristic wide overhangs, horizontal bands of windows and geometric ornaments.

John Stewart Settlement House. 1501 Massachusetts. Listed on the National Register of Historic Places.

ART AND ARTISTS.

Atrium Gallery. 1100 West 6th (885-4264). In Gary Mental Health Center.

Gallery Northwest. Indiana University-Northwest. 3400 Broadway (980-6500).

CEMETERY.

Waldheim. Grant at 20th. Graves of Gary pioneers.

COLLEGES AND UNIVERSITIES.

Indiana University-Northwest. 3400 Broadway (887-0111).

Indiana Vocational and Technical College-Gary. 1440 East 35th (887-9646).

FARM AND FARM PRODUCE.

Chase Street Produce. 35th and Chase (884-3169). April 1-Christmas. Pick your own vegetables at a long time truck farm. Also sells flowers, hams, ham hocks, bacon.

Don Ewen Produce. 35th and Grant (884-6397). April 1 to Christmas. Pick your own or purchase. Also flowers, ham hocks.

HISTORICAL COLLECTION.

Calumet Regional Archives. 3rd floor, Library Building, Indiana University-Northwest. 3400 Broadway (980-6628). Growing storehouse of regional records, memorabilia and photographs. Exhibits.

Indiana Room, Gary Public Library. 220 West 5th (886-2484). Books and memorabilia about the dunes and the Calumet area.

MOVIE.

Ridge Plaza Cinema I and II. 5900 West Ridge (923-9100).

MUSIC.

Blue Room Lounge. 1654 West 11th (no phone). Jazz matinees every Saturday, 2-6.

Mona's Lounge. 1537 Broadway (882-6550). Live jazz every Saturday night, l0-3. Bring your own horn.

RECREATION.

Golf. Calumet Golf Club. 3920 West Ridge (980-9484). 9 holes.

North Gleason Park. 3200 Jefferson (944-1541). April 15-October 15. 9 holes.

South Gleason Park. 3400 Jefferson (944-6517). April 15-October 15. 18 holes.

Parks. Gateway Park. 4th and Broadway. A real bowling green, an old-fashioned steam engine and an architectural treasure, all on one site.

Lake Etta County Park. 3100 Clark (769-PARK). 75 acres. Daily, April 1-October 1, 7 a.m.-dusk. Picnicking, fishing* for catfish and panfish, food for sale, nature interpretation.

See Indiana Dunes National Lakeshore section for information on the Gary area of the park.

South Gleason Park. 3400 Jefferson (944-6417). Beauiful flower shows in the greehouses, usually in May and November.

Restaurants.

Calvary Institutional Church. 230 Virginia (883-4422). 6-8:30. Breakfast, lunch, dinner. Soul food. Open to the public.

Davis Seafood. 3405 West 15th (944-8555). Thursday, Saturday, 11-7; Friday, 11-9; Sunday, 12-7. Smorgasboard. Soul food.

Miller's Restaurant in The Boy's Club. 225 West 5th (882-3303). Daily, 6-6. Soul food. Open to the public.

Shop.

Joyce Sportswear. 2100 East 15th (883-9681). Factory open to the public on Saturday mornings only. Arrive at 8 a.m. for bargains in women's sportswear.

Theater.

Theatre Northwest. Indiana University-Northwest. 3400 Broadway (980-6808). Student productions.

The Company Playhouse. Broadway, north of Ridge (no phone). Amateur productions of high caliber.

Special Event.

Steel City Fest. Contact Dr. Vernon Smith (885-5437) for date. Multi-ethnic entertainment and food. Amateur boxing, fun run, magic show, arts and crafts booths.

Special Facilities.

Chamber of Commerce. 504 Broadway (885-7407).

Methodist Hospital. 600 Grant (886-4000).

St. Mary's Medical Center. 540 Tyler (882-9411).

Gary Municipal Airport. Industrial Highway (994-1663). Heliocopter flights to O'Hare Airport.

Genesis Convention Center. One Genesis Center Plaza (882-5505). New $13,000,000 facility with giant exhibition hall. Call for schedule of activities.

GRIFFITH
(17,026 population)

Griffith owes its existence to the location of nine railroad crossings on Broad Street, and most of its early settlers were German railroad workers. Marshland originally surrounded the town forcing its pioneers to travel by boat from Highland to Merrillville.

The land boom anticipated to follow Chicago's 1893 Columbian Exposition, never materialized. Instead Griffith grew slowly until after World War II when it developed as a residential suburb of Gary and Hammond.

To See and Do
MOVIE.
Griffith Park Cinema I and II. 236 West Ridge (923-4300).

MUSEUM.
Grand Trunk Depot Museum. 201 South Broad (924-2155). June-August, Wednesday, 10-2, Sunday, 2-4. Railroad memorabilia and Griffith historical items housed in an old renovated railroad station.

MUSIC.
Rick's Cafe. 520 East Main (924-9669). Jazz.

RECREATION.
Bikeway. Signed route passes through quiet residential streets crossing a minimum of railroad tracks and busy thoroughfares. It provides dirct access to three parks. Obtain a map from the Northwestern Indiana Regional Planning Commission (939-1080).

Golf. Griffith Golf Center. 1901 North Cline (923-3223). April 1-November 1. 18 holes.

Parks. Hoosier Prairie State Nature Preserve. See Indiana Dunes National Lakeshore section for description.

Oak Ridge Prairie County Park. 301 South Colfax (769-PARK). Daily, 7 a.m.-dusk. 595 acres with cross country skiing, jogging, hiking, and nature trails, picnic shelters, and sledding, tubeing and volleyball facilities.

Tennis. Mansard Racquet Club. 1111 Reyome (972-1050).

RESTAURANTS.

Herman and Mary's Steak House. 216 South Broad (924-9685 or 924-4850). Bar. Dancing and entertainment on weekends.

Magma Restaurant. 101 North Broad (924-6454). Monday-Thursday, 5:30 a.m.-1 a.m.; Friday and Saturday, never closes; Sunday, open until 10 p.m. Unpretentious, frequented by locals, home cooking.

Pagoda Inn. 1207 East Ridge (923-7170). Monday-Thursday, 11:30-9:30; Friday, 11:30-11; Saturday, 3-11; Sunday, 3-9:30 p.m. Extensive menu. Bar.

San Remo. 112 East Ridge (838-6000). Monday-Saturday, 4:30-midnight; Sunday, noon to 8. Bar.

Sherlock's Holme. 921 West 45th (924-2200). Sunday-Thursday, 11-10; Friday-Saturday, 11-midnight. Bar. Large establishment with fireplaces in each room. Lake perch and prime rib.

SPECIAL FACILITIES.

Chamber of Commerce. 102 North Broad (924-2155).
Griffith Airport. 1715 East Main (924-0207).

HAMMOND
(93,714 population)

Hammond, the oldest city in the Calumet Region, remained until 1850 an area of sand ridges and swamps. Its first permanent settler, a Prussian tailor named Ernest Hohman, escaped from a cholera epidemic in Chicago to build the Hohman Inn. Today the American Steel Foundries plant sits on the site of the Inn.

George Hammond, a Detroit butcher, who perfected the method of shipping beef in refrigerated railroad cars, located his slaughterhouse across from the Inn. Few in the sparse population complained about the stench. From 1869 on the

Hammond plant proved an enormous success shipping hundreds of thousands of pounds of meat as far away as Europe. It employed more than 1,500 men in the most important industry in the area. After a fire gutted the plant in 1901, the operation moved to the Chicago Stockyards. However the city has become and remains a commercial hub for the area. Presently it ranks as Indiana's sixth largest city.

The nation's first professional football team formed in Hammond and the first automatic potato digger was invented in the city. Alvah Roebuck worked as a local jeweler but left town after a school janitor stole his girl friend. Richard Heine, the janitor, later became a millionaire banker, and the jilted Roebuck teamed up with Sears to found the chain that bears both their names.

To See and Do

ANTIQUES.

John David's. 6660 Indianapolis (845-4088). Also collectibles. Auction, Saturday night.

2nd Time Around. 810 169th (932-1275). Also reproductions.

ARCHITECTURE.

Forest Avenue Homes. 6600-7300 blocks. Architect L. Crosy Bernard Sr. designed these privately owned residences between 1920 and 1940 using natural materials of stone and wood in a variety of historical styles.

Grand Boulevard. Designed by the noted landscape architect Jens Jensen.

Joseph Hess School House. 7205 Kennedy in Hessville Park (845-4155). Built in 1869, this little old red school house contains furnishings of the period.

ART AND ARTISTS.

Bicentennial Library Gallery. Second floor, Student-Faculty Library Center, Purdue University Calumet. 2233 171st (844-0520). Art shows.

Hammond Public Library. 564 State (931-5100). Art shows.

COLLEGES AND UNIVERSITIES.

Purdue University Calumet. 2233 171st (844-0520).

FLEA MARKET.

International Bazaar. First floor and basement of former Goldblatt store, Sibley and Hohman (enter on Sibley). Saturday and Sunday, 8-5. Big selection of new, old and distressed merchandise with a few antiques available.

HISTORICAL COLLECTION.

Calumet Room, Hammond Public Library. 564 State (931-5000). Local and Indiana memorabilia and artifacts.

Purdue University Calumet Archives. Purdue University Calumet. 2233 171st (844-0520). Mostly Hammond and Munster records and photographs.

HISTORIC SITES.

Monument of 1821. State line, one mile south of Lake Michigan. Marks Indiana-Illinois border.

Site of northwest Indiana's first industry. The George Hammond Meat Packing Plant stood west of Hohman Avenue and north of the Grand Calumet River.

MOVIES.

Hammond Outdoor Theatre. Borman Expressway and Indianapolis Boulevard (844-0219).

Kennedy Theatre. 6735 Kennedy (844-9769). Good for oldies.

RECREATION.

Boats-Launching Area. Wolf Lake-Forsythe Park. 121st and Calumet (932-0093).

Fishing. Commonwealth Edison State Line Power Station. 103rd at Lake Michigan (659-0036). Fishing allowed from breakwater.

Hammond Water Filtration Plant. Calumet at Lake Michigan (853-6439). Fishing allowed from rip-rap covered shore surrounding plant.

Wolf Lake-Forsythe Park. 121st and Calumet (932-0093). Both shore and pier fishing.

Parks. Dowling Park. Kennedy and Borman Expressway. Picnicking, tennis.

Gibson Woods Nature Preserve. 6201 Parrish (769-9030). Nature Center, interpretive nature trails.

Lakefront Park. Calumet at Lake Michigan (853-6379). Fishing, picnicking, boating, public boat ramp, water skiing. No swimming.

Riverside Park. Calumet and Borman Expressway. Picnicking alongside the Little Calumet River in thick woods.

Wolf Lake-Forsyth Park. 121st and Calumet (932-0093) A park extending over the Illinois State line. Swimming, fishing, picnicking, boating, water sports, ice-skating, ice-fishing.

RESTAURANTS.

Cam-Lan. 132 Sibley (931-5115). Monday-Saturday, 11-9. Chinese menu.

Cataldi. 576 State (931-0200). Monday-Thursday, 11-10; Friday-Saturday, 11-11. Has served Italian food for 50 years at this location. Bar.

El Taco Real. 935 Hoffman (932-8333). Tuesday-Thursday, 11-11; Friday, 11-2; Saturday, noon-midnight. Superior Mexican food. Bar.

Purdue University Calumet. 2233 171st (844-0520). Has an excellent cafeteria on campus.

Phil Smidt and Son. 1205 North Calumet (659-0025). Monday-Thursday, 11:15-9:30; Friday-Saturday, 11:15-11:30. For generations one of the best known restaurants in the Calumet region. Fish and frog legs are specialties. All you can eat. Bar.

SHOPS.

Army and Navy Surplus Store. 5134 Hohman (932-9010). Gigantic stock. Wonderful place to browse.

Import Food Market. 120 Sibley (932-7711). Greek delicacies.

Indiana Botanic Gardens. 626 177th (931-2480). An assortment of herbs imported from the four corners of the globe.

Queen Ann Chocolates. 604 Hoffman (932-2400). Monday-Friday, 8:30-3:45. Hard to find. Turn west off Calumet at White Castle. Factory store with spectacular sales. Kids will love the candy.

Solan's Greenhouse. 6804 Columbia (932-8257). Nice quality at low prices.

THEATER AND ENTERTAINMENT CENTER.

Civic Center. Sohl between Carroll and Highland (932-0093). Events such as professional basketball games, cat and dog shows and the circus take place here. Accessible for handicapped.

SPECIAL EVENTS.

A Taste of Yesterday. Hessville Park, 7205 Kennedy (844-7627). Last Saturday before July 4th, 10-10. Tours of Little Red Schoolhouse. Entertainment on outdoor stage. Arts and crafts booths, demonstration of candy-making. Food for sale.

International Cultural Festival and Arts and Crafts Fair. Outside of the Howard Branch, Hammond Public Library, 7047 Grand (931-5100, ext. 273). Second weekend in September, 10-6. Dancing and music of various countries, ethnic foods, arts and crafts booths.

SPECIAL FACILITIES.

Chamber of Commerce. 429 Fayette (931-1000).

St. Margaret Hospital. 5454 Hohman (932-2300).

HIGHLAND
(29,935 population)

Another of the bedroom communities of the Calumet Region, Highland calls itself the largest town in Indiana. Dutch settlers founded Highland and the Town Hall building decorations show their influence. Dutch names still abound. Once a thriving truck farming section, today residences occupy the land.

To See and Do

ANTIQUES.

Main Street Antiques. 9219 Indianapolis (838-9560). Several dealers display here.

ARCHITECTURE.

Highway of Flags Servicemen's Memorial. Ridge and Indianapolis. Beautiful flower displays.

FARM AND FARM PRODUCE.

Jansen's Michigan Fruit Market. 2122 Ridge (838-0300). An open air stand with big selection of fruits, vegetables and flowers. Closes for the winter on Christmas eve.

Zandstra Brothers Farm. 10240 Wicker Park (836-1095). Pick your own strawberries and vegetables.

MOVIE.

Town Theatre. 8618 Kennedy (838-1222). Northwest Indiana's only foreign film cinema. Serves coffee and cake at intermission.

RECREATION.

Dancing-Square. American Legion Hall. Ridge and 2nd. First, third and fifth Sundays, 7:30-10:30 (844-0850); second and fourth Sundays, 6:30 p.m. (924-0221).

Lincoln Community Center. 2450 Lincoln. Second and fourth Saturdays, 8-10:30 (996-4081); Monday, 7:30-9:30 (838-9184).

Golf. Wicker Park Golf Course. Rt. 6 at Rt. 41 (838-9809). Open according to weather. 18 holes.

Parks. Hoosier State Nature Preserve. See Indiana Dunes National Lakeshore section for description.

Wicker Park. Rts. 6 and Rt. 41 (932-2530). Daily, dawn to dusk. Outdoor swimming pool, picnic areas, biking and hiking trails, tennis, small amusement park. Ice-skating, snowmobiling, cross country skiing. Large and lovely grounds.

Racquetball. Sports Illustrated Court Club. 3150 45th (924-0698).

Sports 2000. 2945 Jewett (923-0703).

Shooting Range and Indoor Tennis Courts. Hansen's Sports. 3750 Ridge (838-7495).

RESTAURANTS.

Miner-Dunn. 8490 Indianapolis (923-3313). Daily, 6-10. A diner serving excellent hamburgers.

Town Club. 2904 45th (924-5227). Monday-Friday, 11-midnight; Saturday, 5-midnight. Bar. Good boneless perch. Don't miss weekly tacos luncheon. Reservations a must for dinner.

Brumm's Bloomin' Barn. 2540 45th (924-1000). Attractive store with nice gifts.

Cranberry Cove. 2933 Highway (923-8529). Good selection of items imported from many countries.

Mary Ann Garden Center. 3405 Ridge (838-0015). Nice plants.

SPECIAL FACILITY.

Chamber of Commerce. 8536 Kennedy (923-3666).

HOBART
(22,987 population)

Situated on a rise of land through which the Deep River meanders, for centuries the Indians used the land around Hobart as berrying and hunting grounds. Relics of their dancing and burial sites discovered here.

The development of modern Hobart began with George Earle who platted the town in 1845. Damming the Deep River, he built a grist and saw mill which made the town into a commercial center for pioneer farmers. Timber cut at the mill ended up on Chicago's first paved street, Lake Street. Earle's home contained the first art gallery in northern Indiana.

Hobart soon became a stop on the important stagecoach routes and eventually Lake County's first railroad center. Deposits of clay found nearby led to the establishment of profitable brickyards. Today the high school football team has the nickname of "Brickies" as a recollection of that bygone era.

The town has become a predominantly residential community with a few small industries. Midwest Industries, a leading supplier of model airplanes, calls Hobart home base.

To See and Do

ANTIQUES.

Corner House Antiques. 1005 South Lincoln (no phone).

Hobart Road Antique Shop. 402 East Hobart (942-3942).

The Antique & Collector's Shop. 515 East Third (no phone). Furniture, glassware, china.

ARCHITECTURE.

First Unitarian Church (1876). Main and 5th. Still in use.

Hobart Public Library. 100 Main (942-2243). A handsome modern glass and concrete building overlooking the Deep River.

The Pennsylvania Railroad bridge over the Deep River (1845). Stone arch construction. Listed in the Historic American Engineering Record.

FARMS AND FARM PRODUCE.

Along Rt. 6 east of Rt. 51, a number of open air stands carry an abundance of home grown plants, fruits and vegetables in season as well as other farm products. Some also offer pick your own fields. Among the biggest: Jansen's, corner of Rt. 51 and Rt. 6 (962-1224); Johnson's, one-half mile east of Rt. 51 on Rt. 6 (962-1383); Remus, three-eighths of a mile east of Rt. 51 on Rt. 6 (962-2213); and Sapper's, 1175 South Lake Park (942-6423).

Shilo Arabian Farms. 6900 Ainsworth (942-3753). Reputedly the largest such breeding farm in the world. Call for an appointment to tour.

MOVIE.

Art Theatre. 230 Main (942-1670).

MUSEUM.

Hobart Historical Museum (c. 1915). 706 East 4th (942-5536). Saturdays, 10-3. Call to arrange tours at other times. Housed in a Tudor Revival style building. One of the last Carnegie libraries built. Listed on the National Register of Historic Places. The museum contains some local Indian relics, memoriabilia of Hobart history, 523 dolls comprising the Chapman collection and a fascinating assemblage of craftsmen's tools.

RECREATION.

Bicycle Rental. Hobart Schwinn 840 East Third (942-3492).

Bikeway. Signed route passes through quiet residential streets, Fred Rose Park and along the shores of Lake George. Obtain map from Northwestern Indiana Regional Planning Commission (923-1080).

Golf. Cressmoor Country Club. 601 North Wisconsin (942-7424). 18 holes.

Indian Ridge Lake Country Club. 6363 Grand (942-6850). Mid-March to first snow. 18 holes.

Parks. Robinson Park*. 5200 Liverpool (942-9321). June-August. Lake with sandy beach, swimming, hiking and jogging trail, fishing, picnicking, boating, archery and camping.

Fred Rose Park. 20 acres of woodland on Lake George, 8th off Wisconsin (942-9431). Lighted tennis courts, picnic shelters. Public boat ramp*, ice-skating, ice-fishing, fishing.

RESTAURANTS.

Country Lounge. 3700 Montgomery (942-2623). Daily, 11-12:30. Bar. Good shrimp de jonghe.

Indian Ridge Supper Club. At Indian Ridge Country Club. 6363 Grand (342-0666). Lunch and dinner, Tuesday-Saturday. Bar.

SPECIAL EVENT.

Hobart holds a bang-up, old-fashioned celebration on the Fourth of July weekend. Art show, watermelon and pie-eating contests, pig roast, ice cream social, carnival, barbecue, flea market, parade, fireworks. Call the Chamber of Commerce (942-5774) for more information.

SPECIAL FACILITIES.

Chamber of Commerce. 18 East Ridge (942-5774).

Hobart Airport. 3600 North Lake Park (962-9400). Charter flights.

St. Mary's Medical Center. 1500 South Lake Park (942-0551).

LAKE STATION
(14,294 population)

Archeologists have found artifacts of Indian dancing floors

and burial grounds around Lake Station. Centuries later when the railroads built their transcontinental tracks through Lake County, modern settlement began.

In 1851 the Michigan Central Railroad built roundhouses, shops and a depot which it named Lake Station. The company required all trains to stop at the depot so passengers could eat at the station restaurant. For the next 15 years Lake Station remained a busy rail and shipping center. After the Civil War it settled into somnambulism until the population of Gary began to expand to its borders. In 1908 the town changed its name to East Gary. Several years ago it reverted back to its original name and today continues as a small residential and commercial center.

To See and Do

ANTIQUES.
The Barn. Difficult to find. Take Rt. 51 five miles south of Alternate Rt. 6. Turn right (east) onto East 33rd and continue for about a mile (962-9697). Country and imported furniture.
Spinning Wheel Antiques. 3424 Parkside (962-5145). Superb glass.

ART AND ARTISTS.
Inola Frum (962-1511). Restoration.

HISTORICAL MARKER.
Rt. 51, just south of ramp to I-94. Marks the route to the Potawatomi Trail from old Lake Station southwesterly to the Indiana ceremonial grounds at Merrillville.

NATURE CENTER.
Deep River Nature Center. 3100 Liverpool (962-3579). Operated by the Gary Public Schools as one of the few outdoor education centers administered by school systems in the United States. On a 144 acre tract, the facilities include a 40 acre lake, a wilderness area, hiking trails, a library, mess hall and classroom buildings. Students come by bus to learn about a world vastly different from their urban surroundings. Visits by the public only by appointment.

RECREATION.

Hay Rides. William Remus. Rt. 6 (962-2213).

Park. Riverview Park. Rt. 51, overlooking Deep River.

SPECIAL FACILITY.

The Chamber of Commerce (962-1196) has no office but gives out information by phone.

LEROY
(245 population)

To See and Do
RECREATION.

Park. Stoney Run County Park*. East on Rt. 8 to County Line Road, north to 450S, left one-half mile (787-2020, ext. 391). Open 7 a.m.-dusk. 296 acres of mature forest, ponds and open meadows. A natural area flourishing with wild life. Picnicking, jogging, fitness, hiking, orienteering, and horse-back riding trails, fishing for perch, bluegill and catfish, ice-skating, cross country skiing, hay rides*, primitive camping*, softball, volleyball, soccer and frisbee equipment and other recreation equipment rental*. Parking fee.

SPECIAL EVENT.

Bluegrass Festival. Stoney Run County Park. 145th and Union. Continuous musical entertainment of the foot stompin', knee slappin' variety. Fiddle, banjo and hollerin' contests. Food for sale. Bring chairs or blankets. Advance sale of tickets at discount. For dates and details, call 769-PARK.

LOWELL
(5,827 population)

Named after Lowell, Massachusetts, Lowell, Indiana has experienced a population surge in the past two decades as Lake County residents have sought its rural atmosphere. A handsome old town surrounded by rich farm country, Lowell has an ambiance which mushrooming subdivisions threaten to destroy. Once Belanger racing cars, which won countless chamionships, came from Lowell. Today antique stores abound.

To See and Do

ARCHITECTURE.

Melvin A. Halsted House (1850). 201 East Main. Built by the founder of Lowell, it stands today as the oldest brick home in Lake County. Listed on the National Register of Historic Places.

Lowell Senior High School. East of town on Rt. 2. Designed by the Shaver Partnership of Michigan City in l969, this modern building houses 1,000 students. A modular structure with open classrooms, pits and other educational advances, it radiates a friendly atmosphere.

MOVIE.

Polo Theater. 133 Mill (696-8246 or 696-7244).

NATURE PRESERVE.

German Methodist Cemetery Prairie Nature Preserve. This one acre remnant preserves the only black soil prairie remaining in Indiana. Contains 60 species of prairie plants making it the most botanically diverse acre in the state. Viewing from outside fence only. Call the Nature Conservancy (988-7547) for more information.

RECREATION.

Dancing-Square. Oak Hill School. 195 Oakly (696-8842 or 696-0123). Second and fourth Fridays, 8-10:30. Beginner lessons, Thursdays, 7:30-9:30.

Park. Buckley Homestead County Park. 3606 Bellshaw (769-PARK). The newest of Lake County's parks, Buckley Farm, provides an authentic locale for a "living history" farm. Here visitors can see and participate in farm life as practiced from the middle 1800 to the early 1900's. One room schoolhouse and log cabin on property. Costumed interpreters. Special programs scheduled.

SPECIAL EVENTS.

Buckley Homestead Days*. Buckley Homestead County Park. 3606 Bellshaw. First weekend in October. Festival recreating turn of century farm life. Hayrides. Demonstrations of rush weaving, rag rug, soap, and button making, spinning. Civil War encampment with muzzle loading and battle reenactment. Food and crafts for sale. Call (769-PARK) for date and details.

Old-Fashioned Day. Throughout town. Second Saturday in June, 9-5. Art show in Evergreen Park. Ice-cream social starting at noon at Three Creeks Monument Park, displays of handcraft. Buckley Homestead open. Call Chamber of Commerce (696-0231) for more information.

Oktoberfest. First weekend in October. American Legion Grounds, 108 1/2 Commercial. Thursday, community auction; Friday, 8-11, harvest stomp; Saturday and Sunday, continuous entertainment, biergarten, arts and crafts exhibit, clowns, antique show, children's activities, pig roast. Coincides with Buckley Homestead days. Call Chamber of Commerce (696-0231) for more information.

Chamber of Commerce. 136 West Commercial (696-0231).

MERRILLVILLE
(27,677 population)

Until very recently Merrillville's claim to fame rested on its past history as an important Indian village. With the banishment of the Potawatomi, the area became farm land. However its central location resulted in 16 wagon trails passing through as pioneers journied to settle Chicago, the rich farming lands of southern Illinois and the Kankakee area. Merrillville's prime asset—that central location—also led developers in the early 1970's to chose the intersection of Rt. 30 and the new north-south superhighway, I-65, as the site of South Lake Mall, a giant regional shopping center. In the past decade Merrillville has become the number one shopping mecca of all northwest Indiana.

Malls and more malls have brought traffic jams, food franchises galore and an entertainment complex that rivals those of Chicago. The range of shopping opportunities amazes even the inveterate buyer. Unfortunately Merrillville's prosperity has drained downtown Gary and most of the other older retail centers in the region. In 1971 Merrillville incorporated as a town though its identity remains that of a gigantic shopping center.

To See and Do

ANTIQUES.
The Carriage House. 420 West 73rd (769-2169). Owner Harry Brown salvages, restores and releads old stained glass, terra cotta, fret and iron work.

ARCHITECTURE.
SS Constantine and Helen Greek Orthodox Cathe-

dral. 8000 Madison (769-2481). This Byzantine-style structure stands on 37 acres. The denomination's only cathedral in the state. Covered with mosaics and murals, the church's design includes a rotunda 100 feet in diameter and 50 feet high. Call to arrange a group tour.

Lake County Reference Library. Rt. 30 east of Rt. 55 (769-6123). A modern glass building with a large collection of Indiana historical materials.

ART AND ARTISTS.

D'Cameo Gallery. 7849 Taft (769-2882). Oils, watercolors, lithographs.

Robert Hoffman (769-3416). Painter.

Trachtenberg Gallery. 430 West 73rd (769-8018). Graphics, fiber art, art glass.

ENTERTAINMENT CENTER.

Holiday Plaza. I-65 and Rt. 30 (769-6311). A giant complex with a Holiday Inn, a Holidrome with indoor pool, sauna and children's playground, a convention center and the 3,100 seat Holiday Star Theatre (769-6600). Nationally known entertainers including rock performers, comedians and singers appear regularly drawing audiences from the entire Chicago metropolitan area.

FLEA MARKET.

Dealers Flea Market. 5201 Broadway. Daily, l0-5.

HISTORICAL MARKER.

Homer Iddings School. 7749 Van Buren (769-6373). Commemorates the Great Sauk Trail's route through Merrillville.

LODGING.

La Quinta Motor Inn. 8210 Louisiana (736-2879). 122 rooms. Highly recommended.

MOVIES.

Crossroads Cinema I and II. 6180 Broadway (980-0558).

Southlake Mall Cinema I-IV. 2479 Southlake Mall (730-2652).

Y & W Twin I-III (outdoor). 6600 South Broadway (769-2203).

RECREATION.

Golf. Broadmoor Golf Course. 4300 West 81st (769-5444). 18 holes.

Turkey Creek Golf Course. 6400 Harrison (980-5170). 6-dusk. 18 holes. Bar.

Health Clubs. Admirals Health Club. 1000 East 80th Place (769-8406).

Back Yard Health Club. 240 West 79th (769-3366).

Nautilus Fitness Center. 8328 Colorado (769-7117).

Park. Hidden Lake Park. 63rd and Broadway. 60 acres, beach, swimming, ice-skating.

Ski-Rental. Brown's Sporting Goods. 2278 Southlake Mall (769-9075).

Camp-Land. Rt. 30 and Madison (769-8496).

Tennis. Southlake Tennis Club. 8328 Colorado (769-6378).

RESTAURANTS.

Angelo's Sicilian Cart. 1515 East 82nd (769-2429). Daily, 11-3; Sunday brunch, 11-3. Italian and American cuisine.

Bon Femme Cafe. 6 West 79th in Liberty Square Mall (no phone). Monday-Thursday, 8-6; Friday and Saturday, 8-10. Tiny, serves good soups, crepes and quiche. Wine. Sells sourdough bread sometimes.

El-Mar's. 7404 Broadway (769-5000). Monday-Saturday, 11-11. Sunday brunch, noon-3; dinner, noon-8. Dancing, Friday-Saturday, 8-12. Bar. Tasty American food.

SHOPS.

Century Plaza Mall. Rt. 30 and Broadway. A collection of off-price stores, of which the local branches of the Burlington Coat Factory and Service Merchandise offer good buys.

Great Western Boot Outlet. Rts. 30 and 65 (no phone). Factory outlet for boots.

Quality Discount Apparel. 6136 Broadway (980-3980). In Crossroads Shopping Plaza. High quality men's slacks and suits at considerably less than retail. Smaller selection of women's skirts and suits.

Italian Festival. Michael Angelo Hall Picnic Grounds. 6220 Broadway (980-9410). Last week in June. Thursday-Saturday, 5-midnight; Sunday, 1-midnight. Gourmet Italian food, carnival, Italian bake sale, bingo. For further information, call 736-2020.

Merrillville Grecian Festival. At SS Constantine and Helen Greek Orthodox Cathedral. 8000 Madison (769-8421). Second weekend in July. Friday, 6-12; Saturday-Sunday, noon-midnight. Featuring Greek dancing, foods, handicrafts. Outdoor taverna with wine tasting. Icons for sale.

Merrillville Serbfest*. St. Elijah Serbian Orthodox Church. 8700 Taft (769-2122). Third weekend in June. Friday, 6-midnight; Saturday-Monday, noon-midnight. Serbian dancing, bands, food, games, house and handcrafts.

Merrillville Summer Festival*. Hidden Lake Park (769-2111). July 4th. Continuous entertainment. Carnival rides, food, games. Hot air balloon race. Arts and crafts booths.

SPECIAL FACILITIES.

Chamber of Commerce. 78 West 80th Place (769-8180).

Methodist Hospital. 8701 Broadway (738-5500).

Ross Clinic. 6100 Harrison (980-6000).

MILLER
(included in Gary's population).

Now part of Gary, Miller began as a stagecoach stop on the Chicago-Detroit run. Its first settlers found the area so wild that they reported an eagle perched on every dune. A fisherman named Carr and his wife squatted on the beach and their heirs fought for possession with the United States Steel Corporation for 40 years. A black man named Davey Crockett fled to Miller during the Civil War.

Before the turn of the century, Miller served as a fishing distribution center when Lake Michigan teemed with sturgeon and white fish. The community was also an important shipping center for ice from the Lake and sand mined from the dunes.

In addition, the Miller dunes became world famous in 1896 when Octave Chanute made the first successful flight in a heavier than air craft there. Orville Wright subsequently credited Chanute with building the prototype of the plane which the Wright Brothers flew four years later at Kitty Hawk. A marker commemorating Chanute's flights is located in the grassy area south of the Marquette Park pavillion. The Miller dunes also served as the location of several silent movies including "The Conquest of Mexico" and "Lost in the Sudan".

To See and Do

ARCHITECTURE.

Miller Town Hall. Junction of Miller, Grand and Old Hobart. Listed on the National Register of Historic Places.

ART AND ARTISTS.

Dale Fleming. (938-3834). Dunescapes.

Frame Gallery. 621 South Lake (938-6303). Posters.

Gary Art League Gallery. 607 South Lake (938-1308). Exhibits of local artists.

Statue of Father Marquette. In Marquette Park.

Toni Lane (938-0471). Drawings, photographs.

MOVIE.

Dunes Cinema I and II. 8090 East Rt. 20 (938-0700).

RECREATION.

Beach. Lake Street Beach. Lake Street at Lake Michigan. Parking charge.

Boats-Launching Area. Lake Street at Lake Michigan. Public ramp. Parking charge.

Parks. Marquette Park. Marquette and Grand (844-9404). U.S. Steel gave this 24l acres of scenic dunelands to the city of Gary in 1921 for the first instance of public preservation of the dunes. This sadly underused park includes a fine 2 1/2 mile sandy bathing beach with life guards, fishing lagoon, tennis courts, picnic area, concession stands, picturesque bridges and a pavillion. The noted Chicago architect Jens Jensen designed the park and did a masterful job of preserving the dunescape. Bird enthusiasts find watching waterfowl migrants especially good at the pavillion lagoon. Ample parking. Parking*.

See Indiana Dunes National Lakeshore section for information on Miller area of park.

RESTAURANTS.

Beach Cafe. 903 North Shelby (886-9090). Monday-Saturday, 11-11. Specializes in fish.

Golden Coin. Rt. 20 and Clay (989-8357). Monday-Saturday, 11-midnight. Steaks. Bar. Good service.

SHOP.

Wilco. 6300 Miller (938-6631). Good Greek bakery in a supermarket, also known for its fresh fruits and vegetables.

SPECIAL EVENT.

Art Show. Miller School grounds, Lake Street. First weekend in June. Annual event with arts and crafts for sale, auction, refreshments. Call 938-1308 for details.

10K Run. Course begins and ends at Marquette Park and winds through town. Held annually in June as part of the Gold Cup Series. Call 938-7040 for further information.

MUNSTER
(20,671 population)

Travellers to and from Fort Dearborn often stopped at the Brass Tavern located where Munster now stands. This hostelry built in 1847 by Allen and Julia Brass had the first telegraph station in Lake County. News of President Lincoln's assassination first reached the area through a message sent to the station.

Munster's early Dutch settlers became prosperous truck farmers and the area remained predominantly truck farms until after World War II. Then Munster rapidly changed into a residential bedroom community. Today it has become the most affluent of Lake County's suburbs and a thriving, shopping center.

To See and Do

ART AND ARTISTS.

Mike Daumer (972-1167). Painter.

Mike Gibbs (923-9573). Dunes photographer.

Northern Indiana Art Association. 8317 Calumet (836-1839). Permanent collection. Art shows. Sales and rental gallery. Gift shop. Theatrical and musical performances.

Margaret Oberle (836-5623). Jewelry design, fabrication.

Town Gallery. 27 Ridge (836-6230). Features local artists working in all media. Primitives.

HISTORICAL MARKER.

Columbia and Ridge. The site of the Brass Tavern.

FARM AND FARM PRODUCE.

Herr Farm. 10219 White Oak (924-9351). Pick your own or purchase home grown vegetables from farm stand.

RECREATION.

Health Club. Dynasty. 9245 Calumet (836-2000).

Park. Bieker Woods. Ridge and Columbia. 6 1/2 acres of woodland with walking trails and foot bridges. A nature sanctuary lovingly preserved by the Kaske and Bieker families.

RELIGIOUS SITE.

Carmelite Hall. 1628 Ridge (838-9257). Old church with Byzantine-type murals. Grotto in gardens.

RESTAURANTS.

Bombay Bicycle Club. 9201 Calumet (836-9114). Monday-Saturday, 11:30-midnight; Sunday, 11:30-10. Large, very attractive decor. Bar.

Giovanni's Restaurant. 603 Ridge (836-6220). Full menu, Monday-Friday, 11-11:30; Saturday, 5-11:30. Pizza and sandwiches available to midnight. Bar. Good Italian food.

Gold Rush. 1745 45th (974-6630). Monday-Thursday, 11-1; Friday-Saturday, 11-2; Sunday, 11-11. Bar. Very good salad bar.

Schoops Hamburgers. 215 Ridge (836-6233). Monday-Saturday, 10-11. Their double cheese 'burgers taste special.

Star Delicatessen. 229 Ridge (836-9224). Monday-Saturday, 9-6. Take-outs.

The Charley Horse. 8317 Calumet (836-6100). Monday-Thursday, 11-1; Friday, 11-2; Saturday, noon-2; Sunday, noon-11. Sports motif.

SHOPS.

Big Red Sports. 921-A Ridge (836-8088). Athletic shoes and clothing at discount.

Barton Imports. 419 Ridge (836-2115). Nice gifts and collectibles.

Bruna Christopher. 417 Ridge (836-2015). Expensive jewelry and gifts including dolls and accessories.

Joe Hirsch. 8250 Hohman (836-8888). If your taste runs to expensive, classic clothes, this store has a good selection both for men and women.

Munster Sausage Company. 615 Ridge (836-9050). Superior, home-made Italian and Polish sausage.

The Fabric Shop. 427 Ridge (836-8080). The stock includes exquisite imported materials.

THEATER.

The Gallery Players. Community company performs at the Northern Indiana Arts Association. 8317 Calumet (836-1839). Call for schedule.

SPECIAL FACILITIES.

Chamber of Commerce. 8250 Hohman (836-5549).
Community Hospital. 901 MacArthur (836-1600).
Hammond Clinic. 7905 Calumet (836-5300).

SCHERERVILLE
(13,209 population)

A crossroads for several Indian trails, Schererville became an established community during pioneer days, when settlers used these same trails to trek west in their covered wagons. Some of them got as far as Schererville and stayed. The town's most illustrious settler, A.N. Hart, purchased 18,000 acres of swamp land. To make his property usable he embarked on a massive road and ditch building operation.

Wherever he put a ditch, eventually there would be Hart, traveling in his one-horse buggy, hoe in hand, to keep the ditch free from obstructions. Sadly and ironically the ditch builder lost his life when one of his ditches collapsed on him.

To See and Do

ANTIQUES.
Landmark Antiques. 119 Junction (322-4534 or 923-0429). Country antiques displayed in a converted railroad station.

ARCHITECTURE.
Nicholas Scherer home. 33 Wilhelm. Originl house of the town's founder.

RECREATION.
Amusement Park. Sauzer's Kiddie Land. Rts. 41 and 30 (865-8160). May-September, Monday-Friday, noon-10; Saturday-Sunday, 10-10. September-October, Saturday-Sunday only, noon-10.

Golf. Scherwood Golf Club. 600 East Joliet (865-2554). 18 holes.

Health Club. Omni Health Center. Rt. 41, two miles north of Rt. 30 (865-6969) or (865-6363). Tennis, raquetball, handball. Tours.

RESTAURANT.
Teibel's. Rt. 30 at Rt. 41 (865-2000). Daily, 11-10. Famous for chicken. Huge crowds. Bar.

SHOP.
Preferred Stock. Highland Department Store outlet. Rt. 30 and Rt. 41 (865-2593).

SPECIAL FACILITY.
Chamber of Commerce. 139 East Joliet (322-5412).

WHITING
(5,638 population)

Until 1884 when the Standard Oil Trust built its refinery,

Whiting remained an isolated area of swamps and sand dunes, almost entirely encircled by water. The company came to Whiting because of this isolation. It had constructed a pipe line from its Lima, Ohio oil field to Chicago in order to supply the growing midwest market. However Lima crude had a high sulpher content and the citizens of South Chicago wanted no part of the stench in their neighborhood. So Standard Oil needed an alternate site along the pipeline.

Cheap land, low taxes, use of an unlimited amount of free water from Lake Michigan to cool its distilleries, and no citizens to complain about the foul odors, made Whiting an ideal location for a refinery. In ensuing years, Standard Oil scientists invented the thermal cracking process at the plant which doubled the amount of gasoline derived from crude oil.

Standard Oil remains a major employer in Whiting to this day though its research laboratory has moved elsewhere. Whiting never became a true company town. Standard wisely refrained from building company housing or controlling the commercial establishments. Union Carbide and American Smelting & Refining and other oil firms have also established major plants in Whiting.

Whiting's citizenry includes the descendents of many immigrants who found employment in the refineries, including the largest Turkish settlement in the United States. Today Whiting remains a heavily industrial community whose miles of gas tanks and piping are well-known to drivers entering or leaving Chicago. The city also has a vibrant downtown section which bustles with customers.

To See and Do

ANTIQUES.

Granny's General Store. 1309 Community Court (659-7538). Antiques, collectibles, handmade gifts. Nice selection of china and dolls.

ARCHITECTURE.

Whiting Community Center (1923). 1938 Clark (659-0860). Built with a gift of $1,000,000 from Standard Oil of Indiana and John D. Rockefeller, Jr. Indoor swimming pool.

COLLEGES AND UNIVERSITIES.

Calumet College. 2400 New York (473-7700). Located in former Standard Oil Research Laboratory buildings.

RECREATION.

Parks. Whihala Beach County Park. 117th and Park at Lake Michigan (769-PARK). 9 acres with a 1,500 foot life guarded bathing beach, bath house, concession stand, fishing and picnic areas. Outdoor seating plaza has umbrella shaded tables overlooking beach. Accessibility for handicapped. Interpretive nature programs in summer. Public boat lanching ramps*. Parking*.

Whiting Park. 117th off Indianapolis (659-0860). 40 acres with a 1,500 foot sandy beach on Lake Michigan but swimming prohibited. Fishing pier, pavillion, tennis courts, skeet shooting and picnic tables*. Food available from Memorial Day to Labor Day.

RESTAURANTS.

Condes. 1440 Indianapolis (659-6300). Daily, 11-midnight. Greek specialities. Bar.

Granny's Tearoom. 1950 Indianapolis. Daily, 6-11. Breakfast, lunch, dinner. Home made soup, bread and pastries.

Vogel's. 1250 Indianapolis (659-1250). Tuesday-Thursday, 10-11:30; Friday-Saturday, 10:30-midnight. Specializes in frog legs and perch.

SHOPS.

Anne's Linens. 1419 119th (659-1628). Very nice selection. Reasonable prices. Many seconds.

Kitchens of Sara Lee. 1749 Indianapolis (659-5108). Monday-Thursday, 9-5:30; Friday, 9-6; Saturday, 9-5. Factory outlet. Heaven for those with a sweet tooth.

THEATER.

Marion Theatre Guild. 1844 Lincoln (659-2118). A good community company which gives weekend performances in its own theater. Call for schedule.

SPECIAL EVENT.

Crafts and Peddlers' Mart. Temple and Community

Courts. Last Saturday in July; rain date, last Sunday, 10-6. Arts and crafts booths, food, baked goods.

Lakefront Festival. First week in July with good parade. Call Chamber of Commerce (659-0292) for further details.

Oktoberfest. 119th Street. First weekend in October. Thursday-Friday, 9-8; Saturday, 9-5. Pumpkin carving contest, entertainment, ethnic food.

SPECIAL FACILITY.

Chamber of Commerce. 1312 119th (659-0292).

LAPORTE COUNTY
(108,632 population)

Westward bound pioneers, after travelling for days through thickly forested country, found a natural opening to a 20 mile stretch of rich prairie. They named this territory LaPorte, roughly translated as The Gateway. Originally LaPorte County encompassed all of northwest Indiana. Today it extends from the Michigan state line and the Lake Michigan shoreline on the north to the KankakeeRiver on the south, and from Porter County on the west to St. Joseph County on the east. Its 607 square miles include a heavily settled area built on levelled sand dunes, a moraine section dotted with small lakes and rolling hills on which orchards and vineyards produce millions of pounds of fruit annually, a large prairie band, and a vast acreage drained from the Kankakee marshes now transformed into superb farms.

The LaPorte County Fruit Growers Association publishes a handy map and guide listing locations and harvest schedules. Be sure to get one at any of the member farms. From mid-June to October locally grown apples, cherries, pears, peaches, plums, blueberries, apricots, strawberries, cider, honey and grapes come on the market. Many of the farms let buyers pick their own at substantial savings.

The LaPorte County Convention and Visitors Bureau located at the intersection of Rts. 20/35 and Meer (872-5055) can provide the latest information about any of the material

LAPORTE COUNTY

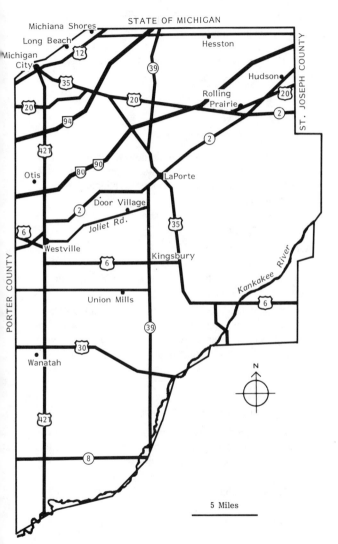

included in this section. The Visitors Bureau can be reached directly off Exit 40 of I-94. Open summers, daily-8:30-4:30; Monday-Friday, rest of year.

The Bureau also operates a hot line (872-0031) which provides information about weather and water conditions during the fishing season. In winter months, the hot line provides snow base and weather forecasts for skiers and snowmobilers.

DOOR VILLAGE
(included in LaPorte's population)

Tiny Door Village stands on the location where the early pioneers of northern Indiana first saw the opening from forest to prairie. The grasses and flowers grew so tall that they hid a man on horseback.

To See and Do
ARCHITECTURE.

Octagonal Barn. Left side of Rt. 35, 1.8 miles south of LaPorte County Court House. Huge Door Village sign on barn. View only from road.

Cemetery. Door Village Cemetery. South on Rt. 39 from LaPorte, west on Joliet Road for two miles. A marker commemorates the messenger sent from Fort Dearborn to warn the early settlers of an Indian uprising.

HESSTON
(Included in Rolling Prairie's population)

In this crossroads hamlet, the intersection is referred to as "State and Madison". For a dot on the map, however, this community has four attractions well worth visiting.

To See and Do
CEMETERY.

Posey Chapel Cemetery. 1000N, two miles east of Fail

Road, north side of road. This old cemetery sits on a high knoll which offers a glorious view of both dune and orchard country. In the 1800's a monthly circuit-riding preacher served the church on this site. It burned down in 1972.

GARDEN.

Hesston Gardens. 215E off 1000N (778-2421). Father Joseph Sokolski has created these gardens, as a labor of love, over the past 50 years. He welcomes visitors to this charming place, sells antiques to support his avocation and also holds Sunday Mass at 10 in a tiny Greek Orthodox chapel in the woods. Don't miss his icon collection. Free will offering.

MUSEUM.

LaPorte County Steam Society*. 1000N east of Rt. 39 (778-2783). Open weekends only, June-October; Saturday and Sunday, 1-6 through September; Sundays only, 1-6 in October. Local train buffs and summer residents have joined together to develop this nostalgic steam museum on a 155 acre site. They've collected a bevy of old-time steam engines and cars and laid track for the little "Flying Dutchman" railroad. The public can ride on this authentic narrow gauge railroad as well as on several others, all with open cars. There's even a train on a 3 1/2 inch track to watch whiz by.

On July 4th and Labor Day weekends bang-up celebrations of steam power take place. The museum has quite an assemblage of old-time steam driven machines many of which they operate only on these days. Old fashioned farm dinners available.

RESTAURANT.

Heston Bar. Fail Road at l000N (778-2938). Tuesday-Saturday, lunch; dinner, 5-9. Bar. Very popular.

HUDSON
(447 population)

The first town settled in LaPorte County, Hudson today bears little trace of its interesting past. Here, one of its pioneer inhabitants, the Reverend Isaac McCoy, established a Baptist mission for the Potawatomi Indians.

The South Shore Railroad once owned nearby Hudson Lake. In the 1920's, excursion trains brought thousands of Chicagoans here for giant picnics. The casino where famous dance bands played still stands on the lake's edge. Today Hudson Lake continues as a summer resort with fishing, boating, boat rental and picnicking available to the general public.

KINGSBURY
(no residential population)

During World War II, the army built a large ordnance plant here on a 23,000 acre site. Architect John Lloyd Wright designed residences for the army personnel some of which still stand forlorn and empty. An industrial park now occupies a portion of the plant site; the federal government has turned another part of the tract over to the State of Indiana for a fish and wildlife sanctuary. (See information about the Kingsbury State Fish and Wildlife Area in the chapter on The Kankakee.)

To See and Do

RECREATION.
    Park. White Oaks County Park. Pin Oak and Hupp. Hiking, picnicking in wooded area. l2 acres.

LAPORTE
(21,796 population)

The county seat since the town's founding in 1832, LaPorte cherishes its old sandstone court house in the midst of downtown. In early years, especially during the Civil War, whenever the bell rang the residents would gather to hear the news.

Today neither a modern addition to the court house nor a huge viaduct entrance to downtown from the north match the architectural distinction of the old court house or the lovely residential section with its huge old-fashioned mansions, large avenues and five lakes. LaPorte's past includes having had the first medical school in the Midwest within its borders. In 1842, four local men, including the father of the Mayo brothers, founded LaPorte University. However Mrs. Belle Guness wins the prize as the most famous past resident. She, at the turn of the century, lured 13 men to her farm north of town with the promise of marriage and killed them all before disappearing.

Today even as LaPorte's industrial base shrinks, the city continues as a thriving commercial center.

To See and Do

ANTIQUES.

Coachman Antique Mall. 500 Lincolnway (326-5933). Daily, 9-5. Three floors and 17,000 square feet of space jammed with antiques of all descriptions shown by numerous dealers.

Memorable Antiques. 607 Michigan (326-7276). Very nice old furniture and good glassware.

Walnut Hill Antiques. 613 Michigan (326-1099). Furniture, both unfinished and redone.

ARCHITECTURE.

815 Division (1840). The first frame house in LaPorte. Moved to this location at a later date.

Garwood House. Small Road, .6 mile east of 500W. Tan brick and gabled home on the south side of the road. The first house in the county built with a furnace. The top floor ballroom used to take two days to heat up before a dance.

LaPorte Commercial Historic District. 20 blocks of downtown west of the Court House in which many buildings constructed from 1870 to 1914 during the city's industrial and commercial heyday still stand. Some restoration work has taken place. Listed on the National Register of Historic Places. Contact the Chamber of Commerce (362-3178) for a map and more information.

Methodist Church. Harrison and Clay. Originally a Quaker meeting house.

Orr-Richter Mansion. 4076 West Small, .8 mile east of

500W (362-5008). A red brick home on the south side of the road. Built by the son of Indian fighter General William Orr, this Victorian Gothic home has a central tower and pointed arch windows. Beautifully restored, a choice antique shop now occupies its first floor. Open Friday-Sunday only.

Pinehurst Hall (1853). 3042 North Rt. 35. Two and a half story red brick mansion. Listed on the National Register of Historic Places.

Swan-Anderson House (1870). 1020 Indiana. A white frame Italianate home with lovely tall windows.

ART AND ARTISTS.

Charlotte Bass (369-1400). Quilter.

Farmhouse Studio. 2215 East 350N (326-5525). Silk-screen textiles and wall coverings.

Jack and Joyce Keane (326-7468). Paintings and drawings.

ARTISAN.

Elwyn Ames. 400N off Fail Road (325-8368). It's great sport to watch this blacksmith and horse trainer at work on summer evenings.

CEMETERY.

Union Chapel Cemetery. North Side of Rt. 6 between Rts. 39 and 421. The first white settler of LaPorte County, Mimam Benedict, is buried here.

FARMS AND FARM PRODUCE.

Garwood Orchards. 5911 West 50S (362-4385). Off Rt. 2 between LaPorte and Rt. 421. July 1-November 1, 8-7:30 p.m.; November 1-February 15, 8-5:30 p.m. Very popular. For the past century, the Garwoods have owned this farm which now has 80 acres of fruit trees, 40 acres devoted to vegetables and, best of all, 15 acres producing wonderful raspberries. For four months, pick-your-own lovers find this heaven, starting with red raspberries and continuing through the growing season to apples with many varieties of vegetables available. A large selection of produce for sale at the farm store, an operating cider mill on the premises.

John Hancock Fruit Farm. Fail Road (778-2096). Beautiful gardens. Sells delicious varieties of apples, vegetables and plants.

MOVIES.

LaPorte Cinema Quad. 608 Colfax (362-7569).
LaPorte Deluxe Drive-In. Rt. 2 East (362-4013).

MUSEUM.

LaPorte County Historical Society now occupies new spacious quarters in the Court House addition (362-7061). Monday-Friday, 10-4:30; also first Sunday of the month, 1-4. A vast and fascinating potpourri of pioneer and Indian artifacts, the W. A. Jones collection of native Kankakee birds and the largest assemblage of antique American firearms in the United States.

RECREATION.

Boats-Launching Areas. Loogys Landing. 229 Holton (362-7620).

Stone Lake. In Soldier's Memorial Park, Rt.35, (362-9746). Public ramp.

Boats-Rentals. Holiday Boat Sales. 1350 Pine Lake (362-4423). Also launching ramp, bait, fishing equipment.

Camping. Cutty's Campground. 4004 Rt. 39 (362-5111). April 1-October 15. 400 campsites. Children's fishing lake, 2 heated pools, 20 acre hiking trail, planned activities, lookout tower, food, store, shuffleboard, volleyball and basketball courts.

Willow Lake Campground. 0353 East 900N (778-4113). Picnicking, lake swimming, canoeing, hiking. 120 campsites.

Golf. Beechwood Golf Course. Woodlawn (362-2651). April 1-November 1. 18 holes.

Briarleaf Golf Club. 3233 North Rt. 39 (362-1992). 18 holes.

Lakes. Clear Lake. Truesdale (326-0600). 106 acres, fishing, ice-fishing, public launch ramp.

Fishtrap Lake. Off McClung Road (326-9600). 70 acres, fishing, ice-skating, ice-fishing.

Lower Fish Lake*. Rt. 4 (324-6401). Southeast of LaPorte. 134 acres, fishing.

North and South Pine Lakes. On either side of Waverly

(326-9600). Swimming, Memorial Day-Labor Day, life-guards, 11-7, fishing, concession stand, picnicking, water skiing, ice skating, boating, public launch area*.

Stone Lake. In Soldiers Memorial Park (326-9600). Picnicking, fishing, rowboat rental, sail and pontoon boating.

Upper Fish Lake*. Rt. 4 (325-8385). Southeast of LaPorte. 139 acres, swimming, fishing, boat rental.

Parks. Kesling Park. 18th off Kingsbury (326-9600). 90 acres of open fields. Picnic shelters*, tennis, handball, baseball diamonds, soccer fields, paved fitness trail, play areas.

Fox Park. Truesdale and Pine Lake Avenue (326-9600). 60 acres bordering Clear Lake. Picnic shelters*, band shell, oncerts, July-August, on Wednesday evenings; tennis,hiking, picnicking, lighted softball and baseball diamonds.

Soldiers Memorial Park. Waverly (326-9600). Parking*, picic shelters*, recreational shelters*, hiking, kiddie playground.

Skiing. Ski Valley. Forrester. Five miles west of city and north of Rt.2 (362-1212). Monday-Friday, 6-10 p.m.; Saturday, 10-10; Sunday, 10-6. Six rope tows, T-bar tow. Beginning, intermediate, advanced trails, lighted night skiing, equipment rental.

RESTAURANTS.

Ole's Meat, Fish & Liquor Company. 502 State (362-8270). Lunch, Monday-Friday, 11-2:30; dinner, Monday-Thursday, 5-10, Friday-Saturday, 5-11. Bar.

Tangerine. Across from the old Court House on Michigan (326-8000). Lunch, Tuesday-Friday, 11-2; dinner, Monday-Thursday, 5-9, Friday-Saturday, 5-10; Sunday brunch, 10-2. Striking decor in art deco style. Bar.

The Timbers. In LaPorte Holiday Inn. 444 Pine Lake (362-8040). Daily, 6-10. Nightly entertainment. Bar. Attractive stone fireplace and massive wooden beams.

Tom's Landing. 304 Detroit (362-2916). Overlooking Clear Lake. Bar.

SHOPS.

Bernacchi Greenhouses. 1010 Fox (362-6202). Thousands of plants growing in a maze of greenhouses. Many varieties, mostly for the wholesale and retail holiday trades. Try not to miss the May 1 or December 1 tours for a visual and aromatic treat. Retail shop, Mondays-Saturdays, 9-5. Outdoor shop, Monday-Friday, 9-5, Saturday, 9-noon in spring and summer months.

Boulder Hill Vineyard. 3366 West 400N (326-7341). Daily, August 15-September 30, 10-8; rest of the year, Friday, 1-8; Saturday, 9-6, Sunday, noon-6. Grows only French hybrid grapes. Pick your own and have them crushed on the premises.

Sages Ice Cream. 204 2nd (362-2252). Tuesday-Saturday, 9:30-8:30; Sunday, 12:30-8:30. An old fashioned ice cream parlor which began serving home-made quality ice cream a century ago. The original fixtures still remain as does the penny candy counter of grandma's day and the friendliness and service associated with that era.

THEATER.

LaPorte Little Theater Company. Old St. John Lutheran Church, 218 A (362-5113). Community company with productions from October to May.

SPECIAL EVENTS.

July 4th Parade. An old fashioned parade down LaPorte's main street, Lincolnway, attracts over 100 units. Followed by musical entertainment at the Fox Lake Bandshell, fireworks at Clear Lake after dusk.

LaPorte County Fair*. Rt. 2 at 150N (362-2647). Held annually the second week in August. An old-time fair with lots of animals and produce on display, amusements.

SPECIAL FACILITIES.

Chamber of Commerce. 609 Michigan (362-3178).

LaPorte Community Hospital. 1007 Lincolnway (362-1234).

Maple City Airport. 2020 150W (362-7018). Charter flights.

LONG BEACH
(included in Michigan City's population)

MICHIANA SHORES
(1197 population)

After World War I, developers began building summer communities east of Michigan City. Today Long Beach, Duneland Beach, Shoreland Hills and Michiana Shores stretch to the Michigan state line. Michiana Shores straddles Michigan and Indiana and has a preponderence of log cabin type homes, many of which have become year-round residences. Drive along Lake Shore Drive to view the area as well as the ever-changing lake.

To See and Do

ANTIQUES.

Artisans Art and Antiques. 505 El Portal (872-2612) Saturday and Sunday, 10-6; Wednesday, 6-9. Nice selection of furniture and art.

ARCHITECTURE.

Bavarian-style house. 2704 Lake Shore, Long Beach. An 18 year old German architect built this gingerbread, gabled house. Note the stones on the roof to fend off wind damage.

John Lloyd Wright structures. Discover scattered throughout Long Beach and Duneland Beach residences and public buildings designed by Frank's son, John. They bear the Prairie School imprint. Experts considered them his best work. Contact the Community Center for the Arts, Eighth and Spring (872-6829) for more information.

ART AND ARTISTS.

Dave and Pat Dabbert (879-7201). Potters.
Gertrude Harbert (874-6374). Painter.
Karl Warren (872-8550). Painter.

LODGING.

Duneland Beach Inn. 3311 Potawatomi, Duneland Beach (874-7729). Once Mrs. Eser's boarding house, this small country inn provides bed and breakfast for its guests and Sunday brunch from March 15 to Christmas for the public. Private beach, good cross country skiing. Picks up guests at South Shore station in Michigan City.

126

Horseback Riding. Michiana Riding Academy. 3848 Academy (872-2114). Daily, 9-dusk. Pleasant wooded trails. Also horse and sleigh rides, boarding, instruction in dressage.

THEATER.

Dunes Summer Theater. Oakdale, Michiana Shores (879-8782). Summer stock each weekend in July and August performed by talented amateurs. Also children's plays and classes for children in the arts and the theater.

MICHIGAN CITY
(36,850 population)

Once larger than Chicago, this community at the mouth of Trail Creek along Lake Michigan has successively functioned as a booming port, a railroad and manufacturing center and a well-known resort town. Today, with its industrial and commercial base declining, Michigan City increasingly relies on its spectacular lakefront to help bolster its economy.

Changing patterns of transportation determined the city's history. For centuries, Indians paddled northward on Trail Creek to reach Lake Michigan. Father Marquette met here with the Potawatomi on his explorations in the 1670's. After Indiana became a state in 1826, the Trail Creek outlet to the Lake became Michigan City's harbor. The new Michigan Road connected the small community with the rest of the state all the way to the Wabash River. (A marker on the County Court House lawn at the corner of Rt. 12 and Washington shows where the road began.) Platted in 1832, Michigan City soon became a thriving community and a stagecoach stop on the Detroit to Chicago run. Beginning in 1836, federal funds to dredge the harbor helped make the town a busier place than Chicago. During the days of sail and steam ships, millions of feet of lumber, vast quantities of farm produce and thousands of pounds of fish left from the Michigan City piers.

In the mid 1850's, the railroad era began. With three railroad lines running through the city, available cheap prison labor (from the State prison located nearby) and the proximity of raw materials such as sand, clay, marl and lumber, Michigan City became an important manufacturing center. A major railroad car manufacturing plant, which became part of the Pullman empire, operated for over a century. In 1907 it ranked as the largest manufacturer in Indiana as well as the largest freight car plant in the country.

By 1900 Michigan City also functioned as a playground for Chicagoans. Excursion boats brought them across the Lake for one day trips or to vacation in summer cottages and hotels. The resort period lasted throughout the 1920's. From the lake, these visitors could see a spectacular natural landmark, the Hoosier Slide, a 184-foot high sand dune on the western side of the harbor. Once the largest sand mountain in the United States, it disappeared by 1920 mined to supply Indiana's glass factories and for other industrial uses as well as to provide a base for the Illinois Central Railroad tracks in Chicago. On that site today, a public utility cooling tower dominates the landscape.

Michigan City's port now functions as a haven for pleasure boats. An extensive redevelopment project to spruce up the city's North End has left blocks of empty land. Like other older industrial communities, Michigan City's industrial and commercial preeminence is fading. Its lakefront has become a prime tourist attraction with boating and outstanding salmon and trout fishing luring visitors to the city.

To See and Do

ANTIQUES.

Dorothy's Gift Shop. 404 Franklin (872-7164). Unpretentious, but especially good for local memorabilia.

Min's Treasure and Trash. 827 Franklin Square (874-3719). An apt name for a store where collectibles predominate but a "jewel" sometimes appears.

Old Pieces and Antiques. 631 Pine (879-7090). A house filled with an eclectic collection.

ARCHITECTURE.

Arndt House. 1305 Washington. A turn of the century

mansion typical of the spacious Victorian homes once predominant in this section of the city. Beautifully restored.

Barker Center. 631 Washington (872-0159). Monday-Friday, 10-3; Saturday, 11-3. The home of a turn-of-the-century railroad magnate, who hosted Vanderbilts, Clays and Fricks in his opulent mansion. The 38 room building contains many of the original furnishings as well as Aubusson tapestries. Note the remarkable continuity of design in the plaster, marble and wood decorations in the downstairs rooms and enjoy the beautiful Italianate gardens. Given to the city by the Barker family, it now serves as an elegant setting for social affairs. Listed on the National Register of Historic Places.

Brewery. York and East Michigan. An imaginative complex of offices and shops in the old Zorn beer plant that architect Ken Fryar has remodelled.

Michigan City Public Library. 4th and Franklin (879-4561). Winner of several national awards for design, this ultra-modern structure combines lots of glass, an interior atrium garden, exposed ductwork and bright colors into a sparkling home for books.

Mullen School. 100 Manny Court in the Sheridan Beach section (872-5783). Designed by the Shaver Partnership, this lovely building nestles in a spectacular dunes setting. The school has open classrooms radiating from a central library pit and bright graphics on the walls.

Porter-Kerrigan Home. 913 Washington. Restoration of this 22 room Romanesque Revival house with its massive carved porch and tower is underway. Note the varied skyline of dormers, roof peaks and chimneys.

Tonn & Blank Building. 126 East 5th. A handsome adaptive use of the old post ffice. Listed on the National Register of Historic Places.

Vail House. 404 Vail. To see the results of restoration, drive by this 1880's red brick home.

Waterford Inn. Johnson and Wozniak at I-94 overpass. Old stage coach hostelry on the Detroit to Chicago route.

Michigan City has a number of other old homes which have been or are being restored. Call the Michigan City Planning Department (872-9471) for more information.

Art and Artists.

Community Center for the Arts. 8th and Spring (872-6829). Tuesday-Friday, 9-5; Saturday, Noon-5; Sunday, 2-5. Housed in the old library building, the Center sponsors exhibits of local, regional and national art work, art classes, art tours. Gift shop. Listed on the National Register of Historic Places.

JoJo Bendix (872-6575). Weaver of clothing and modern designs.

Elizabeth Fleming (879-9446). Figure painting, oil, ink.

Richard Hunt's outdoor sculpture, "Hybrid Figure". In front of Restaurant Management building, 101 West 2nd.

Joe Jansek (872-7459). "Joe the Welder." Sculptor. Semi-representational animals and non-representational works created out of cast-off scrap metal.

Connie Kassell (879-6741). Staind glass, graphics.

Farms and Farm Produce.

Arndt's Orchards. 1875 North Wozniak (872-0122). Apples and cider.

Kintzele. 11366 West Earl (874-4779). Fresh and inexpensive vegetables from a truck farm.

N.W.D. Blueberry Ranch. 640 Freyer (872-7477). Pick your own or purchase.

Radke. 8999 West 200N (872-3140). Apples, pears, vegetables.

Flea Markets.

Anxious Al's. East Rt. 20, one-and-one-half miles east of Franklin Street (874-4130). A vast potpouri of everything and anything from antique nails to heavy machinery.

Wildwood Park Flea Market. 4938 Rt. 20 (879-5660). Friday-Sunday.

Gardens.

Jean Cook. 7757 North 600W (874-5081). Her fields of rainbow colored mums herald fall. Choose your plants and have them dug up for you. Reasonable.

International Friendship Gardens*. Liberty Trail (874-3664). Daily, 9-9. This memorial to world peace, created in 1934, occupies 100 acres east of the city and has a large variety of flora planted in the styles of various countries including specimens given by such celebrities as the late King Gustav of Sweden, Paderewski and Mussolini. Occasional concerts during the summer. Run-down but showing remnants of its original beauty.

Carl Pauley. 121 Top Flight (872-3379). More lilies, in more varieties, than one ever imagined.

Leo Sharp. 303 Fir (879-7638). A wonderful summertime display.

Viola Shawley. 212 South Roeske (872-3430). Grows and sells a huge variety of flowers.

HISTORICAL COLLECTION.

Indiana Room, Michigan City Public Library. 4th and Franklin (879-4561).

HISTORICAL MARKERS.

Commemorates the Battle of Trail Creek fought in the Revolutionary War. On lawn in front of Memorial Park Clubhouse. East 8th and Liberty Trail (872-8934).

Camp Anderson. The site of a Civil War camp. On the Neighborhood Center building, 1702 Michigan.

(Installation of other historical markers occurred as part of the city's sesquicentennial observance in 1983. The Michigan City Historical Society (872-6133) can provide a list.)

LODGING.

Creekwood Inn. 600W (872-8357). From exit 40B on I-94 go north to first intersection. Turn left on 600W, first left hand driveway. New bed and breakfast country inn on 30 acre rustic site. l2 individually furnished double guest rooms, all with bath and tv.

MOVIES.

Dunes Plaza Cinema I-VI. 100 Dunes Plaza, Rt. 20 (874-4281).

Marquette Theatre I-IV. Marquette Mall, Rt. 20 (872-9101).

212 Outdoor Theatre. Rt. 212 (872-1472).

MUSEUM.

Lighthouse Museum*. At the bend of the harbor to the west near the entrance to Washington Park (872-6133). Summer, Tuesday-Sunday, 1-5; winter, 1-3:30. Closed on holidays. Once used to guide ships in and out of the Michigan City harbor. The Michigan City Historical Society has painstakingly restored the building. Contains a fascinating collection of memorabilia of an older Indiana with displays of books, maps, photographs, ships and nautical life. Special exhibits. Gift shop.

MUSIC.

Mirage Lounge. In Holiday Inn. 5820 South Franklin (879-0311). Live entertainment in lovely art deco setting. Dancing. Tuesday-Saturday. Adjoining the Windrift Restaurant where the art deco theme continues.

Sloan's. In Howard Johnson Motel. 4122 South Franklin (874-7203). Wednesday,Friday-Saturday nights, 9-2. Dancing. Jazz, rock bands.

NATURE PRESERVE.

Barker Woods Nature Preserve. This 30 acre green oasis contains many trees, shrubs and flowers more commonly found farther north. Not open to the public. Property of The Nature Conservancy. For more information, call Midwest Office, National Audubon Society (879-3227).

RECREATION.

Boats-Charter. (For fishing on Lake Michigan). Contact LaPorte County Convention and Visitors Bureau (872-5055) for a listing of available charter boats.

Boats-Launching Areas. B&E Marine. Washington Park (879-8301).

Georg Boats and Motors. 83 North Franklin (872-8608).

South Lake Marine. 6th at bridge (872-7201).

Sprague Marina. Trail Creek (872-1712). 4 ramps free to Michigan City residents only with boats 25 feet and under.

Washington Park Marina*. Washington Park Basin (872-1712). 5 ramps; 1 for Hobie Cats only. Available for boats 25 feet and under.

Camping. KOA Campgrounds. Rt. 421, 4 miles south of Rt. 20 (872-7600).

Dancing-Square. Memorial Park. 8th and Liberty Trail (872-5642). Alternate Fridays, 8-11.

Fishing. At NIPSCO Generating Station's warm water discharge. Wabash and Water (872-1712). From steel walkway along Trail Creek or from breakwall. Dawn to dusk. For adults and children over 13 accompanied by an adult.

Trail Creek. Michigan and Chapala, about four miles southeast of Rt. 12.

Washington Park. From breakwater.

Golf. Michigan City North Municipal Golf Course. North Warnke (879-3478). March 15-December 1. 18 holes.

Michigan City South Municipal Golf Course. Wolf and East Michigan (872-2121). March 15-December 1. 18 holes.

Health Club. Northwest Racquet Club. 301 Kieffer (879-4401). Tennis, racquetball.

Park. Mount Baldy and Pinhook Bog. See Indiana Dunes National Lakeshore section for description.

Scuba Diving. Michigan City Scuba Center. 510 East 2nd (874-8979). Lessons, rental equipment.

The Lakefront. Over the years, Michigan City has developed its Lake Michigan shoreline into a wonderful recreational area, undoubtedly the biggest and best in these parts. In the summer months it teams with boaters, swimmers and just plain folks watching the hustle and bustle of a huge marina. Colorful and exciting, it's fun from early morning to late at night. There's a mile long, clean and safe swimming beach at the eastern end with life guards on duty.

The 90 acre Washington Park at the foot of Franklin (879-8393) adjoins the beach. Picnic shelters, fitness course, tennis courts, restored old fashioned band stand. During the summer months, on Thursday evenings at 8 p.m. in the bicentennial amphitheater, the Municipal Band gives concerts, occasionally with soloists.

A small friendly zoo* stands across from park. Open during the summer, daily, 10-6; winter, Monday-Friday, 10-3:30.

To the east of the zoo, during the Depression, the W.P.A. built a limestone observation tower now restored. Visitors can climb up its scenic stairway and spiral staircase to get a beautiful view of the lake and the Chicago skyline as well as a panorama of the shoreline. Open on the same schedule as the zoo.

(Non-Michigan City residents must pay a fee if they park in Washington Park. This regulation is strictly enforced.)

The Michigan City Port Authority owns and operates the busy harbor in Washington Park. During the summer months, 1,600 boats use its facilities. You can watch big and small sailing and power boats tie up to its docks. Try not to miss seeing the graceful craft in the Columbia Yacht Club and the Tri-State Races when they come in and moor. The Michigan City Yacht Club located to the west of the Lighthouse Museum serves as host.

The Coast Guard Station faces the Lake across from the Yacht Club. The Washington Park Marina, 418 slips, stretches to the east. The largest on the southern shore of Lake Michigan.

RESTAURANTS.

Maxine and Heine's. 521 Franklin (879-9068). Monday-Saturday, 4-midnight. Bar. Serves German food in a tavern setting with a huge TV screen. An old favorite with the football crowd. Every man for himself after the Notre Dame-Purdue game.

Panda. 3801 Franklin (872-7566). Monday-Friday, Saturday, 11:30-9:30; Sunday, 4-10. Chinese food.

The Pub. 723 Franklin Square (872-8631). Lunch, Monday-Friday, 11-3; dinner, Monday-Thursday, 5-10; Friday-Saturday, 5-11. Downtown eating place. Bar. Expensive.

SHOPS.

Anko. 731 Franklin Square (874-5555). LaPorte County's own high fashion designer of women's clothes. Pick off the rack or have an outfit made up especially for you. Also Dutch hand-knit sweaters.

Bortz Feed Store. 519 Chicago (874-4188). Monday-Saturday, 8-5:30. Also Sundays in May and June when they sell great quantities of flats of flower plants. An old fashioned feed and seed store at the same location for half a century.

Burnham Glove. 1608 Tennessee (874-5206). Factory store selling tremendous variety of gloves at lower than retail prices. If they make a glove for a special purpose, or in a special size, Burnham has it.

Furness Fisheries. 2nd at the Trail Creek bridge (874-4761). One of the few remaining Lake Michigan fishing families sells locally caught trout, salmon and perch in season as well as delicious smoked fish.

Great Lakes Duck Farm. Rt. 2 (874-6622). Baby ducks galore at Easter time.

Jaymar-Ruby. 209 West Michigan (879-6336). Factory outlet store. Carries huge stock of men's sportswear and suits. Good buys.

Parco. 502 Rt. 20 West (879-4431). Factory outlet store for fancy cookies baked on premises.

The Mart. 650 East Rt. 20 (874-6236). Several dealers offer discounted merchandise. Especially good for famous name, high quality men's and women's sportswear. Some samples.

SPECIAL EVENTS.

Drum and Bugle Corps Contest*. Ames Field. First Sunday in August. Largest competition in mid-west. Draws top bands from all over the country.

In-Water Boat Show*. Last week in August. Port Authority Basin (872-5335). Largest display of marine craft on the Great Lakes. Hundreds of boats for sailors and would-be sailors to inspect.

Lakefront Art Festival*. Washington Park (872-1829). Third weekend in August, 10-dusk. A combined effort of the Community Center for the Arts and the Michigan City Art League. Juried art show, food for sale, supervised painting for kids. Donation suggested.

Lakefront Music Festival.* Bicentennial Amphitheatre, Washington Park (879-6440). Last weekend in June. Noon-midnight. Folk, rock, blue grass music, art exhibit, arts and crafts booths, food.

Lighthouse Treasurama. On the grounds of the Old Lighthouse Museum. Washington Park (872-6311). Last Saturday in July, 10-4. A fun way to spend a summertime Saturday. Home baked goods, books, collectibles, flea market, food, and some antiques.

Library Book Sale. Twice yearly the Michigan City Public Library (879-4561) holds a giant sale of donated and discarded books. Build up a personal library for a pittance. Call for times and dates.

Miss Indiana Pageant finals*. Rogers High School. Last Thursday-Saturday in June. Tickets available in advance at Marquette Mall or at the door.

Oktoberfest. Washington Park. Labor Day weekend. Friday, 5-1; Saturday-Sunday, 1-1; Monday, 1-8. Four days of ethnic foods for sale, ethnic entertainment, carnival rides and booths, folk and rock music. Draws crowds.

Sinai Temple Sale. 2800 Franklin (874-4477). Yearly enormous offering of used clothing, books, furniture, linens. Crowds line up to get in. Bargains galore. Call for date.

Summer Festival. Saturday after July 4th for a week. Sidewalk sales, a big parade and a kiddie parade, entertainment, athletic contests. Second Saturday, Fun Day in Washington Park; second Sunday, fireworks at dusk. Call 872-2162 for further information.

THEATER.

Footlight Players. Johnson (874-4035). Amateur theater group performs in three productions yearly.

Festival Players. Canterbury Theater. 907 Franklin (874-4269). Wednesday-Saturday evening performances, Wednesday matinee. Semi-professional resident company presents summer stock in an attractively remodelled century old church.

SPECIAL FACILITIES.

Chamber of Commerce. 711 Franklin (874-6221). Monday-Friday, 9-5.

Joe Phillips Airport. Michigan (872-5571). Charter flights as well as regularly scheduled flights to Chicago's O'Hare Airport.

Memorial Hospital. 5th and Pine (879-0202).

Municipal Airport. South Franklin (879-0291). Charter flights.

St. Anthony Hospital. 301 West Homer (879-8511).

OTIS
(200 population)

A tiny hamlet whose nearby farms belong to second and third generation Poles. Otis has an attractive Catholic Church. See nearby the old Eight-Square Cemetery on the LaPorte-Porter County Road south of Burdick Road.

ROLLING PRAIRIE
(540 population)

Three Indiana trails crossed near this town on the southwest fork of the Sauk Trail. On one, Indians walked from Illinois to Detroit to collect annuities from the British for their support in the Revolutionary War and the War of 1812. Another route connected Fort Wayne and Fort Dearborn, and the third went north to Michigan City, then east to the mouth of the Chicago River. (A historical marker on Rt. 20 in the rest area on the south side of the road commemorates all three.)

Settled in the early 1830's, the community has remained a thriving farm town ever since.

To See and Do

ARCHITECTURE.

Foster-Shuck House (c. 1833). Jimmerson Shores Road, north of Rt. 20. Greek Revival style.

Provolot-McGuire House (c. 1843). Byron Road north of Rt. 20. Built by Ezekial Provolot, the town's founder. Notice its center entrance and pronounced pilasters. Representative of many homes built in the area by settlers from Ohio.

FARMS AND FARM PRODUCE.

Quail Ridge Farms. 3382 East 1000N (778-2194). Exotic varieties of fruits and vegetables, unusual plants, a spectacular herb garden, and a store filled with books, oriental items, interesting collectibles—all this and more await the visitor to this expanding operation. The animals, from ducks to goats, will enchant children; adults will find much to please their eye and palate.

Sun Acre Fruit Farm. 300E, 4.2 miles north of Rt. 20 (778-2483). To savor the LaPorte County's flavorful fruits in the wintertime, this farm freezes much of its crops.

RECREATION.
Camping. Rolling Timbers Park and Campground. 5502 East Rt. 2 (778-2498).

Golf. Valley Hills Golf Course. 3544 East Rt. 2 (778-2823). 9 holes.

Lakes. Hog Lake*. Two-and-a-half miles north of town on Rt. 425E, west one-half miles on 700N (778-2241). 59 acres with public fishing, boat rental, tent camping, public launch ramp, ice fishing.
   Rolling Timbers Lake.* Two miles east of town, south of Rt. 2 (778-4107). Fishing, picnicking.
   Saugany Lake.* East on Rt. 2 near intersection of Rt. 20 (778-2926). 74 acres, swimming, fishing.

UNION MILLS
(469 population)

Once the center of Indian Mound country, Union Mills is now a small town in the midst of farm lands.

To See and Do
AUCTION.
   111 Hamilton (767-2407). Saturday nights at 7. Furniture, glassware, collectibles and a few antiques.

SHOP.
   Ed Klein's Saddle Shop. South on Rt. 39 between Rts. 6 and 30 (767-2640). Tuesday-Thursday, 8-5; Monday and Friday, 8-9; Saturday, 8-noon. One of the vanishing breed of leather craftsmen who learned his trade from an old harness maker.

WANATAH
(879 population)

A center for farm equipment and supplies, this community

dates back to 1865 and for a while thrived as a railroad hub. The Indian name means "knee-deep-in-mud". To this day Hog Creek periodically overflows its banks.

To See and Do

FARMS AND FARM PRODUCE.

Pinney-Purdue Experimental Farms. North side of Rt. 30 at 100N (733-2379). Purdue University's College of Agriculture conducts agronomy research on this 450 acre farm with its century old farmhouse. Open House Day in July with demonstrations of farming techniques and crafts. Call farm for date.

Siegesmund Berry Farm. Four-and-a-half-miles south of town on Rt. 421, one mile east on 900W (733-2259). Blueberries.

Tidholm's Strawberry Farm. Three-and-a-half miles south of town on 1550S (733-2560). 40 acres of strawberries and blueberries.

RECREATION.

Camping. KOA Campground. Rt 30, Hanna (797-2395). (Three miles east of Wanatah.)

SPECIAL EVENT.

Summer Festival*. Third weekend in July. Pit beef barbeque, horse-pulling contest, art show, childrens' rides, sports.

WESTVILLE

(2,887 population)

Home of a unit of the state prison system, and of the Purdue-North Central campus (north on Rt. 421). There are two historical markers in Westville: one north of town on Rt. 421 indicating the Old Sauk Trail and the other on West Main Street at the railroad tracks commemorating a stop of the Lincoln funeral train.

To See and Do

ARCHITECTURE.

Forrester House. East of town on Rt. 2. An old red brick home with a handsome cupola and two staircases, one for men and one for women.

ART AND ARTISTS.

Tony Popp (926-4764). Metal sculptor.

COLLEGES AND UNIVERSITIES.

Purdue University-North Central Campus. Rt. 421 north of town (872-0527).

RECREATION.

Lake. Clear Lake*. North of Rt. 2 on Porter-LaPorte County Line Road (872-9363). 17 acres with swimming, fishing, picnicking, boat rental, launch ramp. Open only to seasonal subscribers.

ST. JOSEPH COUNTY
(241,617 population)

Father Marquette came to St. Joseph County in 1675, when on his last and fatal expedition, he portaged near South Bend from the Kankakee River to the St. Joseph River, making this the first county in Indiana ever seen by a European. The two rivers have dominated the county's development from Indian days. They provided the main transportation routes for tribes from Canada and the northern United States to the south. Both the Kankakee and the St. Joseph originate in St. Joseph County, the former flowing to the Gulf of St. Lawrence and the latter to the Gulf of Mexico.

The valley of the St. Joseph River makes up the northern portion of the county and that of the Kankakee, the southern section. The Valparaiso Moraine's eastern edge extends into St. Joseph County accounting for its many glaciated lakes and rolling countryside dotted with fruit farms.

The county's fertile soil attracted pioneer settlers. Many

ST. JOSEPH COUNTY

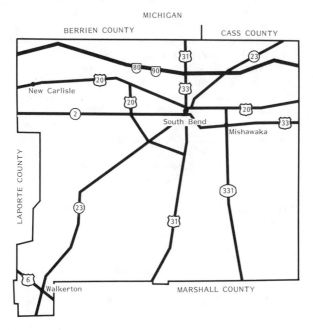

settled the Terre Coupe Prairie, north of South Bend. Today this rich farm area yields bumper crops of corn and soy beans. Other pioneers traded with the Indians and became merchants and small businessmen.

St. Joseph organized as a county in 1830 and originally covered all of northern Indiana to the Illinois border; today its 459 square miles extend from Elkhart County on the east to LaPorte County on the west and from Marshall County on the south to Berrien County, Michigan on the north.

The waters of the St. Joseph River provided an early source of power for industry. Factories developed in the Mishawaka-South Bend area, the county's only urban center, after the discovery of bog iron close to the river bed. The two cities, on opposite banks of the river, functioned for more than a century as major manufacturing centers, especially in the transportation field. Now, like other older industrial cities, they have turned to commercial, service and retail operations.

MISHAWAKA
(40,201 population)

Mishawaka, the Princess city, gets its name from the daughter of Shawnee Chief Elkhart. She chose "Dead Shot," a white trapper her suitor over his jealous Indian rival Grey Wolf. Tribal wars followed as a result, but in the end, "Dead Shot" won the lady and named the St. Joseph River town after her.

The city's history dates from the discovery of bog iron deposits in the 1830's. Settlers poured in to mine the ore. They built the first blast furnace in Indiana which attracted much industry. The industry attracted workers and soon waves of migration brought Italians, Poles and Belgians. At various times, plows, wagons, farm implements, windmills, woolens and Amplex and Simplex cars have originated here. Today Mishawaka serves as home to Bendix, Dodge and Wheelabrater.

To See and Do

ANTIQUES.

100 Center. Lincolnway West (Rt. 33) (256-6611). Five shops covering the gamut from giftie items to costly antiques.

Architectural Tour.

100 Beiger Heritage Corporation. 317 Lincolnway East (256-0365). Mishawaka's active historic preservation group will provide tours of important old historic sites by arrangement.

Architecture.

Beiger Mansion. 117 Lincolnway West. Restoration now underway after partial destruction in a 1975 fire. Listed on the National Register of Historic Places.

Dodge House. 415 Lincolnway East. Listed on the National Register of Historic Places.

William B. Hosford Residence. 722 Lincolnway. Listed on the National Register of Historic Places.

Hutchinson-Schindler Home (c. 1900-1910). 810 Lincolnway East. Large graceful frame houseypical of the turn of the century.

Merrifield-Cass House (c. 1837). 816 Lincolnway East. Originally one story, this house expanded during the Civil War. Porch with Gothic carpentry added in 1871.

Kamm and Schellinger Brewery. 100 Center Street. Old plant now adapted to commercial use.

Niles-Weiss Home (c. 1837). 410 Lincolnway East. Renaissance-type house with handsome curved staircase and marble fireplaces. Now the home of the Mishawaka Children's Museum.

St. Joseph Church (c. 1893). Corner of Third and Mill Streets. Gothic and German influence. Oldest Catholic congregation in city. Hand-carved communion rail. Stained glass window of Last Supper displayed at Chicago's Columbian Exposition in 1893.

Fish Hatchery.

Twin Branch State Fish Hatchery. 13200 East Jefferson (255-4199). Open daily, year round, 8-4. Armed with a self-guide brochure, visitors may view the broodstock raceways, incubators, rearing raceways and other areas designed to produce 225,000 seven-inch steelhead out and 425,000 three-inch chinook salmon annually.

Movies.

Town and Country. 2340 Hickory (259-9090).

University Park Cinema, University Park Mall. 6501 Grape (277-2223).

MUSEUM.

Mishawaka Children's Museum. 410 Lincolnway East (259-3475). Monday-Friday, noon-4; other times by appointment. One of three such museums in Indiana, it has a hands-on policy allowing kids to stroke the mastodon bones and rock the Indian baby dolls. Collection has a historic preservation flavor.

MUSIC AND THEATER.

Bethel College Goodman Auditorium. 1001 McKinley (259-8511). A variety of programs and productions throughout the year suit all tastes. Call for schedule.

NATURE CENTER.

South Bend Audubon Society Nature Sanctuary. Clover Road off Dragoon Trail (291-2830). Guided tours on Sundays only, 1-5.

RECREATION.

Boats-Launching Areas. St. Joseph River, Mishawaka Central Park (255-6610).

Pleasant Lake*. Golden Lake Road and 370W about ten miles south of Mishawaka near Lakeville.

Golf. Eberhart-Petro Municipal Course. 801 North State (255-5508). 18 holes.

Family Golf Center. 303 East Day (256-2800). 18 hole miniature.

Putt Putt Golf and Games. 3615 North Main (259-4171). Three 18 hole miniatures.

Parks. Battell Park. Mishawaka Avenue four blocks west of Main (255-6610). Beautiful rock garden around steps leading to St. Joseph River. Goldfish pond.

Merrifield Park and Recreation Complex. East Mishawaka Avenue (255-6610). Bordered by the St. Joseph River, this park boasts an olympic sized swimming pool, a refrigerated ice rink, boat launch, ball diamonds, and much, much more.

Tennis. Battell Park. 301 West Mishawaka. Three lighted outdoor courts.

Merrifield Recreation Complex. 1000 East Mishawaka (255-6777). Three lighted outdoor courts.

RESTAURANTS.

Band Organ. 211 East Day (259-0050). Tuesday-Thursday, 5-10; Friday and Saturday, 11:30-2 and 5-midnight; Sunday, noon-10. Pizza, salads and sandwiches play second fiddle to the tunes belted out by the 24-rank 1926 Wurlitzer theater pipe organ featured here.

Doc Pierce's. 120 North Main (255-7737). Lunch, Monday-Saturday, 11-2; dinner, Monday-Thursday, 5-11; Friday and Saturday, 5-1. A local favorite for Tiffany lamped decor as well as for well-prepared standards, steak, onion soup, sea food and the like. Good service. Bar.

New Yorktowne Deli. 106 North Main (259-6600). Breakfast, lunch and dinner; closed Saturday. A good variety of deli specialties to eat in or take out. Bagels, croissants and other goodies baked on the site.

Papa Joe's Casa de Pasta. 1209 South Union (255-0890). From Lincolnway and State in downtown Mishawaka, go south on State to 13th. Left (west) on 13th to Union. Friday and Saturday, 5-10; group parties on other days by special arrangement. Specializing in authentic Italian dishes, all with homemade pasta. Absolutely incredible decor. Wine and beer. Moderately priced.

SHOPS.

100 Center. 700 Lincolnway West (Rt. 33) (259-7861). The old (1853) Kammes Brewery on the St. Joseph River, now houses a large, interesting shopping, dining and entertainment complex utilizing five old brewery buildings as well as a few new ones. You can see movies in the old boiler house or choose some art or crafts in former storage rooms that once held hops and malt. In all, 40 shops, five restaurants and a movie theater occupy the space. The old machinery converts to outdoor sculpture. Paddleboat trips along the river in summer. Tours available.

Watson's Part II. Lower level, 100 Center (259-2105). A branch of the famous plate collector's paradise in New Carlisle.

Arts and Crafts Fair. 100 Center, Rt. 33 (256-9626). July. Over 150 exhibitors from all around the nation bring their crafts and music.

NEW CARLISLE
(1,439 population)

Once a stop for stagecoaches on the Chicago-Detroit run, New Carlisle now serves as a trading center for farmers in the surrounding area. Richard Carlisle, a Philadelphian, gave the town his name in 1830, and named its streets after his native city. Schuyler Colfax, the nation's Vice President under Ulysses Grant, lived here as a teenager. So did Elias Baldwin. Then in the 1849 Gold Rush, he went west, hit it big in the Comstock Lode, and country-wide became known as "Lucky Baldwin."

New Carlisle also enjoyed a bit of fame because of its Opera House, built in 1873. Although the 1870 census listed the town's population as 500, a New York agent misread or miscopied the figure as 5,000. As a result, for a number of years, touring New York opera companies included New Carlisle in their circuit.

To See and Do

Hamilton Church. Walnut and Old Chicago Roads. Greek Revival. Begun in 1838, the church burned down before completion. The townspeople rebuilt and dedicated it in 1843.

Hubbard House (c. 1881). Southwest corner of Cherry and Front Streets. Notice ceiling-to-floor windows. Elaborate exterior decoration with applied wood porch details and chalet-style gables.

Methodist Church (now Apostolic) (c. 1870). Front Street.

Olive Chapel (c. 1870). Two miles south of town at junction of Timothy and Rt. 2.

Art and Artists.

Anthony J. Droege II. (654-7485). Oil painter.

Cemeteries.

Hamilton Cemetery. Old Chicago Road. Graves of soldiers dating back to Revolutionary War.

Town Cemetery. Rt. 20 west of town. Organized in 1863.

Recreation.

Camping. Mini-Mountain Campground. Rt. 2 (654-3431). Open year round.

Park. Bendix Woods County Park (*weekends). Rt. 2 south of town (641-3155). Once the proving grounds for the Studebaker Company, then sold to the Bendix Corporation who, in turn, gave it to the county. This lovely area includes prairie and a hardwood forest. The churches of Michiana raised the money for a "whispering woods trail" for the handicapped and blind. It features ramps, plants selected for their delicious aromas and cassettes to inform blind visitors. Today the park also has four miles of hiking trails, a fine nature center offering varied activities, picnic areas, downhill ski slopes, an inner tubing run, ponds, horseshoe courts, ice skating, cross country skiing and tobogganing. This park provides such a wealth of facilities and programs it's best to check with Program Activities (277-8142) for activities, fees and hours.

Restaurant.

Miller's Home Cafe. 110 East Michigan (Rt. 20) (654-3431). Tuesday-Thursday, 4-8; Friday and Saturday, 4-8:30; Sunday 11:30-7:30. Also lunches. Home cooked smorgasbord modestly priced.

Shop.

Watson's. 135 East Michigan (654-3511). This place for plate people describes itself as an old-fashioned shop in an old-fashioned town but don't believe it. If limited edition collector plates appeal, Watson's carries the most complete stock anywhere: B & G, Goebel, Royal Doulton and many more. Headquarters of one of the largest collector's clubs around. Other unique items as well.

Historical Days. Michigan Street. Last week in July. Flea market, circus parade, costume contest, beer garden and historical reenactments. Tours of historical sites. Call Public Library (654-3046) for information.

Maple Syrup Program and Pancake and Sausage Breakfast. * Glen Bauer Shelter, Bendix Woods County Park (654-3158). March. Sugar bush tours, forestry field day.

Winter Festival. Bendix Woods County Park (654-3155). January. Ski and inner tube races, snow games, torch light ski parade.

SOUTH BEND
(109,727 population)

Now enjoying an architectural and cultural renaissance, the city that lies in the south bend of the St. Joseph River has had its ups and downs. Originally Indians lived in villages along the St. Joseph River. These tribes paddled up and down and portaged over to the Kankakee, thus connecting the two major water systems of North America. In 1679 Robert LaSalle arrived here with the Jesuit Father Louis Hennepin to see this link between the St. Lawrence Basin and the Mississippi River.

Two fur traders, Pierre Navarre and Alexis Coquillard, first settled the area. Coquillard together with Lathrop M. Taylor founded the town first called Southhold and then South Bend. With the discovery of iron ore in Mishawaka, South Bend got its first real growth spurt. Five young brothers named Studebaker opened their wagon works in 1852. Their business soon became the largest of its kind in the world. They built carriages for the White House, covered wagons for the pioneers and wagons for the Union Army. From 1902 to 1963 they built automobiles for everyone.

James Oliver manufactured the chilled plow in South Bend. This tool played a vital role in breaking the prairie of the Midwest and the plains.

During the Civil War, South Benders helped runaway slaves on their escape route to Canada. In addition to a large influx of blacks, South Bend has had repeated waves of ethnic migration: Germans, Poles, Hungarians, Russians, Belgians and Irish.

The Irish, of course, made their headquarters at the University of Notre Dame du Lac, a college founded in 1842 by Father Edward Sorin. (A reproduction of his log cabin stands on the campus next to the original College building.) When the "Fighting Irish" football team has a home game, traffic jams Rt. 31 from sun-up to sun-down. The football frenzy probably reached its zenith under Knute Rockne, the late, great coach who, in his prime, allegedly walked the streets of South Bend arguing football strategy with everyone from barbers to retail clerks. In the past few decades, particularly under President Theodore M. Hesburgh, Notre Dame has taken its place as an important intellectual center. The university has given the city a measure of sophistication and a sphere of regional influence extending beyond Indiana into Michigan.

After a period of blight and decay, South Bend has undertaken major urban renewal projects. On the east bank of the St. Joseph River, developers have turned three old warehouses into an exciting shopping and restaurant complex. Downtown, Century Center, a theater and entertainment facility, exemplifies the renaissance. Today, many industries as well as such educational institutions as Saint Mary's College, Holy Cross Junior College and the regional campuses of both Indiana University and the Indiana Vocational and Technical College call South Bend home. And finally, and perhaps a bit bumpily, the South Shore Railroad makes its last stop in South Bend.

To See and Do

ANTIQUES.
*South Bend Antique Mart.** 4H Fairgrounds. Intersection of Jackson and South Ironwood (291-0075). Held some Sundays in good weather months, 8-4:30. Over 150 dealers bring goods of every description and ply their wares. Under roof stalls; food available. Call for dates.
Thieves Market. 2309 E. Edison (233-9820). Weekends

only 10-6. Forty-six antique dealers display their collections in individual stalls all housed under one roof.

The Wooden Indian. 50877 1/2 Rt. 31 North and Greenacre (277-3892). Sunday-Thursday 10-6; Friday and Saturday, 10-8. Authentic Indian artifacts and art work both modern and old. Everything from blankets and tomahawks to gold, silver and beadwork.

ARCHITECTURAL TOURS.

South Bend Heritage Corporation (289-1066). A new group dedicated to neighborhood preservation rather than that of single historic sites. Group tours available by arrangement.

Southhold Restoration. 502 West Washington (234-3441). Tours of South Bend historic sites. Call for schedule.

ARCHITECTURE.

Bartlett House. 720 West Washington (1850). Marker on front lawn. Indians bent the tree here to mark their ancient trail. Bartlett's grandfather signed the Declaration of Independence. Federal style, one of the oldest brick houses in the city, it has two-foot thick foundations, hand hewn walnut beams, half-inch thick aprons and sills of cast iron. Unique. The house has secret passages for the family to escape in case of Indian attack. When Bartlett retired he used brick from the oven in his commercial bakery to pave the walk.

Chapin Park Historic District. Roughly bounded by the St. Joseph River, Main, Madison, Rex, Lindsay and William Streets and Leland and Portage Avenues. Listed on the National Register of Historic Places.

Chapin-Willis House (1855). 407 West Navarre. Frame with arched windows. One of only 50 examples of Gothic Revival in the United States.

Horatio Chapin House. 601 Park. Listed on the National Register of Historic Places.

Cushing House (1882). 508 West Washington. Front doors of this house took first prize at Chicago's 1893 World's Fair. Italian style house, long narrow windows, fine woodwork.

James A. Judie House. 1515 East Jefferson. Listed on the National Register of Historic Places.

Chauncey N. Lawton House. 405 West Wayne. Listed on the National Register of Historic Places.

Main and South Quadrangles. University of Notre Dame. Off Rts 80-94. Listed on the National Register of Historic Places.

Old Courthouse Museum (c. 1855). 112 South Lafayette. Greek Revival. One of the few remaining examples of Chicago architect John Van Osdel's work. Moved to this site in 1897. Museum since 1907. Originally a courthouse. Listed on the National Register of Historic Places.

Joseph D. Oliver House. 808 Washington. Listed on the National Register of Historic Places.

Saint Paul's Memorial Methodist Church (1901). 1001 West Colfax. Gift of Clement Studebaker and his wife who bought the stained glass windows while visiting the Mayer and Company glass works in Munich. Note the window of St Paul preaching from Mars Hill. Baptismal font by Roman marble workers of the twelfth or thirteenth century.

Tippecanoe Place. 620 West Washington. Former digs of Clement Studebaker who made a bundle in the wagon business back before the turn of the century. The 40 room, 20 fireplaced fieldstone mansion has been lovingly, elegantly restored and turned into a restaurant. A must see whether you want to eat or not. Listed on the National Register of Historic Places.

West Washington Historic District. Roughly bounded by Main Street, Western and La Salle Avenues and McPherson Street. Listed on the National Register of Historic Places, this makes a satisfying tour for history and architecture buffs. Contact the Historic Preservation Commission 284-9798 for information.

Frank Lloyd Wright Homes. Two of Indiana's five Wright homes are here:

Avalon Grotto-De Rhoades House (1906). 705 West Washington. This, in Wright's Prairie style, has long, low eaves and leaded glass windows. Viewing from the street only.

Herman T. Mossberg House (1951). 1404 Ridgedale. Example of late Wright work.

ART AND ARTISTS.

Baldoni Fine Arts. 411 Hickory (287-6661).

Hibel Art Gallery. 602 North Michigan (233-2232). Original lithographs, oils and porcelains.

Moreau-Hammes Galleries. Saint Mary's College (284-4854). Monday-Friday 9:30-noon and 1-3; Sunday 1-3.

Snite Museum of Art. University of Notre Dame (239-5466). Tuesday-Friday, 10-4; Weekends 1-4. Opened in 1980 this center exhibits major international and American works running from ancient and medieval through 20th century.

Century Center. 120 South St. Joseph (284-9102). Tuesday-Sunday, 1-5. Both permanent collection and current exhibits, classes, museum shop. The center houses the Warner Gallery on the street level which presents major exhibits by national and international artists and the Woman's Art League Upper Level Gallery which features monthly shows of work by local and regional artists.

FARM.

Martin Blad Mint Farm. 58995 Rt. 123 (234-7271). This 2,500 acre peppermint farm, one of the largest in the country, sells in bulk to Wrigley. Call for an appointment to visit in July to see this big and growing industry from the ground up. The highly mechanized Blad farm has bright yellow mint wagons, specially designed to haul the newly harvested crop into the mint press building. The wagons act as cook pots for 50 minutes while the oil is separated, picked up like steam, guided through coils and pumped into 55 gallon containers.

GARDENS.

Fragrance Garden. Leeper Park, 900 block of North Michigan Street (284-9405).

Morris Conservatory and Muessel-Ellison Tropical Gardens. Mishawaka Avenue (284-9442). Daily, 9-9. Three major flowering shows a year. Arizona Desert Garden features a worldwide selection of more than 300 varieties of cactus.

HISTORICAL SITES.

Highland Cemetery. 2557 Portage. Here stands an oak tree called the Council Oak, allegedly 700 years old. On this site, during the French and Indian War, LaSalle convinced the Miami and Illinois tribes to side with the French against the Iroquois.

Pierre Navarre Cabin. Leeper Park. 900 block of North Michigan Street (Rt. 31) (284-9405). Pierre Navarre, a French fur trader, built a combination home and trading post on the north bank of the St. Joseph River. His cabin now stands here and visitors can get a real flavor of the settler's life in 1820. They can also see the Powell Home, the dwelling of South Bend's first black settler.

LODGINGS.

Bed and Breakfast. Home of Marge Chomyn (233-7791). Marge has three bedrooms available just 11 minutes from Notre Dame. Shared bath, full breakfast, modest prices.

Morris Inn. On Notre Dame campus (234-0141). 91 rooms, restaurant, 18 hole golf course with putting green.

MOVIES.

Forum Cinema. 52709 Rt. 31 North (277-1522).
River Park Theater. 2929 Mishawaka (288-8488).
Scottsdale Theater. 1153 Scottsdale Mall (291-4583).

MUSEUMS.

Discovery Hall Museum. * 120 South St. Joseph, Century Center (284-9714). Tuesday-Friday, 10-4:30; Saturday, 10-4; Sunday 1-4; Tuesdays free. Displays and exhibits telling of the community's industrial history through the products of Bendix, Birdsell, Oliver, South Bend Range.

Old Courthouse Museum. 112 South Lafayette (284-9664). Monday-Friday 9-5; Sunday 1-5. Previously called the Northern Indiana Historical Society Museum, and housed in the former St. Joseph County Courthouse, this museum concentrates on exhibits of pioneer tools, toys, powder horns, newspaper presses, fire engines and Indiana, particularly South Bend, lore. Many costumes and photos. It also boasts a genealogy library consisting of 4,000 old books. A good resource for roots seekers.

Studebaker Exhibit.* 520 South Lafayette (284-9108). Tuesday-Friday, 11-4; Saturday, 10-4; Sunday, 1-4; Tuesday free. Now under the auspices of the Discovery Hall Museum, the 1919 building (originally built as a factory dealership) contains 25 Studebaker products including four presidential carriages and the last Studebaker car ever made.

MUSIC.

Saint Mary's College. (284-4176). Check for monthly schedule.

South Bend Symphony. Morris Civic Auditorium. 211 North Michigan. Call South Bend Symphony (232-6343) for schedule.

NATURE PRESERVES.

Spicer Lake Nature Preserve. County Line Road three and 3/4 miles north of Rt. 20, just east of the LaPorte-St. Joseph County line and just south of the Indiana-Michigan border (277-4828). A melting block of ice left behind when the last glacier left Indiana created this pothole lake. It illustrates the stages of succession from open water to swamp forest and abounds in vegetation typical of each stage.

Swamp Rose Nature Preserve. Northeast corner Potato Creek State Recreation Area. 25601 Rt.4, 13 miles southwest of South Bend (656-8186). Another glacial remnant, with profuse quantities of swamp rose, marsh marigold, blue flag, jewelweed and bittercress; also dense colonies of rushes, sedges, cattails and grasses. On higher ground a hardwood forest predominates.

RECREATION.

Boats-Charter. 1602 Ewing (289-1905).

Boats-Launching Areas. St. Patrick's Farm. St. Joseph River. Two miles north on Laurel off Auten (277-8142). Public ramp.

St. Joseph River. Northwest of South Bend on Riverside Drive. Public ramp.

Golf. Ebel Park Municipal Course. 26595 Auten, seven miles west of city (272-4009). April-November. 18 holes.

Erskine Park Course. 4200 Miami (291-0156). April-November. 18 holes.

Playland Golf Center. 1715 Lincolnway East (288-0033). 9 holes, 18 hole miniature, driving range. Night lighted. March 15-December 1.

Robin Hood Course. 20099 New Road, seven miles south of city (291-2450). March 15-December 1. 9 holes.

Studebaker Course. 718 East Calvert (237-9136). March 15-November 30. 9 holes.

Parks. Potato Creek State Recreation Area. 25601 Rt. 4, 13 miles southwest of South Bend (656-8186). Open daily, year round from 7 a.m.-11 p.m. The result of 30 years of effort by self-taught naturalist, Darcy Worster and others, Potato Creek became a state park in 1977. Worster Lake, named in recognition of his efforts, is a major attraction in the park offering anglers a year round chance to reel in bass, bluegill, crappie, channel catfish and once and a while brown trout. The park also has 287 family campsites, a 70 site horsemen's campground. Housekeeping cabins rented Saturday to Saturday June through August; Friday and Saturday nights together only in April, May, September and October. Bike Trail, beach and lake swimming, cross country skiing, nature preserve.

Potawatomi Park. 2105 Mishawaka (284-9401). 60 acres including recreation and picnic areas, tennis courts, pool, gardens and zoo. A new learning center houses a zoo lab, aquaria, six major animal exhibits and a classroom.

Rum Village Park. 1304 West Ewing (284-9455). Sunday-Friday 10-5. A 160 acre park containing a 55 acre nature woodland. Picnicking, nature trails. The southwest portion of the park contains the Nature Center and natural history exhibits. Rum Village Park also features Safetyville, a simulated city for kids 5-12 which stresses bike, pedestrian and automobile safety. Monday-Friday 8:30-2:30; other times by appointment. Call 284-9496.

St. Patrick's County Park (*weekends). 50650 Laurel (277-4828). Canoe rental, beach swimming, fishing, inner tubing and cross-country skiing.

Tennis. Leeper Park Tennis Center. Michigan at Park (284-9405). 15 outdoor lighted courts.

Potawatomi Park. Mishawaka at Greenlawn (284-9401). Four outdoor lighted courts.

RELIGIOUS SITE.

Lourdes Grotto. University of Notre Dame. A replica of the famous French shrine where millions have gone over the centuries to pray for a cure.

RESTAURANTS.

Captain Alexander's Moonraker. 320 East Colfax (234-4477). Dinner, daily; Sunday brunch. Seafood specialties, nautical decor, river view. Good salad bar and homemade bread. Bar, entertainment, dancing.

East Bank Emporium. 121 South Niles (234-9000). Lunch and dinner, Monday-Saturday. Attractive eatery in a well-restored old warehouse overlooking the river. Bar.

Eddie's. 1345 North Ironwood (232-5861). Lunch and dinner, daily. This old standby has stood the test of time. Simply prepared favorites from land and sea. Bar.

Lee's Grill and Barbecue. 1132 South Bend (237-9167). Dinner, Tuesday-Saturday. Casual student ambience; spicy sauce and cold beer.

Morris Inn. Notre Dame campus (234-0141). Breakfast, lunch and dinner, daily. American favorites in the beef and fish line.

Senor Kelly's. 119 North Michigan (234-5389). Lunch and dinner, daily. An incongruous assortment of Irish and Mexican fare voted top drawer by native South Benders. Accomodates large groups in the heart of downtown.

Tippecanoe Place. 620 West Washington (234-9077). Lunch and dinner Monday-Friday; dinner Saturday and Sunday; Sunday brunch. Located in the old Studebaker mansion and worth a meal for the privilege of seeing the exquisite restoration. Sumptuous Sunday brunch.

SHOPS.

Farmers' Market. 760 South Eddy (282-1259). Tuesday and Thursday, 7-2; Saturday, 7-3; open Fridays in summer. Large, colorful market with 125 stalls selling fruit, vegetables, meat, fowl, hickory smoked bacon, mushrooms, flowers, superb baked goods and even rocks, fossils and some pets. In the coldest weather the Amish plain people come in with their apples and tomatoes protected by individual newspaper wrappings.

South Bend Cut Glass Company. 225 South Michigan (288-0347). Owned and operated by glass cutter Richard L. Martin. Visitors can watch him cut his unique designs into glass by holding it against a grinding wheel. In addition to Martin's original patterns, the shop carries Fostoria, Lenox and Imperial crystal as well as glassware from Europe including Rumania, Poland and Turkey.

SPECIAL EVENTS.

Firefly Festival. St. Patrick's County Park. 50651 Laurel (277-4828). Summer entertainment for the first three weeks in July including orchestral and band concerts, theater.

4-H Fair. Jackson and Lakewood Streets (291-4870). First week in August. The largest of its kind in Indiana. Animal and craft exhibits during the day, entertainment at night.

Gem, Mineral and Jewelry Festival. Athletic and Convocation Center, University of Notre Dame. September. Displays and working demonstrations of jewelry-making. Sales, silent auction. Call 293-5030 for information.

North Liberty Potato Creek Festival. Downtown City Park. Mid-August. Everything from arts and crafts to helicopter rides and sky diving exhibitions. Contact Chamber of Commerce, 234-0051, for information.

South Bend Ethnic Festival. River Bend Plaza Downtown (284-9328). Weekend closest to July 4. Ethnic food, crafts and antiques for sale. Dancers, hot air balloon race, children's theater, mime.

Zoofest. Potawatomi Park, 2105 Mishawaka Avenue (288-8133). June. Circus acts, camel rides, wagon rides and a frontier village.

THEATERS AND ENTERTAINMENT.

Broadway Theater League. 211 North Michigan (234-4044). Presents Broadway hits from September to June at the Morris Civic Auditorium. Call or write for schedule.

Century Center. 120 South St. Joseph (284-9711). Designed by Philip Johnson and opened in 1977, Century Center overlooks a stretch of white water rapids on the St. Joseph

River and provides a view of Mark di Suvero's sculpture "Keepers of the Fire." It contains convention and banquet facilities, theaters, recital halls, art galeries and a museum. The complex also has an island park. Noon Whitewater concert series.

Century Center/Century Productions. 120 South St. Joseph (284-9111). Well known celebrities from the worlds of music, stage and tv.

Notre Dame Athletic and Convocation Center (283-7353). Two and a half acres. Seats 12,000 for trade shows, football and hockey games and dances.

O'Laughlin Auditorium. Saint Mary's College (284-4141). Theater productions and big name attractions. Call for schedule.

South Bend Civic Theater. 701 Portage (233-0683). Amateur theatricals.

UNIVERSITY CAMPUSES.

University of Notre Dame du Lac. Rt. 31 (293-7367). Largest Roman Catholic University in the United States. Guided tours available. Special attractions: famous Golden Dome, Lobund sterile laboratory, original chapel, Lourdes Grotto reproduction, Stepan Center with geodesic dome (largest building of its kind in the world), over two million volume library with exterior murals, all on 1,700 handsome acres containing magnificent old trees of many species.

Saint Mary's College. Rt. 31 (284-4000). Has especially fine mosaics in its Church of Loretto.

ZOO.*

Potawatomi Park. 2000 Wall (288-8133). Open daily, summer 10-6:30; winter, 10-5:50; free Saturday, 10-12. A greatly expanded collection of animals.

SPECIAL FACILITIES.

Chamber of Commerce's Convention and Visitor's Bureau. 320 West Jefferson (234-0051).

Memorial Hospital. 615 West Michigan (234-9041).

St. Joseph's Medical Center. 811 East Madison (237-7111).

Michiana Regional Airport. 4535 Terminal Drive (233-

2185). Serviced by Piedmont, Britt, United Air Lines. United Limo (234-6600) provides bus service from airport, Notre Dame and other locations to O'Hare Airport in Chicago.

BERRIEN COUNTY
(171,276 population)

Michigan's most southwesterly county, Berrien, extends from the Indiana border northward 25 miles along Lake Michigan. Its 576 square miles include an enormously productive fruit growing region of rolling country dotted with inland lakes and level plain used for wheat growing. Summer colonies dot the sandy bluffs of Berrien's lake shore. Both St. Joseph and New Buffalo have good harbors.

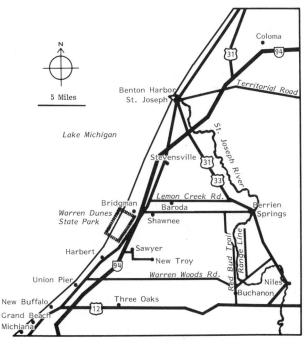

The Miami Indians, and later from 1710 to 1838 the Potawatomi, once called Berrien County home. White men had known the area 150 years earlier. The famous French explorers, Marquette and LaSalle, visited the St. Joseph region in the 1670's. Here Frenchmen established a trading post to which the Indians brought furs to sell. At the start of the nineteenth century, Berrien County still belonged to the Potawatomi, but the Indians lost it because they sided with the British during the War of 1812. Organized in 1829, Berrien County gets its name from John M. Berrien, a Georgian who served as Attorney-General under President Andrew Jackson.

Pioneer settlers in the county's western section found a hardwood forest. Thus logging became an important industry that resulted in woodworking plants throughout the county. Settlers in the interior found that the combination of soil and climate produced high yields of fruit. The first orchards date from the late 1820's; since then, the industry has continued to flourish.

By the turn of the century, as the lumber supply dwindled, Berrien County began its resort business. Daily excursion boats from Chicago brought visitors to the hotels that lined the lakefront. Developers built summer home colonies, both modest and opulent. Today the area continues to attract a large to tourist business with its beaches, harbors, sports and increasing emphasis on winter activities.

BARODA
(627 population)

One of the loveliest drives in the whole area runs through rolling country side along Lemon Creek Road from Baroda to Berrien Springs. The vineyards and orchards, beautiful any time of the year, show off best at blossom time in May and harvest time in the fall.

To See and Do

ANTIQUES.
Shawnee Road Antique Shop. Shawnee Road (422-

1382). Daily, 1-5. A huge stock of rough and refinished antiques, furniture, primitives and glassware in two buildings.

FARMS AND FARM PRODUCE.

Mead's Farm Market. 1885 Shawnee (422-1562).

Zavoral's Farm Market. 7811 Stevensville-Baroda Road (422-1007).

RECREATION.

Cross Country Skiing. Tabor Hill Winery. Mt. Tabor Road (422-1161). See shop for directions. Scenic trails through the vineyards.

RESTAURANTS.

Bill's Tap. 8906 First (422-1141). Specializes in fresh perch, barbecued ribs and prime rib.

Tabor Hill Restaurant. Mt. Tabor Road (422-1165). (See shop for directions). Lunch, Tuesday-Saturday, 11:30-4:30; dinner, Wednesday-Saturday, 6-9:30; Sunday brunch, 11:-6. Reservations recommended. New dining room at the Tabor Hill winery with a view of the countryside and vineyards. Outdoor seating in warm weather.

SHOP.

Tabor Hill Vineyard and Winecellar. Mt. Tabor Road (422-1161). From I-94, Exit 16 (Bridgman) turn right on Lake Street and continue through Bridgman. (Lake Street becomes Shawnee Road outside of town.) Follow Shawnee to Hill's Road. After the cemetery, turn right onto Mt. Tabor Road. Many blue and white signs will guide you. Tours and tastings Monday-Saturday, 11-5; Sundays, noon-6. Each tour lasts about 25 minutes; special arrangements by appointment. Four Chicagoans started the winery in 1968, choosing the area for its temperate growing season, abundant moisture and sandy clay soil. They started with hybrid vines from France. Now the winery makes both red and white, some prize winners.

SPECIAL EVENT.

Annual Blessing of the Harvest. Tabor Hill Winery. Mt. Tabor Road (422-1161). Weekend after Labor Day. Eat, drink and stomp grapes. Call for exact dates.

BENTON HARBOR-ST. JOSEPH
(24,329 population)

These towns once looked alike and acted alike. They both had an abundance of blossoms in the spring and tourists in the summer. But the recession of the 1980's has taken its toll on Benton Harbor which now suffers from urban blight and decay. The St. Joseph River separates them and the traveller can cross the bridge leading from Benton Harbor's Main Street to St. Joseph's Wayne Street. The two towns have a history almost three centuries old. Father Marquette came up the St. Joseph River about 1675. The explorer Robert de La-Salle arrived soon after and built Fort Miami at the river's mouth. Over the years, the fort became an important trade center with the Indians of southwestern Michigan. In turn, four flags flew over it: Spanish, French, British and American. Eventually the fort became a trading post and the trading post became St. Joseph. Settlers who couldn't afford land at St. Joseph built a new community, Benton Harbor.

As they grew, Benton Harbor and St. Joseph had periodic feuds over size, boundaries and settlers. Finally they cemented their friendship when they realized they shared a common economic interest in tourism, orchards, shoreline and industries. While Benton Harbor's manufacturing has declined sharply in recent years, both towns hope for a comeback in the near future.

Benjamin Franklin Purnell (King Ben), one of the most colorful of local citizens bought 130 acres in Benton Harbor for a commune. His House of David in its heyday had great success in baseball.

To See and Do

ARBORETUM.
Margaret Upton Arboretum. At the foot of State on the St. Joseph River, St. Joseph. Scenic view of the harbor and river.

ART AND ARTISTS.
Krasl Art Center. 707 Lake, St. Joseph (983-0271).

Monday-Thursday, 10-4; Friday, 10-1; Saturday, 10-4; Sunday, 1-4. Operated by the St. Joseph Art Association, this complex houses three galleries, educational rooms, studios and a shop. It features a high quality mix of tours, classes, films, programs and exhibits.

FARMS AND FARM PRODUCE.

Benton Harbor Fruit Market. 1891 Territorial (925-0681). May 1-November 1, 9-5. The largest non-citrus cash-to-grower market in the world. Each grower acts as his own auctioneer. The farmers of three counties bring their produce, consisting of many kinds of fruits, vegetables and plants.

FLEA MARKET.

Community Expo Flea Market. Rt.139 and Napier, Benton Harbor. Weekends 9-5.

MOVIES.

Fairplain Cinemas I-V. Fairplain Plaza, corner of Napier and M-139, Benton Harbor (927-4862).

St. Joseph Auto Drive-in Theater. 4023 Red Arrow Highway, St. Joseph (429-3926).

Southtown Twin Theaters. 815 St. Joseph Street, St. Joseph (983-3233).

MUSEUMS.

Fort Miami Heritage Society. 116 State, St. Joseph (983-1191 or 983-1375). Tuesdays, 9:30-1; Thursdays, 1:30-4. Walking tours include the indoor collection and historical monuments and sites in Lake Front Park.

The Josephine Morton Memorial House. 501 Territorial, Benton Harbor (925-7201). April-October, Thursdays, 1-4; Sundays, 2-4. Guided tours upon request with one week's advance notice. Built in 1849, this large white frame house (with adjoining barn) now has rooms depicting different periods of history. Costumed guide conducts tours. Note particularly the porch, called the Indian Hotel because the Potawatomi slept here as they came through town selling their blankets. Demonstrations of carding and spinning of wool on request. Run by the Ft. Miami Heritage Society.

MUSIC.

Band Concerts. Lake Bluff Park, Lakebluff Avenue, St. Joseph. Every Sunday in summer at 2:30 and 7:30. Played by the St. Joseph Municipal Band.

NATURE CENTER.

Sarett Nature Center. Benton Center Road, Benton Harbor (927-4832). This beautiful, off-the-beaten-track, 175 acre wildlife sanctuary and educational center offers field trips, lectures, craft classes and exhibits. Its name comes from poet, teacher and nature lover, Lew Sarett. Belonging to the Michigan Audubon Society, the facility features observation platforms where children can watch a variety of birds and small mammals feeding. Hiking and cross country skiing. Good book shop. No pets, picnics or radios.

RECREATION.

Beaches. Lion's Beach at the end of Pine, St Joseph. Swimming, picnicking.

Rocky Gap. Rocky Gap Road and Lake Michigan northwest of town, Benton Harbor. Swimming, picnicking.

Silver Beach. Broad Street below Lake Boulevard. St Joseph. Swimming, boating.

Tiscornia Beach. Park Road off Ridgeway, St. Joseph. Swimming, boating, picnicking.

Boats-Charter. Fisher's Charter. 100 Main, St. Joseph (849-0249 or 849-1763 or 983-4051).

Ken Neidlinger (925-2558).

Ted Ryzner (429-5033).

Boats-Launching Areas. Benton Harbor Launch. Riverview Drive (925-7601).

Benton Township Launch. Behind Ramada Inn, 798 Ferguson, Benton Harbor (925-0616).

Riverview Park. Niles Avenue, St. Joseph.

St. Joseph Township Launch. Riverbend Drive, St. Joseph.

Boats-Marinas. Pier 1000 Marina. 1000 Riverview, Benton Harbor (927-4471). 220 slips on the St. Joseph River.

Lasalle Landing Marina. 143 Industrial, St. Joseph (982-0812).

Whispering Willows Marina. 2383 Niles, St. Joseph (429-9811). Take I-94 to exit 27 (Niles Avenue). Go one and 7/10 miles north on Rt. 33. Boat rentals, fishing boat charters.

Boats-Rental. Wolf Enterprises. 1207 Ann, St. Joseph (983-1008). Canoe rental.

Golf. Blossom Trail. 1565 Britain, Benton Harbor (925-4591). 18 holes.

Wyndivicke Country Club. 3711 Niles Avenue, St. Joseph (429-6210).

Horseback Riding. Stockbridge Stable. 1995 Dickinson, St. Joseph 429-9892).

Parks. Lake Bluff Park. Lakebluff, between Park and State, St. Joseph. Beautiful view. Historical monuments, band concerts in summer.

River Front Park. Riverview Drive, Benton Harbor. Fishing boat launch.

Riverview Park. Niles Avenue, St Joseph. Picnicking, boat launch.

RESTAURANTS.

Captain's Table. 655 Riverview, Benton Harbor (927-2421). Breakfast 7-1; lunch, 11:30-2; dinner, Monday-Thursday, 5-10; Friday and Saturday, 5-11; Sunday, 6-10 in season. Dancing, live entertainment. Bar.

Holly's Landing. 105 North Main, St. Joseph (983-2334). Monday-Saturday, 11-midnight; Sunday, 12-12. Bar.

Bill Knapp's. Rt. 139 at I-94, Benton Harbor (925-3212). Monday-Thursday and Sunday, 11-10; Friday and Saturday, 11-midnight. Bar.

SPECIAL EVENTS.

Art Fair. Lake Bluff Park, Lakebluff Avenue, St. Joseph. Two days each July. 150 artists and their work draw upwards of 50,000 visitors. One of the better regional art shows.

Blossomtime. Blossomtime Inc., 151 East Napier, Benton Harbor (926-7397). First week in May. Don't miss the area's biggest festival and the oldest in all of Michigan. A week of activities including the Blessing of the Blossoms, the

Grand Floral Parade, carnival, youth parade and more. Close to three quarters of a million visitors attend each year. The Blossom Trail, actually four motor trails covering 125 miles and 52,000 lovely acres, wanders through orchards of apples, peaches, pears, plums, grapes and every kind of berry.

St. Joseph River Venetian Festival. St. Joseph/Benton Harbor on the St. Joseph River (983-7917). Mid-summer. Featuring water activities on the river and its banks.

Tri-State Regatta. Labor Day Weekend. A Chicago-St. Joseph-Michigan City sailboat race that's just stunning when the wind makes the spinnakers fly.

Western Amateur Golf Tournament. Point O'Woods Country Club. 1516 Roslin, Benton Harbor (944-1433). August. This private club opens to the public for the event that draws the world's best amateurs.

TOURS.

Heath Company. Hilltop Road, Benton Harbor (982-3200). June 1-August 31, Monday-Friday at 10 and 1:30. Makes home electronic kits for the do-it-yourselfer, small business computers and robots.

Nye's Apple Barn. 4716 Hollywood, St. Joseph (983-6602). Grows and sells apples and provides visitors with tours of the orchards.

Whirlpool Company. Upton, Benton Harbor (926-5000). Tours. Call for appointment.

SPECIAL FACILITIES.

Twin Cities Area Chamber of Commerce. 685 West Main, Benton Harbor (925-0044).

Memorial Hospital. 2611 Morton, St. Joseph (983-1551).

Mercy Hospital. 960 Agara, Benton Harbor (925-8811).

Ross Field. West Main, Benton Harbor (927-3194). Scheduled daily flights to Chicago and Detroit by commercial airlines. Charters flights.

BERRIEN SPRINGS
(2,042 population)

Today this area comprises the heart of the county's fruit

growing belt. One hundred thirty years ago Indian tribes travelling the Sauk Trail passed through here on their way to Detroit.

To See and Do

ANTIQUES.

Berrien Springs Antique Market. Fairgrounds, Rts. 31-33 between the Indiana Toll Road and I-94 (927-3997). First Sunday of the month June-October, 8-4:30. Annual event begun in 1983 draws over 300 dealers showing everything from baseball cards to bronzes.

ARCHITECTURE.

Berrien County Courthouse (1839). North Cass and West Union. Now part of the Courthouse Museum complex. Greek Revival building of red brick and white wood has hand hewn timbers. Listed on the National Register of Historic Places.

FARMS AND FARM PRODUCE.

Blossoms End Market. Exits 22-28 on I-94-Scottsdale (429-9310 or 422-2378). U-pick or buy fruits. Also cider, grape juice, firewood.

Edge of Meadow Farm. Hinchman (471-1831). Fresh eggs only. Call first.

Family Pear Market. 1901 St. Joseph (471-5603).

Pagel Dave Produce. Shawnee (471-7117).

Stover's Farm. Arden (471-1401). U-pick fruits and vegetables in season.

GARDEN.

Peg Bormann's Herbs and Flowers. 273 Hinchman (473-1356). Large assortment of herbs for sale and flowers for viewing. Peg grows them to dry and sell to florists. She also makes moth preventers and potpourris and loves to share her recipes.

LODGING.

Pennellwood Resort. Range Line Road (473-2511). American plan cottages with full line of facilities and activities. On Lake Chapin. Pool or lake swimming, boating, sports. Supervised activities for kids.

MUSEUM.

Berrien County Historical Association. Rt. 31 (North Cass) and Union (471-1202). Open all year. Tuesday-Friday, 9-4; Saturday and Sunday, 1-5. Located in the oldest courthouse in Michigan (1839). Exhibits depicting the history of Berrien County together with a log cabin (c. 1830) and a reproduction of a turn of the century blacksmith's shop.

NATURE CENTER.

Love Creek Nature Center. Huckleberry (471-2617). Trails open dawn to dusk, daily. Building open, Wednesday-Friday, 9-5; Saturday, 11-5; Sunday, 1-5. This plant and wildlife sanctuary offers a variety of activities: hiking, cross country skiing (rentals available), snowshoeing and programs given by naturalists. Exhibits and bookshop.

RECREATION.

Beaches. Lake Chapin. Near the village. Free public access.

Oronoko Lakes Recreation Area*. Snow Road four miles west of town. Swimming and boating, picnic area.

Camping. Oronoko Lakes Recreation Area. Snow Road four miles west of town (471-7389). Twenty-five rustic campsites. Electricity, showers, fishing, swimming, boating, nature trails, private lake.

Cross Country Skiing. Love Creek Nature Center. Huckleberry (471-2617). Tuesday, Thursday, Saturday. Marked, groomed trails lighted for night skiing. Warming area with hot drinks available. Ski and snowshoe rental. Lessons.

SPECIAL EVENTS.

Berrien County Youth Fair. Fairgrounds (473-4251). Mid-August. Call for schedule and dates. Livestock, thousands of flowers, vegetables and fruits grown by county youngsters. Tractor and horse-pulling contests. Entertainment by well-known rock and stage stars.

Races. Red Bud Trails. Three miles north of town on Red Bud Trail (695-6405). Motorcycle and 4-wheel drive vehicle races on 200 acre site. Call for schedule.

Andrews University. Rt. 31 (471-7771). Open daily except Sunday. A Seventh Day Adventist school, the University operates its own College Wood Products Company on campus (471-3355) which makes early American type furniture. Visitors can watch the process. The University also runs the Apple Valley complex, a bakery, grocery store and flower market. Because the Seventh Day Adventists eat no meat, the food shop features a wide variety of natural foods—soy and peanuts in endless guises, fresh grated coconut, grains galore. The bakery specializes in whole grain breads. Try the extra good cheese and onion.

BRIDGMAN
(2,235 population)

Bridgman has fine high dunes and according to the natives, whispering sands. Unfortunately, industrial sand mining has stripped some of the highest dunes. During the first World War this remote area became a secret meeting place for members of the famous illegal labor group, the International Workers of the World.

To See and Do

RECREATION.

Beach. Weko Beach. Lake Street at Lake Michigan (465-5407). From the Bridgman exit on I-94 go one mile north of town. Swimming, picnicking and boat launching facilities. Municipally owned.

Camping. Warren Dunes State Park.* Red Arrow Highway, west of town (426-4013). 197 campsites near beaches. Electricity, hot and cold water, showers. Area for youth organizations serves 150 people.

Weko Beach. Lake Street (465-5144). 44 developed areas. Electricity, water. 26 tenting areas.

Golf. Pebblewood Country Club. 9794 Jericho (465-5611). 18 holes. Also pub, disco, restaurant.

Hang Gliding. Warren Dunes State Park*. Red Arrow Highway west of town (426-4013). Hang gliders use Tower Hill, a vertical descent of 200 feet. A great spectator sport as well.

Park. Warren Dunes State Park*. Red Arrow Highway, west of town (426-4013). 1,500 acres with two miles of splendid lakefront, fine beaches and large high dunes. The park has facilities for swimming, picnicking, hiking, camping and cross country skiing.

SHOPS.
Little Red Shoe House. 4236 Lake (465-6825). Discount shoes, boots and slippers for the whole family.

Tabor Hill Champagne Cellars. Just off I-94, Exit 16 in Bridgman (465-6566). Open June-September, Monday-Saturday, 10-8; Sunday, noon-8; October-May, Monday-Saturday, 10-5; Sunday, noon-5. Taste the Tabor Hill wines and buy these and others from Michigan wineries at this shop.

BUCHANAN
(5,142 population)

One of the oldest towns in the county, Buchanan once went by the name of McCoy's Creek. Its first settlers arrived in 1833. Now a town with several industries, Buchanan once housed the plant that manufactured the first phonograph needles. It also boasts the only cave in all of Michigan.

To See and Do

ANTIQUES.
Crow's Nest. 108 East Front (695-0837).
The Treasure Mart. 306 Short (695-3175).

ARCHITECTURE.
Front Street. Several blocks of old Greek Revival and Federal style homes.

CAVE.
Bear Cave. * Red Bud Trail four miles north of town (695-

3050). Tours daily, 10-5, Memorial Day-Labor Day. The cave results from the action of water on Tufa rock, a porous rock base over 25,000 years old. Stalactites, petrified vegetation, much of it colored by metallic oxide.

CEMETERY.

Oak Ridge Cemetery. Front Street. Notice monument marking grave of one Joseph Coveney, an atheist whose tomb, erected during his lifetime bears inscriptions from atheistic writings. Coveney had to have his tomb made in England, because no local God-fearing stonecutter would do the job.

FARMS AND FARM PRODUCE.

Phillippi Fruit Farm and Cider Mill. One-fourth mile south of Glendora (422-1700 or 695-3253). Open daily. Some U-pick--apples, cherries, grapes, strawberries, cabbage and tomatoes.

HISTORIC SITE.

Moccasin Bluff Site. Three-quarters mile north of town on Main. Listed on National Register of Historic Places.

NATURE PRESERVE.

Dayton Prairie. Off Dayton Road southwest of Buchanan near the Indiana Border. Twenty acres of unique wet prairie owned and operated by the Michigan Nature Conservancy.

RECREATION.

Beach. Ronnie's Pavilion and Beach. Clear Lake. Swimming and boating.

Boats-Marina. Smitty's Marine. 1240 North Red Bud Trail (695-3501).

Golf. Brookwood Golf Club. 1339 Rynearson (695-7818).

Skiing. Royal Valley Ski Resort. Main State Road, three miles north of town (695-3847). Daily, Thanksgiving to March 15, weather permitting. Monday-Friday, noon-10; Saturday, 10-11; Sunday, 10-6. Check for holiday schedule. Many package deals available for individuals and large groups. Call for details. 15 slopes and trails—25% beginner, 45% intermediate, 30% advanced. Chairlifts, 7 electric tows, rental equipment, night skiing. Lodge, cafeterias, bar.

Herman's Haven. Elm Valley Road (695-6736). Closed Monday. Orchids, all prices, all colors.

Marz Sweet Shop. 205 Front (695-9111). Soda fountain and candies.

Proud's V & S General Store. 120 East Front (695-2250). Specializing in cross country ski equipment. They sell, rent, service and give instruction.

Timberlou. 105 East Front (695-5374). Antique reproductions and country accessories.

THEATER.

Cinema and stage series produced by the Buchanan Fine Arts Council. Write for information at P.O. Box 3, Buchanan 49197.

SPECIAL FACILITIES.

Buchanan Area Chamber of Commerce. 119 Main (695-3291).

Buchanan Community Hospital. 1301 Main (695-3851).

COLOMA
(1,833 population)

A canning center for the rich Michigan farm crops of the surrounding countryside, Coloma sits amongst beautiful rolling terrain. The New Yorkers who first settled the town called it Dickersville. Scarcity of money in those days caused almost everything, including the first store, to operate on the barter system. A town father who tried his hand in the gold rush and returned named the town Coloma, Spanish for a flower that grows on the Pacific slopes.

To See and Do

AMUSEMENT PARK.

Deer Park. Paw Paw Lake (468-4961). Open May 25-Labor Day, 10-6. Deer, llama, bears, monkeys, camels, seals and birds on display. A natural setting where children can see, pet and enjoy many different animals and animal shows.

ANTIQUES.

Millstone Antiques. Martin Road (468-6667). On a farm with a children's playground. Two big barns filled with finished furniture, china, glass, toy trains, gloves and other country items.

ARCHITECTURE.

Community Church (1885). Church Street. Volunteers for the Civil War gathered here to join the Army of the Republic. The church bell comes from a steamship wreck.

FLEA MARKET.

Farmer's Flea Market. Red Arrow Highway east of town. Daily, 9-5. Both indoors and outdoors.

RECREATION.

Beaches. Hagar Shore and Roadside Parks northwest of town on Lake Michigan, off the Blue Star Memorial Highway. Swimming, picnicking.

West Paw Paw Lake. Off Paw Paw Lake Road. Swimming, boating.

Cross Country Skiing. Pine Ridge Ski Shop and Trails. 46th (468-8415). Five miles of marked groomed trails. Group rates, equipment for rent or sale, lessons and night skiing by prior arrangement for groups of six or more.

SHOP.

Cider Mills. Indian Summer Inc. West Street (468-3101). Cider and vinegar.

SPECIAL EVENT.

Coloma Gladiolus Festival (468-3285). First weekend in August. Largest gladiolus show in Michigan. The children's parade and grand parade head a gala line-up of events. Call for schedule.

GRAND BEACH
(227 population)

Grand Beach once hosted Chicago's former mayor, Richard J. Daley and an enclave of his political cronies who weekended and summered there. The small beach community has a John Lloyd Wright house on Station Street. An early example of Wright's work, this house originally started as a summer retreat.

HARBERT
(487 population)

Harbert belongs to a series of old summer colonies originally settled by Chicagoans of Swedish descent. The poet Carl Sandburg once lived here. The Prairie Club of Chicago maintains a permanent camp in the town.

To See and Do

AUCTION.
Big Ed's Auction. 13652 Red Arrow Highway (469-5285). Fridays, 7:30 p.m.

RECREATION.
Beach. Cherry Beach. Between Harbert and Lakeside off Red Arrow Highway. On Lake Michigan.

Boats-Charter. M&M Sport Fishing Charter (469-2759).

RESTAURANT.
Blue Chip Lounge. 13982 Red Arrow Highway (469-5199). Closed Monday. Bar. Entertainment weekends. Dancing—polkas and other old time music.

SHOPS.
Harbert Bakery. 13746 Red Arrow Highway (469-1777). Also known as the Swedish Bakery this shop features Swedish breads and pastries.
Lakeside Vineyard and Winery. 13581 Red Arrow Highway (469-0700). Tours, April-October, Monday-Saturday, 10-4; Sunday, noon-4. Tasting year round, Monday-Saturday, 11-6; Sunday, noon-6. Home of Molly Pitcher Wines and Olson Family Winecellars. Restaurant and winegarden. Sandwiches, fruit, cheese and sausage plates, salads, fondue. Special events, call for schedule.

LAKESIDE
(608 population)

In its early days, Lakeside served as a center for shipping timber, logged nearby, to Chicago and other Great Lakes ports. As a summer resort colony during the past 50 years, Lakeside once had large hotels, now all disappeared. Chicagoans still have summer homes here and families now into the second and third generations enjoy the town's quiet summers.

The property owners' association has planted thousands of bulbs along Main Street, a delight in the spring. On Memorial Day, the town puts on an old fashioned parade ending with speeches at the cemetery.

To See and Do

ANTIQUES.
What Not Shop. 9132 Pier (926-2164). Hand knit items as well as pewter, copper, glass and other country items.

ART AND ARTISTS.
Lakeside Studio. 15263 Lake Shore (469-1377). Call in advance for an appointment. Museums, collectors and universities regularly purchase the prints by famous artists produced here. Very fine but costly items. Housed in an old hotel overlooking the lake.

LODGING.
Pebble House. 15197 Lake Shore (499-1416). 10 rooms, private and shared baths, large continental breakfast, tennis court, beach access, kids over 12, no pets, reservations required.

NATURE PRESERVE.
Robinson Preserve. East Road between Lakeside and Three Oaks. 80 acres of virgin forest and exotic plants. Many species of flora on the endangered list. Managed by The Nature Conservancy.

RECREATION.
Cross Country Skiing. Harbor Country Cross Country Ski Club (469-2181). This club plans excursions to area ski trails. Welcomes new members and interested skiers.

SHOP.
Arts and Crafts of Lakeside. 14876 Red Arrow Highway (469-2771).

NEW BUFFALO (including UNION PIER)
(2,784 population)

New Buffalo, first settled in 1835, got its name because a ship's captain from Buffalo, New York, wrecked his boat on Lake Michigan. While searching for his craft, he found the harbor. The town became a lumbering center and a ship terminus for Lake Michigan travellers. Today New Buffalo has a fine natural harbor and a beach front that offers fishermen and boaters a summer paradise. Developers have big plans for "improving" the shoreline. Southcove and the The Moorings, multi-million dollar marine condo communities, will surely change the scenery. Youth and welfare camps have long used New Buffalo sites.

To See and Do

ANTIQUES.
Heronbrook Quilts (469-0505 or 312-944-5451) by appointment. This New Buffalo area collector buys, sells and displays antique quilts. She has 18 hanging at all times which she rotates with the seasons. Helps "build quilt collections."

FARMS AND FARM PRODUCE.
Janicki Farm Market. 910 West Buffalo (469-0235). Good baked goods as well.

GARDEN.
David Holmes. 13128 Lubke (469-2758). Fine geranium garden. Lake with Canada geese and mallards.

LODGING.
Gordon Beach Inn. 1642 Lakeshore, Union Pier (469-3344). Open all year. 13 rooms, private and shared baths, cottages, continental breakfast, kids ok, no pets. Reservations required.

RECREATION.

Beach. Public beaches on Riviera Road at Lake Michigan. Managed by New Buffalo town and township.

Boats-Charter. New Buffalo Charter Service. 125 North Whittaker (469-1141).

Mari-Ron Charter Service (756-9235).

Skipper's Charter Service. 6 North Whittaker (469-3311).

Striker Sportfishing Charters. P.O. Box 374 (469-1120).

Boats-Launching Area. Public Ramp*. New Buffalo Dock on Lake Michigan.

Boats-Marinas. Oselka Snug Harbor Marina. 514 Oselka (469-2600).

Boats-Rental. Skipper's Landing. 6 North Whittaker (469-0344).

RESTAURANTS.

Lighthouse. 144 North Whittaker (469-5489). Sunday-Thursday, 11-1 a.m.; Friday and Saturday, 11-2:30 a.m.; Sunday brunch. Live entertainment and dancing. Bar.

Little Bohemia. 115 South Whittaker (469-1440). Lunch and dinner, daily. Known for schnitzels, dumplings and sauerkraut. Provides shuttle service from the harbor. Bar.

Redamaks. (The Hamburger That Made New Buffalo Famous). 616 East Buffalo (469-4522). Monday-Thursday, 10:30-10:30; Friday and Saturday, 10-11; Sunday, noon-11. Closed December-March. Hamburgers and all the fixin's. Fish Fry on Fridays. Picnic table service in warm weather. Now has chi chi Chicago branch.

Skip's Other Place. Red Arrow Highway between New Buffalo and Union Pier (469-3330). Open Tuesday-Saturday at 5, Sunday at 3. Like Skip's first place, The Heston Bar. Steaks, fish and the old standbys. Prime rib specialty. Bar.

Theo's Lanes. Rt. 12 (469-0400). Everything from a good sandwich to a meal to go with your bowling. Bar.

SHOP.

Decors. Red Arrow Highway (469-2745). Objets d'art and a few hand-made wood carvings.

NEW TROY
(394 population)

This tiny hamlet, settled in 1836, once had four operating grist mills. Today one of the few originals still operates here. This mill once led the pack by grinding its grain with the new-fangled electricity even though it still had a sod roof and an old sign advertising "Marley's wheat germ for constipation and nervousness." New Troy Mills produces corn meal, buckwheat, graham, whole wheat and pancake flour and sells them on the premises. Open daily (462-3422).

NILES
(13,115 population)

Niles calls itself the City of the Four Flags, since the French, the British, the Spanish and finally the United States have all governed it. Settled for 300 years, Niles stands on a high bluff overlooking the St. Joseph River. It has an even older Indian history; the Sauk Trail forded the St. Joseph River here.

At its French Jesuit mission, the first in the lower Michigan, Wisconsin or Indiana area, priests instructed and baptized thousands of Indians. The French built Fort St. Joseph, south of the city, in 1697. Notre Dame archeologists worked on uncovering the remains of the fort.

The Dodge brothers of auto fame hailed from Niles, as did Ring Lardner and Montgomery Ward.

To See and Do

ANTIQUES.

Carriage Collection. 3116 North 5th (683-3020).

Clevering Antiques. 36 South 5th (638-3674). Daily, 10-5; Sunday, noon-5.

Elsie's Exquisiques. 513 Broadway (684-7034).

Four Flags Antique Mall. Sycamore and 2nd (683-6681). Daily, 10-6; Sunday, noon-5; closed Tuesday. Two floors and over 60 dealers. This high quality establishment attracts big crowds. Good selections.

Ruth's Reliques. 621 South St. Joseph (683-7327). By appointment only.

ARCHITECTURE.

City Hall. 508 East Main (683-4700). Monday-Friday, 8-5. Henry Austin Chapin built this elegant mansion in 1882; his grandchildren donated it to the city. It has 14 rooms, an early elevator, a ballroom, beautiful fireplaces and stained glass windows. Each room uses a different wood for decoration.

Greek Revival houses of the 19th century line Oak Street.

Paine Bank. 1008 Oak. Listed on National Register of Historic Places.

Ring Lardner House (c. 1860). 519 Bond. A Hudson River Gothic, the house perches on a high bluff overlooking the St. Joseph River. Ring Lardner grew up in this home where he began his writing career with a Niles newspaper.

ART AND ARTISTS.

The River House Gallery. 74 North St. Joseph (683-3067). Tuesday-Friday, 12-4:30; Saturday, 10-4; by appointment. Art displays as well as antiques, pottery and hand crafted merchandise made by local residents. Located in an historic Greek Revival house, the gallery also provides tours of this stately mansion built in 1850.

CEMETERY.

Bertrand Catholic Cemetery. Madalene Street. Many old tombstones.

FARMS AND FARM PRODUCE.

McComb Produce Company. 18 Parkway (683-9250).

Shelton's Farm Market. Rt. 33 South at Bell (684-0190). Open all year. Wholesale and retail, fruit, vegetables, cheeses, ethnic foods, candy. Some home made and home grown. Also meat department.

Walker's Fruit Stand. 2278 North 5th (683-6410).

Zelmer Fruit Farms. Rt. 12 and 31 Bypass (684-3111).

HISTORIC MARKERS.

The Grave of Father Allouez, the Jesuit missionary, is

on Bond Street, on a rise overlooking the St. Joseph River.

Fort St. Joseph. Bond Street. A boulder marks the approximate site of the fort and gives dates of its checkered history.

Carey Mission. A boulder at the crossroads of Phillips Road and the Niles-Buchanan Roads, on the west bank of the St. Joseph River, commemorates the Reverend Issac McCoy's aid to the Potawatomi Indians.

Catholic Mission. Clay and Lincoln Streets. Here on the grounds of the Roman Catholic Church the Jesuits ministered to the Indians.

Sauk Trail Crossing. On the west side of St. Joseph River on Rt. 31, the old Sauk Trail forded the river.

LODGING.

Lilac Hill. 1720 Killarney Lane one mile from Rt. 31 bypass (683-2188). Open all year. Two rooms with shared bath available in this private home, full breakfast.

MUSEUM.

Fort St. Joseph Historical Museum. 508 East Main (683-4702). Tuesday-Saturday, 10-4; Sunday, 1-4; closed Mondays and holidays. Call for tours. Self-guide tour sheets to Fort St. Joseph and the Summerville Mounds provided. Located behind City Hall in the former stables of the Chapin Mansion. Displays of Indian and local history.

NATURE CENTER.

Fernwood. 1720 Range Line northwest of the city (695-6688). Buildings open March 1-November 30. Weekdays, 9-5; Saturday, 10-5; Sunday, noon-5. An unusually beautiful hilly nature preserve with springs, pools and streams along the St. Joseph River. Formal gardens, herb and rock and bog gardens, a river trail, an eighteen acre wilderness trail and a self-guided nature trail. Fernwood offers programs and classes in nature study, gardening and arts and crafts. Gift shop.

RECREATION.

Beach. Swimming at Kugler's Beach on Barron Lake northeast of town.

Boats-Charter. Four Flags Charter Service (684-2408).

Boats-Launching Areas. Municipal boat dock. St. Joseph River at Marmont.

Boats-Rental. Can-U-Canoe. 455 Moccasin (695-5866).

Camping. Nub Lake Campground. 1701 Pucker (683-0671). 130 sites on creek and lake. Canoeing, fishing, swimming. Two fireplace pavillion.

Spaulding Campgrounds. 2305 Bell 3 miles southeast of the city (684-1393). Fishing, nature trails, ball diamonds.

Cross Country Skiing. Madeline Bertrand Park. Niles Township south of Niles. Take Rt. 33 south to Stateline Road and west to Laurel for the park entrance. 121 acres now under development. Four cross country ski loops near the St. Joseph River already completed.

Golf. Plym Park. East of Rt. 31 (684-7331). Municipally owned, 9 holes.

Kelly's Sports Land. 2107 South 11th (683-5421). Two 18 hole miniature golf courses.

Horseback Riding. Diamond D Ranch. 3232 Dunning (683-5892). Also hay and sleigh rides.

Larry Smith Stables. 2224 Reum (684-0167).

RESTAURANTS.

Franky's. 1033 Lake (683-7474). Daily except Tuesday, 11:00- midnight; Saturday and Sunday from 4. Italian specialties, sandwiches and snacks. Bar.

Happy House. 3121 South 11th (684-0484). Lunch and dinner, Tuesday-Sunday. Cantonese family restaurant. Pressed duck, sweet and sour shrimp and the like. No liquor served. Take out available.

SHOP.

Fa$hion Outlet Center. 219 East Main (684-4443). Daily, 9:30-6; Friday, 9:30-7:30; Saturday, 9:30-5:30; Closed Sunday. Plain pipe rack family clothing and shoes at discount.

Jay Arrels Sample Outlet. 1400 Niles Road (684-4104). Daily, noon-6; Saturday, 10-2. Luggage, hiking, running and tennis shoes. Jackets and pants.

Paris Candy Company. 220 East Main (683-9792). An

old fashioned ice cream parlor selling home made candies and ice cream.

Fort St. Joseph Days. Riverfront Park. June. Reenactment of Revolutionary War era. Mock battles and simulated family life during a weekend encampment at Riverfront Park.

Four Flags Area Apple Festival. 67th and Lake Street (683-8913). Autumn. An annual celebration of the apple harvest in the St. Joseph Valley. The event includes the crowning of an apple queen, craft and art displays, carnival and apple goodies of every description. Closes with a grand parade. Call for dates and times.

SPECIAL FACILITIES.

Chamber of Commerce, Four Flags Area. 321 East Main (683-3720).

Niles Airways. 2030 Lake (683-3434). Charter Flights.

Pawating Hospital. 31 North St. Joseph (683-5510).

SAWYER
(207 population)

Sawyer is another Lake Michigan summer community with a heavy Swedish influence. Although the recent economic downturn in the Benton Harbor area has diminished Sawyer's year round population, summer residents still enjoy the town's delights.

To See and Do

ANTIQUES.

Olde Tyme Shoppe Antiques. Main (426-8191).

Serendippity Antiques. Red Arrow Highway (426-3636). Much wicker.

FARMS AND FARM PRODUCE.

The Blueberry Patch. Holloway (426-4521 or 545-8125). U-pick.

Schiffer's U-pick Blueberries. Sawyer Road (426-4994).

SHOPS.

The Book Rack. Red Arrow Highway (426-4120). Here's

the place to replenish the summer and leisure reading supply. Paperbacks.

Haalga's. Red Arrow Highway (426-4233). Large selection of Swedish imports.

Schlipp's Pharmacy (426-3487). Has a soda fountain that whips up *REAL* milkshakes.

STEVENSVILLE
(1,268 population)

A bustling community in the midst of Michigan's dune country, Stevensville provides many activities for the visitor.

To See and Do

ANTIQUES.

Bill's Antiques. 7566 Red Arrow Highway (465-3246). Daily, noon-7. A large, choice stock.

J Bit of Everything. 4173 Red Arrow Highway (429-1577).

NATURE CENTERS.

Grand Mere Nature Preserve. John Beers I-94 exit 22, off Thornton Drive (927-4832). 350 acres of dunes, beach, woods, swamps and bogs. Three inland lakes. Good birding here.

Lincoln Township Nature Center. Notre Dame Road (465-6235). New nature center on Lake Michigan offers a look at five different plant communities and migratory birds. Picnic table and enclosed shelter.

RESTAURANTS.

Grande Mere Inn. 5800 Red Arrow Highway (429-3591). Lunch and dinner, Tuesday-Saturday. Good seafood and fish.

Win Schuler. 5000 Red Arrow Highway (429-3273). Monday-Friday, 11-11; Saturday, 11-midnight; Sunday brunch, 10-2:30. Decorated like an old English inn. Specializes in fish, seafood, beef. Very popular. Bar.

Tosi's. 4337 Ridge (429-3689). Lunch, 11-2:30; dinner,

from 5. Closed Sundays and holidays; closed January and February. Now owned by Berghoff of Chicago, Tosi's has kept its bountiful Italian menu and good service. No reservations taken. Always popular and crowded. A long wait for those who come after six. Bar.

SHOPS.

Emlong Nursery. Red Arrow Highway (429-3431). Open daily all year. A large nursery with excellent quality field grown trees and shrubs.

A Bit of Swiss Bakery. On the premises of Tosi's restaurant, 4337 Ridge (429-1661). Monday-Friday, 8 a.m.-10 p.m. Closed January-March. Excellent European pastries and tortes.

THEATERS.

Lakeshore Community Theater. Call Lakeshore High School for information, (429-6131). Summer performances.

Twin City Players. 600 West Glenlord (429-0400). Call for schedule and information.

THREE OAKS
(1,774 population)

In the park at the entrance to Three Oaks stands the first cannon that Admiral Dewey captured at the battle of Manila in 1898. The residents raised more money per capita than any town in the nation. They won the cannon—and a dedication speech by President McKinley. Three giant oaks that stood close together near the site of the post office gave the town its name. Trainmen coming through would look out and say, "There now're the three oaks." The town boasts the nation's largest Flag Day parade.

To See and Do

ANTIQUES.

Jenny's Shop. 9 North Elm (756-7219). Wednesday-Sunday, March-September; weekends only, October-February. If nobody answers, the shop is open.

Rainbow's End. Lakeside Road (756-9291). Excellent selection.

ARCHITECTURE.

Union Meat Market. 23 South Elm. Now Drier's. Listed on National Register of Historic Places.

AUCTION.

Arend's Auction Service. 13815 Red Arrow Highway (469-0522). Monday evenings, call for time. Norma Arend combines auctioning antiques with a social evening. Buy and meet your friends at the same time.

NATURE PRESERVE.

Warren Woods. Entrance off Warren Woods Road (426-4013). 480 acres of virgin woods. The trails lead past a natural spring and across a cable bridge. Picnic in a beautiful and peaceful area. Spectacular fall colors. Cross country skiing. Bird and game sanctuary.

RECREATION.

Biking. Self-guided tour maps of bike trails in Berrien County available from the Three Oaks Spokes Bicycle Club, 303 East Michigan.

Camping. Bob-A-Ron Lake and Park. Warren Woods Road (463-5454). 95 full hook-up sites; 120 primitive sites; fishing and swimming in two man-made lakes. Boat rental. Particularly lovely area with much wildlife and blazing fall color.

RESTAURANTS.

Carpenter's. West Rt.12 (756-6821). Tuesday-Thursday, 11:30-9; Friday and Saturday to 10; Sunday noon-7:30. Evening salad bar. Large modestly priced menu. Wood paneling and old maps on the wall.

Village Pump. 13 South Elm (756-9132). Daily, 11-2 a.m.; Sunday, noon-2 a.m. Grill open 'til 1:30 a.m. daily. Bar.

SHOPS.

Drier's. 23 South Elm (756-3101). Three generations of Driers have run this excellent shop featuring aged cheeses, smoked meats and homemade sausage. The main store has a treasure trove of old pictures, knives, butcher blocks and other generational memorabilia. Drier also has a country store on Rt. M-60.

Gerber's Children's Wear Outlet. West Rt. 12 (756-7311). Factory store for Gerber Babywear Products.

Cross country skiing and snowmobile weekends. Bob-A-Ron Campgrounds. Warren Woods Road (469-3894). January and February.

Maple Syrup Festival. Bob-A-Ron Campgrounds. Warren Woods Road (469-3894). March. Group wagon tours, syrup samples.

KANKAKEE RIVER AREA

The Kankakee River begins at Mud Lake near South Bend, winds through Indiana and Illinois on a southwesterly course, joins the Illinois River and finally flows into the Mississippi. The river gets its name from the Indian "A-ki-ki", meaning wolf, because a band of Mohicans lived on its banks and terrified other tribes in the area.

LaSalle, Marquette and countless other missionaries and explorers meandered through this land. Indian tribes lived and left their burial grounds here. Thousands of settlers later followed trails first marked by the Indians.

The Grand Marsh, a 500,000 acre section, between English Lake and Momence, Illinois became the river's most famous section. For centuries the marsh acted as an immense sponge attracting millions of migrating birds and making the area one of the largest concentrations of waterfowl in the world. Prairie chickens once abounded in this hunter's paradise, as did otter, mink and deer. Wolves, fox, raccoon and some waterfowl comprise the major wildlife survivors today.

Around the turn of the century gentlemen hunters from as far away as England began to come to the Kankakee. These sportsmen, whose wives were known as Kankakee widows, built a number of clubhouses for themselves in the English Lake and Baum's Bridge section; a few abandoned buildings

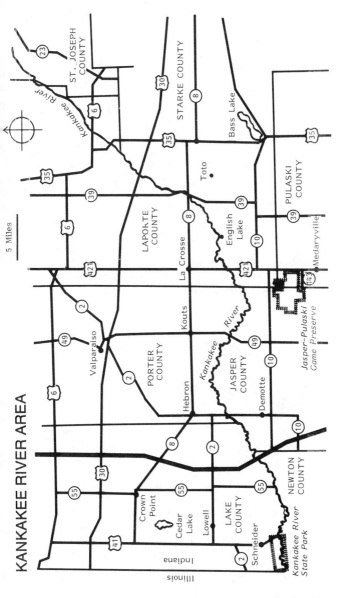

KANKAKEE RIVER AREA

5 Miles

Illinois
Indiana

ST. JOSEPH COUNTY
Kankakee River
STARKE COUNTY
Bass Lake
Toto
English Lake
PULASKI COUNTY
Medaryville
Jasper-Pulaski Game Preserve
LAPORTE COUNTY
La Crosse
Kankakee River
Kouts
Valparaiso
PORTER COUNTY
Hebron
JASPER COUNTY
Demotte
Crown Point
Cedar Lake
Lowell
LAKE COUNTY
Schneider
NEWTON COUNTY
Kankakee River State Park

187

remain. The fraternity included General Lew Wallace who, idling down the river on his houseboat, conceived his most famous book, *Ben Hur.*

Over the years, constant draining of the Kankakee flood plains produced very fertile farm land for the growing of peppermint, corn, potato, onions, blueberries and asparagus. However drainage and clearing of 600,000 acres together with the straightening of the river caused the destruction of the natural flood control for the areas to the south and west. The hunters blasted the wildlife; the great marsh sponge which had attracted the waterfowl disappeared and migrating birds stopped coming; lumbermen timbered the woodlands almost bare. In short a devastation so terrible and so complete occurred that by the 1920's hunters, fishermen, conservationists, legislators and agronomists finally began the slow and painful work of partial restoration of the marsh. No amount of effort can restore its original state of wilderness. Moreover the Kankakee still remains subject to clashes between farmers who want to prevent further flooding of their land and others who object to any more man-made interference with the river and its meandering.

DEMOTTE
(2,559 population)

Demotte calls itself the asparagus capital of the country. Each year farmers in the neighborhood harvest 800 acres of this choice crop. The growers have names like DeVries and Walstra because all of them descended from "wooden shoe" Dutch settlers. The term distinguishes them from Amish Dutch. They work hard, pray devoutly and close up tight on Sunday.

Demotters have grown asparagus for 50 years. In May and June visitors can watch the asparagus carts in the fields. These conveyances, designed by a local blacksmith, hold four to ten pickers, who sit backwards, feet raised, fingers gloved. As they swing on swivel seats, they snap the vegetable spears from the ground. In the past, when children worked as asparagus pickers, school started later in the morning. Now, with a

consolidated school system that ranks classes more important than asparagus, agile housewives have replaced the
youngsters.

To See and Do

FARMS AND FARM PRODUCE.

Eenigenburg Farms. Rt. 231, one-half mile north of town
(987-3500). The Eenigenburg family has several asparagus
farms of its own and in addition hauls half of the entire local
crop. They welcome visitors who can watch the operation,
and at very reasonable prices can buy asparagus, plants and
flowers.

HISTORICAL MARKER.

Rt. 231 at Kankakee River. Commemorates the spot
where LaSalle's expedition stopped en route from South
Bend to the Mississippi River.

RECREATION.

Camping. Lake Holiday Jellystone Park. 11780 West Rt.
10 (345-3132). April-November. Restaurant, grocery, swimming pool, lake swimming, fishing. 674 sites for rvs and
tents.

Oak Lake Campgrounds. I-65 and Rt. 10, Roselawn
(345-3153). Pond swimming, fishing, picnic area, recreation hall. April 15-October 15. 250 sites for tents and rvs.

Pioneer Family Campgrounds. West on Rt. 10 for five
miles from I-65. South one mile on 100 E to 900N (345-
4472). Playground, store, swimming lake. 125 sites for
tents and rvs.

Ramsey Landing Camping. South side of Kankakee River
off Rt. 231 (996-4472).

RESTAURANT.

Forest River Lodge at Ramsey's Landing. South side of
Kankakee River off Rt. 231 (996-4472). Mooring dock for
boaters. Sandwiches, beer.

SPECIAL EVENT.

Art and Craft Fair. On Demotte Elementary School
grounds, Halleck Street. Second Saturday in August, 10-5.

Antiques, flea market, demonstrations, entertainment. Preceeded by marathon race and parade.

ENGLISH LAKE
(60 population)

Fishermen have no trouble finding this tiny hamlet where the Yellow and Kankakee Rivers meet. Trout, walleye and channel fish abound beginning in early March. Non-fishermen can watch the deer drink at the rivers' edge or the wild flowers in bloom everywhere.

The tycoons had their game clubs around here. Even today good duck and goose hunting exists at the Kankakee Wildlife Area to the east.

To see and Do

RECREATION.
   Boats-Launching Area. Public ramp. Shelby: Rt. 55 at the Kankakee River.

   Boats-Rentals. Mrs. James Wickizer. 650W (754-2174).

HEBRON
(2,696 Population)

This town, named for Abraham's Biblical village in Canaan, lies in the valley of the Kankakee, near the once great marshland. Originally a Potawatomi settlement, now Hebron's source of distinction comes from its newspaper, *The Porter County Herald,* the county's official Democratic newspaper and the best source for farm auction ads.

To See and Do

HISTORICAL MARKER.
   Rt. 2, two miles south of Hebron. Here stood "Huiakiki"

(Indiana Town Village), the winter home and largest village of the Potawatomi. They abandoned it when federal troops forced the tribe to leave Indiana and move to a reservation in Kansas.

MUSEUM.
The Stagecoach Inn. Main (996-2700). Obtain the key from the Alyeas auto agency across the street. Restoration of an 1849 hostelry.

RECREATION.
Park. Grand Kankakee Marsh County Park. Rangeline Road, off Rt. 2 east of I-65 (696-9951). January-September, 7-dusk; October-December by special admission for hunting season. 106 acres containing a visitor's center, waterfowl and nature photography blinds, waterfowl habitat areas, picnic shelter, fishing all year except during hunting season, canoeing with rentals available from June to September, cross country skiing, jogging and hiking trails. No vehicles allowed except during hunting season.

RESTAURANT.
Country Kitchen. 20 North Main (996-9221). Monday-Saturday, 6 a.m.-8 p.m.; Sundays, 7 a.m.-8 p.m. Plain but excellent cooking. Home-made pies.

Old Heritage Inn. Main (996-9010). Weekdays, sandwich lunch; dinner, 4:30-10; Saturday until 2 a.m. with dancing. Bar. 100 years old.

KINGSBURY
(no residential population)

To See and Do

FISH HATCHERY.
Mixsawbah State Fish Hatchery. Rt. 104 (369-9591). Daily, 8-4. Salmon and trout hatchery to provide stock for Lake Michigan fishermen. Tours.

RECREATION.
Boats-Launching Area. Kankakee River. Four miles

south of Kingsbury on Rt. 4, three-quarters mile south on Rt. 104, two miles south on Hupp Road, two miles west on Hupp Road and two miles south on River Road. Public ramp.

WILDLIFE AREA.

Kingsbury State Fish and Wildlife Area. East on Rt. 6, south on Rt. 39 (393-3612). On these 5,000 acres, Indiana maintains the only fenced-in wildlife area in the state in order to protect visitors from undetonated shells beyond the fences. (The shells remain from a World War II ordance plant located on the grounds.) Camping, hiking, shooting range, hunting in season for teal, pheasant, rabbit, quail, squirrel and deer. Bucks by bow and arrow only. Training for rabbit and bird dogs.

KNOX

(3,674 population)

The county seat of Starke County, Knox has a handsome, old sandstone courthouse at North Main and East Washington. Notice the griffins which decorate the building.

To See and Do

ANTIQUES.

Rubbi's Antiques. Rt. 5, Bass Lake (772-4984). A very large selection of primarily glass and dishes including collectibles and miscellaneous.

CEMETERY.

Crown Hill Cemetery. East Lake, north of town. Contains the burial plot of Che Ma, reputedly the smallest man in the world. His two feet, four inch height made him three inches shorter than Tom Thumb. This midget came from China in 1881, spent his life working with a circus and retired to Knox where he died at the venerable age of 88.

FISH HATCHERY.

Bass Lake Fish Hatchery. South of Knox on Rt. 35 to Toto Road. Turn east for two miles to Lake Road. Follow Lake Road south to Bass Lake and turn east one-half mile (772-

2353). Open daily to sunset. 18 acres, 15 ponds. The only bass hatchery in the midwest.

MUSEUMS.

Archbishop Andrew Sheptytsky Museum. 700E off Toto Road (772-2411). On the grounds of the St. Andrew's Missionary Apostolate. Sunday, 2-4 or by appointment. Ivan Mestrovic sculptures. Extensive collection of Byzantine icons, examples of Ukrainian folk dolls and eggs.

Starke County Historical Museum. 401 South Main (772-5393). Monday, Saturday-Sunday, 1-4. Located in the home of the late Indiana Governor Henry F. Schreiker. Old dolls, clothing, uniforms, household items and tools on display.

RECREATION.

Beach. Bass Lake State Beach. South of Knox on Rt. 35 to Toto Road. Turn east for two miles to Lake Road. Follow Lake Road south to Bass Lake and turn east for one-half mile (772-2351). Memorial Day weekend-Labor Day, 7-11. 102 acres. Swimming, picnicking, camping, fishing. This natural lake, the fourth largest in Indiana, also has a water ski jump and a slalom course. The Miami and the Potawatomi called Bass Lake "Winchetonoua" meaning beautiful water. An old summer resort, the lake is surrounded by private homes. Public boat ramp.

Boats-Launching Area. Fishburn Marina. Rts. 35 and 10, Bass Lake (772-2243).

WILDLIFE AREA.

Kankakee State Fish and Wildlife Area. Rt. 8 near Rt. 39 (792-4125). 3320 acres. In 1927 Starke and LaPorte County farmers donated tracts of their swamp land to the state. Those gifts began this preserve, one of the oldest in Indiana. Camping, public boat ramp, hunting for ducks and deer, fishing for walleye, northern pike and channel catfish, canoeing, swimming, ice skating. Superior birding.

RESTAURANT.

Courthouse View Lounge. 60 East Washington (772-5535). Lunch, dinner, Mondays-Saturdays, 11-8. Tasty food. Bar.

SHOP.

Toto's. South of Knox on Rt. 35, turn west on Toto Road for 3.7 miles (772-4533). Allegedly the first discount store in the country. Tremendous stock of all sorts of merchandise spread out in several buildings. Located in the middle of nowhere.

SPECIAL EVENT.

Bass Lake Festival. Rts. 35 and 10 (772-3909). Third and fourth weekends in July. Pageant, food sale, arts and crafts booths.

SPECIAL FACILITIES.

Starke Memorial Hospital. 102 East Culver (772-2131).
Starke County Airport. 300N (772-2921).

KOUTS
(7,619 population)

Kouts got its name during the period when the Panhandle Railroad was building a new route from Valparaiso south to the Kankakee River. One evening after a hot day's work, the surveyors stopped at a farm and inquired after dinner and accommodations. The lady of that house engaged in making apple butter wanted no part of guests. At the next farm, however, Bernhardt Kouts and his wife provided bed, board and hospitality. Later when naming the nearby town site, the surveyors honored their hosts.

Germans, Poles and Irish settled Kouts. First they came to work on the railroad and then they stayed on to farm. Kouts' location not far from the Kankakee River also made the town an early gathering place for hunters and fishermen. In 1889, an 80 round world's featherweight boxing championship took place in the town.

To See and Do

ANTIQUES.

American Legacy. 208 East Mentor (766-2654). 18th centry reproductions.

What Not Shop. 224 South Main (962-8789). Country primitives, cloisonnée, better furniture.

ART AND ARTISTS.

Wayne Cooper (766-3807). Painter, mixed media.

FARM AND FARM PRODUCE.

Mrs. Olson's Farm. 501 Indiana (766-3819). For blueberry picking, bring your own containers.

HISTORICAL SITES.

Baum's Bridge. One and a half miles west of Rt. 49 on Rt. 8 to Baum's Bridge Road, then south to the Kankakee River. Built in 1863, this stone bridge crosses the river at the same point as the ford of the Potawotomi Trail. On this site, Father Marquette preached Christianity to the tribe.

Boone Grove. 350W and 650S. In 1912, at the Wark Mound located in this tiny hamlet, University of Illinois archeologists dug up a seated circle of skeletons holding tools and weapons. They removed every prehistoric relic from the mound, one of the oldest Indian burial tombs in the area.

Dunn's Bridge. Rt. 8 to 500E, then turn south to Kankakee River. This walking bridge was made from part of the dome of the Administration Building at the 1893 Columbian Exposition in Chicago.

Tassinong Grove. Baum's Bridge Road north of Kouts between 550S and 600S. Probably the site of a French post established as early as 1673, this tiny settlement's name came from the French word for trading station, "tassements". An Indian gathering place existed here even earlier. Today a marker commemorates the oldest village in northwestern Indiana as well as the location of the first post office (1837).

RECREATION.

Camping. Donna Joe Campground. 1200S and 300E (462-1545). Swimming, fishing, hiking, picnicking, boat rental, boat ramp.

RESTAURANTS.

Baum's Bridge Inn. 3 miles south of Rt. 8 on Baum's Bridge Road (766-9925). Monday-Thursday, 4-9; Friday, 4-10; Saturday, noon-10; Sunday, noon-9. Offers a groaning platter. Bar.

John's Corner Tap. Main (766-9933). Fish fry on Fridays, 4:30-10. Walleye, perch, and other fresh water fish.

Arts and Crafts Festival. Kouts Park. Rts. 8 and 49 (766-3766). Third Saturday in September. Arts and crafts displays, pig relay races, contests, food for sale.

TOURS.

Cargill fertilizer plant. Rt. 8, four and a half miles west of Kouts (766-2234). Young scientists will enjoy this operation.

Heinhold grain elevator. Rt. 49 south across two railroad tracks (766-2234). Five and half days a week visitors can see wheat unloaded at the elevators in July, soy beans and corn in the fall.

Heinhold hog yards. South of the grain elevators on Rt. 49 (766-2221). Call to make arrangements. The largest hog buyer in the world, Heinhold has from 200 to 1,000 hogs in this yard at all times. Bring boots for walking in the yard and a plastic bag for carrying them home.

SPECIAL FACILITY.

Chamber of Commerce. No office (766-2673).

LACROSSE
(713 population)

LaCrosse derives its name from the crossing of the Monon and Pennsylvania Railroads in the town. Actually at one time five railroads came through this village. Early homes perched on stilts to avoid the flooding that came with every rise of the Kankakee River.

In 1868, when the Pennsy wanted to reroute several miles of its right-of-way near La Crosse, it took 36 hours and several hundred men and wagons to accomplish the engineering feat. The Lincoln funeral train stopped at the Monon Depot in town on its way to Michigan City.

To See and Do

ANTIQUES.

Das Antikhaus. One mile south of the intersection of Rts. 421 and 8. Turn three-quarters of a mile west on 2100S (754-2265). Daily, 9-5; Sunday, 1-5. Ring outside great bell.

196

FARM.

LaVern Kreuger's angus farm. 2100S (754-2402). Call for appointment and the family will happily show children their breeding herd.

RECREATION.

Camping. River Bend Campground. 900W and Toto Road, San Pierre (896-3339). April 15-October 15. Grocery, swimming pool, 50 sites.

Fishing. D.J. Bait Shop. Rt. 421 at the Kankakee River (823-3145). Also boat ramp.

MEDARYVILLE
(731 population)

To See and Do

NATURE PRESERVE.

Tefft Savanna Nature Preserve. Northwest portion of the Jasper-Pulaski Fish and Wildlife Area (843-4841). From Rt. 421 turn west on Rt. 143 for 2.1 miles. Past the shooting range turn north on 400E for one mile to larger section of the preserve. Several parking lots on road. No trails. Be sure to check with Jasper-Pulaski property manager before entering as hunting is allowed in season. Contains unusual reptiles, mammals and numerous rare plants. Includes sand dunes, black oak savannas, black and pin oak forest, understory of blueberry and huckleberry plants, sedge meadows and wet prairies and marshes.

TREE NURSERY.

Jasper-Pulaski Tree Nursery. Rt. 421, north of Medary-ville (843-4827). Indiana residents can purchase seedlings of many varieties at bargain prices, and everyone can visit black walnut orchards where genetically healthy specimens grow.

RECREATION.

Camping. Leisure Time Gampgrounds. 1125W and 200N (843-8171). Pond swimming, fishing. Picnic area. Country music on Saturday nights, holiday weekends. May 1-October 1. 150 sites for tents and rvs.

Wildlife Area. Jasper Pulaski State Fish and Wildlife Area. Five miles north of Medaryville on Rts. 421 and 143 (843-4891). 7,585 acres with full camping and picnicking facilities. Fishing and hunting in season. Hiking trails, archery, rifle range. Watch their buffalo herd and hundreds of pheasants. Best of all observe rare sandhill cranes and other birds from an observation platform. The birds stop at Jasper-Pulaski on their migration from Canada to Florida and Texas. Bring binoculars.

SCHNEIDER
(426 population)

To See and Do

NATURE PRESERVE.

Beaver Lake Nature Preserve. In LaSalle State Fish and Wildlife Area. 3 miles north of Enos on Rt. 41, turn east 1 mile and north 1 mile (992-3019). 640 acres. Get permission to enter from LaSalle property manager. Refuge for wildlife and plants of prairie and wetlands.

RECREATION.

Wildlife Area. LaSalle State Fish and Wildlife Area. Turn west off Rt. 4l onto Rt. 10 for one and a half miles (992-3019). 800 acres. Fishing, hunting, picnicking, camping, ice skating, ice-fishing, boat ramp.

Categorical Guide

In this section, the reader will find everything listed by category. For example, if antiques are your interest look after amusement parks and before architecture to discover every antique listing included in the book. When appropriate, the name, address, town and telephone number appears. For more detailed information look in the Community Guide under the town.

AIRPORTS (C = Charter Flights)

Benton Harbor-St. Joseph: Ross Field. West Main, Benton Harbor (927-3194). Also C
Gary: Municipal Airport. Industrial Highway (994-1663). Helicopter service. C
Griffith: Griffith Airport. 1715 East Main (924-0207). C
Hobart: Hobart Airport. 3600 North Lake Park (962-9400). C
Knox: Starke County Airport. 300N (772-2921). C
LaPorte: Maple City Airport. 2020 150W (362-7018). C
Michigan City: Municipal Airport. South Franklin (879-0291). C

Joe Phillips. Michigan Road (872-5571). Scheduled service to O'Hare Airport. Also C.
Niles: Niles Airways. 2030 Lake (683-3434). C
South Bend: Michiana Regional Airport. 4535 Terminal Drive (233-2185). Scheduled bus service to O'Hare Airport.
Valparaiso: Porter County Municipal Airport. East of Rt. 30 on 100N (462-6508). C

AMUSEMENT PARKS

Chesterton: Enchanted Forest. Rt. 20 west of Rt. 49 (926-2161).
Coloma: Deer Park. Paw Paw Lake (468-4961).

Highland: Wicker Park. Ridge and Indianapolis (839-9809).
Schererville: Sauzer's Kiddie Land. Indianapolis and Rt. 30 (865-8160).

ANTIQUES

Baroda: Shawnee Road Antique Shop. Shawnee (422-1382).
Bass Lake: Rubbi's Antiques. Rt. 5 (772-4984).
Berrien Springs: Berrien Springs Antique Market. Fairgrounds, Rts. 31-33 between the Indiana Toll Road and I-94 (927-3997).
Buchanan: Crow's Nest. 108 Front (695-0837).
   The Treasure Mart. 306 Short (695-3175).
Cedar Lake: Bobin's Antiques. 10820 Wicker (365-5320).
Chesterton: Carol's. 214 South Calumet (926-4757).
   Five Gables Antiques. 500 South Calumet (926-7411).
   Kathy's. 530 Indian Oaks Mall (926-1400).
   Russ and Barb's Antiques. 222 Lincoln (926-4937).
   Second Hand Rose. 402 Grant (926-3894).
Coloma: Millstone Antiques. Martin Road (468-6667).
Crown Point: Court House Square Antiques. Lake County Courthouse basement (663-7670).
   Crowntique. 146 North Main (663-9049).
   Dan's. 8703 East 109th (663-4571).
   Liberty Antiques. 2125 South Main (663-9191).
   Main Street Antiques. 930 North Main (663-6547).
   Tudor House Antiques. Lake County Courthouse basement. (663-1309).
Hammond: John David's. 6660 Indianapolis (845-4088).
   2nd Time Around. 810 169th (932-1275).
Highland: Main Street Antiques. 9219 Indianapolis (838-9560).
Hobart: Corner House Antiques. 1005 South Lincoln (no phone).
   Hobart Road Antique Shop. 402 East Hobart (942-3942).
   The Antique & Collector's Shop. 515 East Third (no phone).
Kouts: American Legacy. 208 East Mentor (766-2654).

What Not Shop. 224 South Main (962-8789).

LaCrosse: Das Antikhaus. 2100S (754-2265).

Lakeside: What Not Shop. 9132 Pier (926-2164).

Lake Station: The Barn. East 33rd (962-9697).

Spinning Wheel Antiques. 3424 Parkside (962-5145).

LaPorte: Coachman Antique Mall. 500 Lincolnway (326-5933).

Memorable Antiques. 607 Michigan (326-7276).

Walnut Hill Antiques. 613 Michigan (326-1099).

Lowell: Collector's Corner. 162 West Washington (696-0100).

Eon's Antiques. 140 West Washington (no phone).

Evergreen Antiques. 1115 East 181st (696-0702).

Grandfather's House. 427 East Commercial (696-8559).

Green Acres Antiques. 10506 West Commercial (696-7242).

Hitzeman's Country Haus. 135 West Commercial (696-7121).

John's This and That Shoppe. 146 West Commercial (696-0578).

Lister's Antiques. 20510 Wicker (696-8883).

Lor Jon's. 525 East Main (696-0745).

Tish Antiques. 201 East Commercial (696-6962).

Merrillville: The Carriage House. 420 West 73rd (769-2169).

Michiana Shores: Artisans Art and Antiques. 505 El Portal (872-2612).

Michigan City: Dorothy's Gift Shop. 404 Franklin (872-7164).

Min's Treasure and Trash. 827 Franklin Square (874-3719).

Old Pieces and Antiques. 631 Pine (879-7090).

Mishawaka: 100 Center. Lincolnway West (Rt. 33) (256-6611).

New Buffalo: Heronbrook Quilts (469-0505 or 312-944-5451).

Niles: Carriage Collection. 3116 North 5th (683-3020).

Clevering Antiques. 36 South 5th (638-3674).

Elsie's Exquisiques. 513 Broadway (684-7034).

Four Flags Antique Mall. Sycamore and 2nd (683-6681).
Ruth's Reliques. 621 South St. Joseph (683-7327).
Portage: Portage Antiques. 2532 Portage Mall (763-4154).
Squirrel's Nest. 5674 Sand (762-7441).
Sawyer: Olde Tyme Shoppe Antiques. Main (426-8191).
Serendippity Antiques. Red Arrow Highway (426-3636).
Schererville: Landmark Antiques. 119 Junction (322-4534).
South Bend: South Bend Antique Mart. Fairgrounds, intersection of Jackson and South Ironwood (291-0075).
Thieves Market. 2309 East Edison (233-9820).
The Wooden Indian. 50877 1/2 Rt. 31 North and Greenacre (277-3892).
Stevensville: Bill's Antiques. 7566 Red Arrow Highway (465-3246).
J Bit of Everything. 4173 Red Arrow Highway (429-1577).
Three Oaks: Jenny's Shop. 9 North Elm (756-7219).
Rainbow's End. Lakeside Road (756-9291).
Valparaiso: Marc T. Nielson Country Shop. Old Suman Road (462-9812).
Moulin Rouge Antiques. 39E, 600N (462-0035).
Potpourri. 302 East Jefferson (462-9920).
Uphaus Antique Shop. 349W, 100S (462-2810).
Whiting: Granny's General Store. 1309 Community Court (659-7538).

ARCHITECTURAL TOURS

Mishawaka: Beiger Heritage Corporation. 317 Lincolnway East (256-0365).
South Bend: South Bend Heritage Corporation (289-1066).
Southhold Restoration. 502 West Washington (234-3441).
Valparaiso: Marcella Borcherding, 502 Garfield (462-3474) or Dorcas Luecke. 603 Institute (464-1387).

ARCHITECTURE—Churches

Chesterton: St. Patrick's Church. 312 West Indiana.
Coloma: Community Church. Church Street.
Heston: Greek Orthodox Chapel. Heston Gardens, 100N and 215E.
Hobart: First Unitarian Church. Main and 5th.

LaPorte: Methodist Church, Harrison and Clay.

Merrillville: SS Constantine and Helen Greek Orthodox Church. 8000 Madison (769-2481).

Mishawaka: St. Joseph Church. Corner of Third and Mill Streets.

New Carlisle: Hamilton Church. Walnut and Old Chicago Roads.

Methodist Church (now Apostolic). Front Street.

Olive Chapel. Two miles south of town at junction of Timothy and Rt. 2.

Porter: Augsburg Svenska Skola. North side of Oakhill two miles west of Mineral Springs Road.

Saint John: Pioneer Church. 9400 Wicker.

South Bend: St. Paul's Memorial Methodist Church. 1001 West Colfax.

Church of Loretto, Saint Mary's College.

Valparaiso: Chapel of Resurrection, Valparaiso University.

Immanuel Lutheran Church. 308 North Washington.

ARCHITECTURE—Homes, Inns, Courthouses (1830-1920)

Berrien Springs: Berrien County Courthouse. North Cass and West Union.

Buchanan: Front Street district.

Chesterton: Holmes-Brown Mansion. 700 West Porter.

Friday Farm. Friday Road.

Mansion at Sand Creek Campground. 105N and 350W.

Weller House. 1200 North Road.

Cedar Lake: Lassen Hotel. 7808 West 138th Place.

Crown Point: Lake County Courthouse. Courthouse Square.

Old Homestead. 227 South Court (663-0456 or 663-0590).

Door Village: Octagonal Barn. Rt. 35.

East Chicago: Marktown Historic District. Pine, Riley, Dickey and 129th.

Riley Bank. Chicago and Indianapolis.

Gary: Prairie School houses. West 6th and Fillmore; West 7th and Van Buren.

Gary Land Company Office. 4th and Broadway.

John Stewart Settlement House. 150l Massachusetts.

Hammond: Forest Avenue Homes. 6600-7300 Forest.

Joseph Hess School House. 7205 Kennedy (845-4155).

Grand Boulevard.

Knox: Starke County Courthouse. North Main and East Washington.

LaPorte: 815 Division.

Garwood Home. 60N and 500W.

LaPorte Commercial Historical District. 20 blocks of downtown.

LaPorte County Courthouse. Courthouse Square.

Orr-Richter House. 4076 West Small Road.

Pinehurst Hall. 3042 North Rt. 35.

Swan-Anderson. 1020 Indiana.

Lowell: Melvin A. Halsted House. 201 East Main.

Miller: Miller Town Hall. Miller, Grand and Old Hobart Road.

Long Beach: Bavarian House. 2704 Lake Shore Drive.

John Lloyd Wright buildings. Throughout Long Beach and Duneland Beach.

Michigan City: Arndt House. 1305 Washington.

Barker Center. 631 Washington (872-0159).

Community Center for the Arts building. 8th and Spring (872-6829).

Porter-Kerrigan Home. 913 Washington.

Tonn & Blank Building. 126 East 5th.

Vail House. 404 Vail.

Waterford Inn. Johnson and Wozniak Roads.

Mishawaka: Beiger Mansion. 117 Lincolnway West.

Dodge House. 415 Lincolnway East.

William B. Hosford Residence. 722 Lincolnway.

Hutchinson-Schindler Home. 810 Lincolnway East.

Merrifield-Cass House. 816 Lincolnway East.

Niles-Weiss Home. 410 Lincolnway East.

New Carlisle: Hubbard House. Cherry and Front Streets.

Niles: City Hall. 508 East Main (683-4700).

Greek Revival houses. Oak Street.

Paine Bank. 1008 Oak.

Ring Lardner House. 519 Bond.

Portage: Wolf Homestead. 450N and East Cleveland.
Porter: Beam House. 116 Wagner.

Porter House. 204 Lincoln.
Rolling Prairie: Foster-Shuck Home. Jimmerson Shores Road.

Provolot-McGuire House. Byron Road.
Schererville: Scherer Home. 33 Wilhelm.
South Bend: Bartlett House. 720 West Washington.

Chapin Park Historic District. Roughly bounded by the St. Joseph River, Main, Madison, Rex, Lindsay and William Streets, and Leland and Portage Avenues.

Chapin-Willis House. 407 West Navarre.

Horatio Chapin House. 601 Park.

Cushing House. 508 West Washington.

James A. Judie House. 1515 East Jefferson.

Chauncey N. Lawton House. 405 West Wayne.

Main and South Quadrangles. University of Notre Dame.

Northern Indiana Historical Museum. 112 South Lafayette.

Joseph D. Oliver House. 808 Washington.

West Washington Historic District. Roughly bounded by Main Street, Western and La Salle Avenues and McPherson Street.
Three Oaks: Union Meat Market. 23 South Elm.
Valparaiso: Heritage Hall. Campus Mall, South College Avenue.

Porter County Jail and Sheriff's House. 153 Franklin.

Joseph Robbins Home. 800N and 800W.

Rose-Kuehl Home. 156 South Garfield.
Westville: Forrester Home. Rt. 2.
Whiting: Whiting Community Center. 1938 Clark.

ARCHITECTURE—Modern (1930-1984)

Beverly Shores: Bartlett Houses. Throughout Beverly Shores.

Lustron Houses. Lake Front Drive and Dunbar. Lake Front Drive and State Park Road.
*Gary:*Doll House Fire Station. West 35th at Pierce.

Gary-Hobart Water Tower. 7th and Madison.
Hobart: Public Library. 100 Main.

Merrillville: Lake County Reference Library. Rt. 30.
Michigan City: Public Library. Rt. 12 (879-4561).
   Mullen Elementery School. 100 Manny Court.

ARCHITECTURE—Restorations.

Michigan City: Brewery. East Michigan Boulevard.
Mishawaka: Kamm and Schellinger Brewery. 100 Center Street.
Porter: Joseph Bailly Homestead. Mineral Springs Road between Rts. 12 and 20.
   Chellberg Farm. Mineral Springs Road between Rts. 12 and 20.
South Bend: East Bank Complex. St. Joseph River.
   Tippecanoe Place. 620 West Washington (234-9077).
Valparaiso: Tratebas Mill. Tratebas Road, east of Rt. 49.

ARCHITECTURE—World's Fair Houses

Beverly Shores: House of Tomorrow. Lake Front Drive west of Broadway.
   Old North Church. Beverly Drive west of Broadway.
   Rostone House. North side of Lake Front Drive near Dunbar.
   Armco-Ferrara House. Lake Front Drive one house west of the House of Tomorrow.
   Florida Cypress House. Lake Front Drive east of the House of Tomorrow.
   House of Seven Gables. Pearson.

ARCHITECTURE— Frank Lloyd Wright Houses

South Bend: Avalon Grotto-De Rhoades House. 705 West Washington.
   Herman T. Mossberg House. 1404 Ridgedale.

ART GALLERIES

Chesterton: Chesterton Art Gallery. 115 South 4th (926-4711).
Crown Point: Gallery Ltd. 400 North Main (663-3610).

East Chicago: The Gallery. 5005 Indianapolis (398-6100).
Gary: Atrium Gallery. 1100 West 6th (885-4264).

Gallery Northwest. 3400 Broadway (980-6500).
Hammond: Bicentennial Library Gallery. Purdue University Calumet. 2233 171st (844-0520).

Hammond Public Library. 564 State (931-5100).
Lakeside: Lakeside Studio. 15263 Lake Shore (469-1377).
Michigan City: Community Center for the Arts. 8th and Spring (872-6829).
Merrillville: D'Cameo Gallery. 7849 Taft (769-2882).

Trachtenberg Gallery. 430 West 73rd (769-8018).
Miller: Frame Gallery. 621 South Lake (938-6303).

Gary Art League Gallery. 607 South Lake (938-1308).
Munster: Northern Indiana Art Association. 8317 Calumet (836-1839).

Town Gallery. 27 Ridge (836-6230).
Niles: The River House Gallery. 74 North St. Joseph (683-3067).
St. Joseph: Krasl Art Center. 707 Lake (983-0271).
South Bend: Baldoni Fine Arts. 411 Hickory (287-6661).

Hibel Art Gallery. 602 North Michigan (233-2232).

Moreau-Hammes Galleries. Saint Mary's College (284-4854).

Snite Museum of Art. University of Notre Dame (239-5466).

Art Center. Century Center, 120 South St. Joseph (284-9102).
Valparaiso: Art Barn. 695N, 400E (462-9009).

Porter County Arts Commission. 74 Lincolnway (464-4080).

Sloan Art Gallery. Valparaiso University in the library basement. 651 College (462-5111).

ART—Public

East Chicago: Mural. Baring branch, Public Library. Chicago and Baring (397-2453).
Michigan City: Richard Hunt sculpture. Restaurant Management building. 101 West 2nd.

Miller: Statue of Father Marquette. Marquette Park. Grand Boulevard.

South Bend: Mark di Suvero's sculpture. Viewable from Century Center, 120 South St. Joseph.

Mosaics. Church of Loretto, Saint Mary's College.

Valparaiso: Frederick Frey sculpture. Courthouse Square.

ARTISTS

Painters

Beverly Shores: David Tutwiler (879-5611).

Cedar Lake: Sandra Kozlowski (769-1606).

Chesterton: Evelyn Finnstrom (926-1343).

Kouts: Wayne Cooper (766-3807).

Lake Station: Iola Frum (962-1511). Restoration.

LaPorte: Jack and Joyce Keene (326-7468).

Long Beach: Gertrude Harbert (874-6374).

Karl Warren (872-8550).

Merrillville: Robert Hoffman (769-3416).

Michigan City: Elizabeth Fleming (879-9446).

Miller: Dale Fleming (938-3834).

Toni Lane (938-0471). Also photography.

Munster: Mike Daumer (972-1167).

New Carlisle: Anthony J. Droege II (654-7485).

Ogden Dunes: Lee Hibbs. Box 378. Also photography.

Porter: Ruth Bremner (926-6471).

Kate Brooks (926-6361).

Valparaiso: Marlies Glickauf (462-6657).

Russell Nelson (462-5854).

Harriet Rex Smith (462-4567).

Potters

Chesterton: Loretta Cohn (926-5813).

Hazel Hannell (926-4568).

Long Beach: Dave and Pat Daubert (879-7201).

Ogden Dunes: Charles Chesnul (762-5740).

Portage: Creek Bend Artworks. 5484 Central (762-7925).

Valparaiso: Cheri Hill (464-1159).

Sculptors

Beverly Shores: Kevin Firme (874-4038).
Chesterton: John Mullin (926-8937).
Michigan City: Joe Jansek (872-7459).
Ogden Dunes: James Maples (762-4397).
Valparaiso: Marjory Crawford (926-6224).
Westville: Tony Popp (926-4764).

Weavers

Crown Point: Weaver's Way. 306 East Goldsboro (663-1406).
Michigan City: JoJo Bendix (872-6575).
Ogden Dunes: Karyn Johnson. Box 903.
Valparaiso: Deb Macke (464-2729).
   Kathy O'Neal (938-2936).
   Nancy Searles (462-7405).
   Bob Springsteen (462-8561).

Other Media

Chesterton: Judith Gregurich (926-5645). Stained Glass.
   Skip Hector (926-6030). Dunes photographer.
LaPorte: Charlotte Bass (369-1400). Quilter.
   Farmhouse Studio. 2215 East150N (326-5525). Silkscreen.
Michigan City: Connie Kassell (879-6741). Stained glass, graphics.
Munster: Margaret Oberlie (836-5623). Jewelry.
   Mike Gibbs (923-9573). Dunes photographer.
Valparaiso: Konrad Juestel Studio (462-2348). Prints.

AUCTIONS

Chesterton: Frye Auction Barn. Old Porter Road (926-2501 or 926-3500).
Harbert: Big Ed's Auction. 13652 Red Arrow Highway (469-5285).
Three Oaks: Arend's Auction Service. 13815 Red Arrow Highway (469-0522).
Union Mills: 111 Hamilton (767-2407).

BAND CONCERTS

Michigan City: Washington Park. Pine at Lake Michigan.
Mishawaka: Battell Park. Mishawaka Avenue.
St. Joseph: Lake Front Park. Lakebluff Avenue.

BICYCLE RENTAL

Hobart: Hobart Schwinn. 840 East Third (942-3492).

BIKEWAYS

Crown Point
Griffith
Hobart
Indiana Dunes National Lakeshore.
South Bend: Potato Creek State Recreation Area.
Three Oaks: Bike trail maps. Three Oaks Spokes Bicycle
Club. 303 East Michigan.

BOATS—Launching Ramps (P = Public $ = Pay)

Benton Harbor: Benton Harbor Launch. Riverview Drive. P
  Benton Township Launch. 798 Ferguson (925-0616). P
Cedar Lake: Lake Shore Drive and Cline. P
East Chicago: Jeorse Park. Aldis at Lake Michigan (392-
8320). P
Hammond: Lakefront Park. Calumet at Lake Michigan. P
  Wolf Lake-Forsythe Park. 121st and Calumet. P
Hobart: Fred Rose Park. 8th off Wisconsin. P
Kingsbury: River Road at the Kankakee River. P
Knox: Kankakee State Fish and Wildlife Area. Rt. 8 (792-
4125). P
Kouts: Donna Joe Campground. 1220N and 300E (462-
1545). $
LaCrosse: D.J. Bait Shop. Rt. 421 at Kankakee River (823-
3145). $
LaPorte: Clear Lake. Truesdale. P
  Holiday Boat Sales. 1350 Pine Lake Avenue (362-4423). $
  Loggys Landing. 229 Holton (362-7620). $
  Stone Lake. Rt. 35 (362-9746). P

Michigan City: Goerg Boats and Motors. 83 North Franklin (872-8608). $

South Lake Marine. 6th (872-7201). $

Sprague Marina. Trail Creek (872-1712). P

Washington Park Marina. Washington Park Basin (872-1712). $

Miller: Lake Street at Lake Michigan. P

Mishawaka: Mishawaka Central Park (255-6610). P

Pleasant Lake. Golden Lake Road and 370W. $

New Buffalo: Public Ramp. New Buffalo Dock on Lake Michigan. $

Niles: Municipal Boat dock. St. Joseph River at Marmont. P

St. Joseph: Riverview Park. Niles Avenue. P

St. Joseph Township Launch. Riverbend Drive. P

Rolling Prairie: Hog Lake. 700N (778-2241). P

Schneider: LaSalle State Game and Wildlife Area. Rt. 150 and 150N (992-3019). P

Shelby: Rt. 55 at Kankakee River. P

South Bend: St. Patrick's Farm. Two miles north on Laurel off Auten on the St. Joseph River (277-8142). P

St. Joseph River. Northwest of South Bend on Riverside Drive. P

Valparaiso: Loomis Lake. Burlington Beach Road off Rt. 49 (462-5144). $

Westville: Clear Lake. Porter-LaPorte County Line Road (872-9363). $

Whiting: Whihala Beach County Park. 117th and Park at Lake Michigan (769-PARK). P

BOATS—Marinas

Benton Harbor: Pier 1000 Marina. 1000 Riverview (927-4471).

Buchanan: Smitty's Marine. 1240 North Red Bud Trail (695-3501).

Cedar Lake: Pine Crest Marina. 14415 Lauerman (374-5771).

East Chicago: Jeorse Park. Aldis at Lake Michigan (392-8320).

Knox: Fishburn Marina. Rts. 10 and 35, Bass Lake (772-2243).

LaPorte: Fay's Marina. 908 Pine Lake Avenue (362-1491).
Pine Lake Marina. 816 Pine Lake Avenue (362-8455).

Michigan City: B & E Marine. Washington Park (879-8301).
Goerg Boats and Motors. 83 North Franklin (872-8608).
South Lake Marine. 6th (872-7201).
Sprague Marina. Trail Creek (872-1712).
Washington Park Marina. Washington Park Basin (872-1712).

New Buffalo: Oselka Snug Harbor Marina. 514 Oselka (469-2600).

Portage: Burns Harbor Marine. 1700 Marine (762-2304).
Lefty's Coho Landing. Rt. 12 (762-7761).

St. Joseph: Lasalle Landing Marina. 143 Industrial (982-0812).
Whispering Willows Marina. 2383 Niles (429-9811).

BOATS—Rental

Cedar Lake: Chuck's Pier. 13947 Huseman (374-9832).
Tulip Harbor. 14611 Lauerman (374-6666).
Pincrest Marina. 14415 Lauerman (374-5771).

Deep River: Deep River County Park. County Road 330 (769-9030).

English Lake: Wickizer (754-2174).

Hebron: Grand Kankakee Marsh County Park. Rangeline Road (696-9951).

Hudson: Hudson Lake. Rt. 20.

Kouts: Donna Joe Campground. 1200S and 300E (462-1545).

LaPorte: Holiday Boat Sales. 1350 Pine Lake (362-4423).
Stone Lake. In Soldier's Memorial Park (362-9600).
Upper Fish Lake. Rt. 4 (325-8385).

New Buffalo: Skipper's Landing. 6 North Whittaker (469-0344).

Niles: Can-U-Canoe. 455 Moccasin (695-5866).

Rolling Prairie: Hog Lake. 700N (778-2241).

St. Joseph: Whispering Willows Marina. 2383 Niles (429-9811).

Wolf Enterprises. 1207 Ann (983-1008).
South Bend: St. Patrick's County Park. 50650 Laurel (277-4828).
Three Oaks: Bob-A-Ron Lake and Park. Warren Woods Road (463-5454).
Valparaiso: Lake Eliza. Rt 30 (462-1935).
Loomis Lake. Burlington Beach Road off Rt. 49 (462-5144).
Westville: Clear Lake. Porter-LaPorte County Line Road (872-9363).

BRIDGES

Hobart: Pennsylvania Railroad at Deep River.

CAMPING

Berrien Springs: Oronoko Lakes Recreation Area. Snow Road (471-7389).
Bridgman: Warren Dunes State Park. Red Arrow Highway. (426-4013).
Weko Beach. Lake Street (465-5144).
Cedar Lake: Lemon Lake County Park. 6322 West 133rd (663-7627).
Chesterton: Sand Creek Camp Ground. 1000N, 350E (926-6918).
Crown Point: Fancher Lake Park. South Court and West Greenwood (663-0428).
Demotte: Lake Holliday Jellystone Park. 11780 West Rt. 10 (345-3132).
Oak Lake Campgrounds. I-65 and Rt. 10, Roselawn (345-3153).
Pioneer Family Campgrounds. 900N, Lake Village (345-4472).
Ramsey Landing Camping. Off Rt. 231 at the Kankakee River (996-4472).
Hanna: KOA Campground. Rt. 30 (797-2395).
Hobart: Robinson Park. 53rd and Liverpool (942-5498).
Indiana Dunes State Park: Rt. 49 (926-4520).
Kingsbury: Kingsbury State Fish and Wildlife Area. Rt. 39 (393-3612).

Knox: Bass Lake State Beach. Lake Road (772-2351).

Kankakee State Fish and Wildlife Area: Rt. 8 (792-4125).

Kouts: Donna Joe Campground. 1200N and 300E (462-1545).

LaCrosse: River Bend Campground. 900W and Toto Road, San Pierre (896-3339).

LaPorte: Cutty's Campground. 4004 Rt. 39 (362-5111).

Willow Lake Campgrounds. 0353 East 900N (778-4113).

Leroy: Stoney Run County Park. 450S (787-2020, ext. 391).

Medaryville: Jasper-Pulaski State Fish and Wildlife Area. Rt. 421 (843-4891).

Leisure Time Campgrounds. 1125W and 200N (843-8171).

Michigan City: KOA Campground. Rt. 421 (872-7600).

New Carlisle: Mini-Mountain Campground. Rt. 2 (654-3431).

Niles: Nub Lake Campground. 1701 Pucker (683-0671).

Spaulding Campgrounds. 2305 Bell (684-1393).

Rolling Prairie: Hog Lake. 700N (778-2241).

Rolling Timbers Campground. 5502 East Rt. 2 (778-2498).

San Pierre: Riverbend Campground. 900W and Toto Road (896-3339).

Schneider: LaSalle State Fish and Wildlife Area. Rt. 4l and 150N (992-3019).

South Bend: Potato Creek State Recreation Area. 25601 Rt. 4 (656-8186).

Three Oaks: Bob-A-Ron Lake and Park. Warren Woods Road (463-5454).

Valparaiso: Lake Eliza. Rt. 30 (462-1935).

Rogers-Lakewood Park. Campbell east of Rt. 49 (462-5144).

CAR RACING

Berrien Springs: Red Bud Trails. Three miles north of town on Red Bud Trail (695-6405).

Crown Point: Illiana Speedway. 7211 West Lincoln Highway (322-5311).

CAVES

Buchanan: Bear Cave. Red Bud Trail (695-3050).

CEMETERIES

Buchanan: Oak Ridge Cemetery. Front Street.
Cedar Lake: Indian Mound Cemetery. Front Street.
Crown Point: Civil War Cemetery. Marquette Street.
Deep River: Woodale Cemetery. County Road 330.
Door Village: Door Village Cemetery. Joliet Road.
Furnessville: Furnessville Cemetery. Furnessville Road.
Gary: Waldheim Cemetery. Grant at 20th.
Hesston: Posey Chapel Cemetery. 1000N.
Knox: Crown Hill Cemetery. East Lake.
LaPorte: Union Chapel Cemetery. Rt. 6.
New Carlisle: Hamilton Cemetery. Old Chicago Road.
    Town Cemetery. Rt. 20 west of town.
Niles: Bertrand Catholic Cemetery. Madalene.
Otis: Eight-Square Cemetery. LaPorte-Porter County Line Road.
Porter: Bailly Cemetery, Oakhill Road.
Valparaiso: Quakerdom Cemetery. Rt. 6 east of Jackson Center.

CHAMBERS OF COMMERCE

Benton Harbor: 685 Main (925-0044).
Buchanan: 119 Main (695-3291).
Chesterton: 123 South Calumet (926-5513).
Cedar Lake: 9742 West 133rd (374-6157).
Crown Point: 154 West Joliet (663-1800).
East Chicago: 2001 East Columbus (398-1600).
Gary: 504 Broadway (885-7407).
Griffith: 102 North Broad (924-2155).
Hammond: 429 Fayette (931-1000).
Highland: 8536 Kennedy (923-3666).
Hobart: 18 East Ridge (942-5774).
Kouts: No office (766-2673).
Lake Station: no office (962-1196).
LaPorte: 609 Michigan (362-3178).
Lowell: 136 West Commercial (696-0231).
Merrillville: 78 West 80th Place (769-8180).
Michigan City: 711 Franklin (874-6221).
Munster: 8250 Hohman (836-5549).

Niles: 321 East Main (683-3720).
Portage: Portage Mall (762-3300).
Schererville: 139 East Joliet (322-5412).
South Bend: 320 West Jefferson (234-0051).
Valparaiso: 601 East Lincolnway (462-1105).
Whiting: 1312 119th (659-0292).

COLLEGES AND UNIVERSITIES

Benton Harbor: Lake Michigan College. 2755 East Napier (927-3571).
Berrien Springs: Andrews University. Rt. 31 (471-7771).
Gary: Indiana University-Northwest. 3400 Broadway (887-0111).

Indiana Vocational and Technical College-Gary. 1440 East 35th (887-9646).
Hammond: Purdue University Calumet. 2233 171st (844-0520).
Mishawaka: Bethel College. 1001 McKinley (259-8511).
South Bend: Indiana University South Bend. 1700 Mishawaka (237-4111).

Indiana Vocational and Technical College. 534 West Sample (289-7001).

Saint Mary's College. Rt. 31 (284-4000).

University of Notre Dame. Rt. 31 (293-7367).
Valparaiso: Valparaiso Technical Institute. West Chestnut (462-2191).

Valparaiso University. 651 College (462-5111).
Westville: Purdue University-North Central. Rt. 421 (872-0527).
Whiting: Calumet College. 2400 New York (473-7700).

DANCING (S = Square P = Polkas B = Ballroom)

Cedar Lake: Midway Ballroom. 13130 Lake Shore Drive (374-9667).
Highland: American Legion Hall. Ridge and 2nd (844-0850 or 924-0221). S
Lowell: Oak Hill School. 195 Oakley (696-8842 or 696-0123). S

Michigan City: Memorial Park. 8th and Liberty Trail (872-5642). S

Mirage Lounge. In Holiday Inn, 5820 South Franklin (879-0311). B

Sloan's. In Howard Johnson Motel. 4122 South Franklin (874-7203). B

Portage: Square Jammers. YMCA Annex Garyton, 5341 Central (759-3118).S

Woodland Park Promenaders. 2100 Willowcreek (762-5236 or 926-2778). S

EMERGENCY MEDICAL CARE

Benton Harbor: Mercy Hospital. 960 Agara (925-8811).

Buchanan: Buchanan Community Hospital. 1301 Main (695-3851).

Chesterton: Porter Memorial Hospital Westchester Convenience Center. 700 South Calumet (926-7755).

Crown Point: St. Anthony's Hospital. Main and Franciscan (738-2100).

Dyer-St. John: Our Lady of Mercy Hospital. Lincoln Highway (865-2141).

East Chicago: St. Catherine Hospital. 4321 Fir (392-1700).

Gary: Methodist Hospital. 600 Grant (886-4000).

St. Mary's Medical Center. 540 Tyler (882-9411).

Hammond: St. Margaret Hospital. 5454 Hohman (932-2300).

Hobart: St. Mary's Medical Center. 1500 South Lake Park (942-0551).

Knox: Starke Memorial Hospital. 102 East Culver (772-2131).

LaPorte: LaPorte Hospital. Lincolnway (362-1234).

Merrillville: Methodist Hospital. 8701 Broadway (738-5500).

Ross Clinic. 6100 Harrison (980-6000).

Michigan City: Memorial Hospital. 5th and Pine (879-0202).

St. Anthony Hospital. 301 Homer (879-8511).

Munster: Community Hospital. 901 MacArthur (836-1600).

Hammond Clinic. 7905 Calumet (836-5300).

Niles: Pawating Hospital. 31 North St. Joseph (683-5510).
South Bend: Memorial Hospital. 615 West Michigan (234-9041).

St. Joseph's Medical Center. 811 East Madison (237-7111).
St. Joseph: Memorial Hospital. 2611 Morton (983-1551).
Valparaiso: Porter Memorial Hospital. 814 LaPorte (464-8611).

ENTERTAINMENT CENTERS

Gary: Genesis Convention Center. One Genesis Center Plaza (882-5505).
Hammond: Civic Center. Sohl (932-0093).
Merrillville: Holiday Plaza. I-65 and Rt. 30 (769-6311).
South Bend: Century Center. 120 South St. Joseph (284-9711).

Notre Dame Athletic and Convocation Center. Notre Dame (283-7353).
Valparaiso: Porter County Exposition Center. 215 East Division Road (464-8661). Open 1985.

FAIRS

Berrien Springs: Berrien County Youth Fair. Fairgrounds (473-4251).
Crown Point: Lake County Fair. South Court and West Greenwood (663-0428).
LaPorte: LaPorte County Fair. Rt. 2 at 150N (362-2647).
South Bend: St. Joseph County 4-H Fair. Jackson and Lakewood (291-4870).
Valparaiso: Porter County Fair. 1984-Old Porter County Fair Grounds, Evans and Indiana. 1985-Porter County Exposition Center. 215 East Division (464-8661).

FARM PRODUCE

Baroda: Mead's Farm Market. 1885 Shawnee (422-1562).

Zavoral's Farm Market. 7811 Stevensville-Baroda Road (422-1007).
Benton Harbor: Benton Harbor Fruit Market. 1891 Territorial (925-0681).

Berrien Springs: Blossoms End Market. Exits 22-28 on I-94-Scottsdale (429-9310 or 422-2378).

Edge of Meadow Farm. Hinchman (471-1831).

Family Pear Market. 1901 St. Joseph (471-5603).

Pagel Dave Produce. Shawnee (471-7117).

Stover Farm. Arden (471-1401).

Buchanan: Phillippi Fruit Farm and Cider Mill. One-fourth mile south of Glendora (422-1700 or 695-3253).

Crown Point: Rinkenberger. l09th (663-5019).

Demotte: Eenigenburg. Rt. 231 (987-3500).

Gary: Chase Street Produce. 35th and Chase (884-3169).

Don Ewen Produce. 35th and Grant (884-6397).

Highland: Jansen's Michigan Fruit Market 2122 Ridge (838-0300).

Zandstra Brothers Farm. 10240 Wicker Park (836-1095).

Hobart: Jansen's. Rts. 6 and 51 (962-1224).

Johnson's. Rt. 6 (962-1383).

Remus. Rt. 6 (962-2213).

Sapper's. 1175 South Lake Park (942-6423).

Kouts: Mrs. Olson's. 501 Indiana (766-3819).

LaPorte: Bernacchi Farm Market. 2429 Monroe (362-7416).

Garwood Orchards: Pinola, 50S north of Rt. 2 (362-4385).

John Hancock. Fail Road (778-2096).

Michigan City: Arndt's Orchards. 1875 Wozniak (872-0122).

Kintzele. 11366 Earl (874-4779).

N.W.D. Blueberry Ranch. 640 Fryar (872-7477).

Radke. 8999 West 200N (872-3140).

Munster: Herr Farm. 10219 White Oak (924-9351).

New Buffalo: Janicki Farm Market. 910 West Buffalo (469-0235).

Niles: McComb Produce Company. 18 Parkway (683-9250).

Shelton's Farm Market. Rt. 33 South at Bell (684-0190).

Walker's Fruit Stand. 2278 North 5th (683-6410).

Zelmer Fruit Farms. Rt. 12 and 31 Bypass (684-3111).

Rolling Prairie: Quail Ridge Farms. 3382 East 1000N (778-2194).

Sun Acre Fruit Farm. 300 E (778-2483).

Sawyer: The Blueberry Patch. Holloway (426-4521 or 545-8125).

Schiffer's U-pick Blueberries. Sawyer Road (426-4994).
South Bend: Farmer's Market. 760 South Eddy (282-1259).
St. Joseph: Nye's Apple Barn. 4716 Hollywood (983-6602).
Valparaiso: Anderson Orchards. Rt. 6, east of Rt. 49 (464-4936).

Farmers' Markets. Courthouse Square.
Wanatah: Sieguesmund Berry Farm. 900W (733-2259).

Tidholm's Strawberry Farm. 1550S (733-2560).

FARMS

Hobart: Shilo Arabian Farm. 6900 Ainsworth (942-3753).
LaCrosse: LaVern Kreuger angus farm. 2100S (754-2402).
Medaryville: Jasper-Pulaski Tree Nursery. Rt. 421 (843-4827).
Michigan City: Great Lakes Duck Farm. Rt. 2 (874-6622).
South Bend: Martin Blad Mint Farm. 58995 Rt. 123 (234-7271).
Wanatah. Pinney-Purdue Experimental Farm. Rt. 30 and 100N (733-2379).

FISH HATCHERIES

Bass Lake: Bass Lake State Fish Hatchery. Lake Road (772-2353).
Kingsbury: Mixsawbah State Fish Hatchery. Rt. 104 (369-9591).
Mishawaka: Twin Branch State Fish Hatchery. 13200 East Jefferson (255-4199).

FISHING—Boat Charters

Chesterton: Jack's Gun Shop. Rt. 20 (787-8311).
Harbert: M&M Sport Fishing Charter (469-2759).
Michigan City: Contact LaPorte County Convention and Visitors Bureau (872-5055).
New Buffalo: New Buffalo Charter Service. 125 North Whittaker (469-1141).

Mari-Ron Charter Service (756-9235).

Skipper's Charter Service. 6 North Whittaker (469-3311).

Striker Sportfishing Charters. P.O. Box 374 (469-1120).

Niles: Four Flags Charter Service (684-2408).

South Bend: Charter Boats. 1602 Ewing (289-1905).

St. Joseph: Fisher's Charter. 100 Main (840-0249-or 983-4051).

Ken Neidlinger (925-2558).

Ted Ryzner (429-5033).

FISHING—Information

Lake County: Conservation Officers, Jeff Richwine, Brian Hultquest or Pam Dailey (942-1125).

LaPorte County: Conservation Officers Ken Spence and Tim Theriac (362-6205)

Michigan City: Hot line (872-0031).

Porter County: Conservation Officer Alan Fix (843-1011 or 464-8674).

St. Joseph County: Conservation Officers Stephen Rolewicz or John Mortimore (656-4411).

FISHING—Private Sites

Cedar Lake: Chuck's Pier. 13947 Huseman (374-9832).

Pinecrest Marina. 14415 Lauerman (374-5771).

Hobart: Robinson Park. 53rd at Liverpool (942-5498).

Hudson: Hudson Lake.

Kouts: Donna Joe Campground. 1200S and 300E (462-1545).

D. J. Bait Shop. Rt. 421 at Kankakee (823-3145).

LaPorte: Lower Fish Lake. Rt. 4 (324-6401).

Upper Fish Lake. Rt. 4 (325-8385).

Rolling Prairie: Rolling Timbers Lake. South of Rt. 2 (778-4107).

Saugany Lake. Off Rt. 2 (778-2926).

Valparaiso: Lake Eliza. Rt. 30 (462-1935).

Loomis Lake. Burlington Beach Road (462-5144).

Westville: Clear Lake. Porter-LaPorte County Road (872-9363).

FISHING—Public Sites

Cedar Lake: Cline and Lake Shore Drive.

Lemon Lake County Park. 6322 West 133rd (663-7627).

Crown Point: Fancher Lake Park. South Court and West Greenwood (663-0428).

East Chicago: Jeorse Park. Aldis at Lake Michigan (392-8320).

Gary: Lake Etta County Park. 3100 Clark (769-PARK.)

Hammond: Commonwealth Edison State Line Power Plant. 103rd at Lake Michigan (659-0036).

Hammond Water Filtration Plant. Calumet at Lake Michigan (853-6439).

Wolf Lake-Forsyth Park. 121st and Calumet.

Hebron: Grand Kankakee Marsh County Park. Rangeline Road (696-9951).

Hobart: Rose Park. 8th off Wisconsin (942-9421).

Kingsbury: Kingsbury State Fish and Wildlife Area. Rt. 39 (393-3612).

Knox: Bass Lake State Beach. Lake Road (772-2351).

LaPorte: Clear Lake. Truesdale (326-9600).

Fishtrap Lake. Off McClurg (326-9600).

North and South Pine Lakes. Waverly (326-9600).

Stone Lake. In Soldier's Memorial Park (326-9600).

Leroy: Stoney Run County Park. 450S (787-2020, ext. 391).

Medaryville: Jasper-Pulaski State Fish and Wildlife Area. Rt. 421 (843-4891).

Michigan City: NIPSCO Generating Station. Wabash and Water (872-1712).

Trail Creek. Michigan and Chapala.

Washington Park. From breakwater.

Miller: Marquette Park. Marquette and Grand (844-9404).

Portage: Port of Indiana docks. (926-9711).

Porter: Access to Little Calumet River from Hawthorn Park and Pratt Lake. Waverly south of Rt. 20 at Franklin (926-2771).

Rolling Prairie: Hog Lake. 700N (778-2241).

Schneider: LaSalle State Fish and Wildlife Area. Rt. 41 at 150N (992-3019).

South Bend: Potato Creek State Recreation Area. 25601 Rt. 4 (656-8186).

St. Patrick's County Park. 50650 Laurel (277-4828).

Whiting: Whiting Park. 117th off Indianapolis (659-0860).

GARDENS

Berrien Springs: Peg Bormann's Herbs and Flowers. 273 Hinchman (473-1356).

Chesterton: Mr. and Mrs. Sylvan Cook (926-4029).

Herbs and Wildflowers. 301 Indian Boundary (926-2218).

East Chicago: Washington Park Conservatory. 141st and Grand (392-8320).

Gary: South Gleason Park Conservatory. 3400 Jefferson (944-6517).

Hesston: Heston Gardens. 215E off 1000N (778-2421). Wild flowers.

Michigan City: Jean Cook. 7757 North 600W (874-5081).

International Friendship Gardens. Liberty Trail (874-3664).

Carl Pauley. 121 Top Flight Road (872-3379).

Leo Sharp. 303 Fir (879-7638).

Viola Shawley. 212 South Roeske (872-3430).

Mishawaka: Battell Park. Mishawaka Avenue (255-6610).

New Buffalo: David Holmes. 13128 Lubke (469-2758).

Niles: Fernwood. 1720 Range Line (695-6688).

St. Joseph: Margaret Upton Arboretum. State and the St. Joseph River.

South Bend: Fragrance Garden. Leeper Park, 900 block of North Michigan (284-9405).

Morris Conservatory and Muessel-Ellison Tropical Gardens. Mishawaka Avenue (284-9442).

Valparaiso: Ogden Gardens. Campbell and Harrison.

Edith Podresky (462-3531).

GOLF COURSES

Benton Harbor: Blossom Trail. 1565 Britain (925-4591).

Bridgman: Pebblewood Country Club. 9794 Jericho (465-5611).

Buchanan: Brookwood Golf Club. 1339 Rynearson (695-7818).

Cedar Lake: Monastery. 9728 129th (374-7750).

South Shore. 14400 Lake Shore (374-6070).

Crown Point: Oak Knoll. Rt. 8 (663-3349).

Pheasant Valley. 3834 West 141st (663-5000).

Ringo's Golf Center. 7611 East Lincoln Highway (942-8929).

Summertree. 2323 East 101st (663-0800).

East Chicago: MacArthur. In Tod Park, 142 Hemlock (398-4200, ext. 264).

Gary: Calumet. 3920 Ridge (980-9484).

North Gleason. 3200 Jefferson (944-1541).

South Gleason. 3400 Jefferson (944-6517).

Griffith: Griffith Golf Center. 1901 North Cline (923-3223).

Highland: Wicker Park. Rts. 6 & 41 (838-9809).

Hobart: Cressmoor. 601 North Wisconsin (942-7424).

Indian Ridge. 6363 Grand (942-6850).

LaPorte: Beechwood. Woodlawn (362-2651)

Briarleaf. 3233 North Rt. 39 (362-1992).

Merrillville: Broadmoor. 4300 West 81st (769-5444).

Turkey Creek. 6400 Harrison (980-5170).

Michigan City: Michigan City North Municipal. North Warnke (879-3478).

Michigan City South Municipal. Wolf and East Michigan (872-2121).

Mishawaka: Eberhart-Petro Municipal Course. 801 North State (255-5508).

Family Golf Center. 303 East Day (256-2800).

Putt Putt Golf and Games. 3615 North Main (259-4171).

Niles: Plym Park. East of Rt. 31 (684-7331).

Kelly's Sports Land. 2107 South 11th (683-5421).

Portage: Robbinhurst Golf Course. One mile west of Rt. 149, one-half mile north of Rt. 6 off McCool (762-9711).

South Bend: Ebel Park Municipal Course. 26595 Auten (272-4009).

Erskine Park Course. 4200 Miami (291-0156).

Playland Golf Center. 1715 Lincolnway East (288-0033).

Robin Hood Course. 20099 New Road (291-2450).

Studebaker Course. 718 East Calvert (237-9136).

Rolling Prairie: Valley Hills. 3544 East Rt. 2 (778-2823).
St. John: Lake Hills. 1001 West 85th (365-8601).
   Palmira. 12111 West 109th (365-4331).
St. Joseph: Wyndivicke Country Club. 3711 Niles Avenue (429-6210).
Schererville: Scherwood. 600 Joliet (865-2554).
Valparaiso: Forest Park Golf Course. West Harrison at Yellowstone (462-4411).
   Mink Lake. Rt. 49 (462-2585).

HAY RIDES (H) AND SLEIGH RIDES (S)

Cedar Lake: Lemon Lake County Park. 6322 West 133rd (663-7627). H
Chesterton: Jeff Christiansen. 1081 North 400E (926-6918). S
Crown Point: L. Fox. 4612 East 109th (663-3222). H and S
Deep River: Deep River County Park. County Road 330 (769-9030). H
Lake Station: William Remus. Rt. 6 (962-2213).H
Leroy: Stoney Run County Park. 450S (787-2020, ext. 391). H
Niles: Diamond D Ranch. 3232 Dunning (683-5892). H and S

HISTORICAL MARKERS, SITES

Boone Grove: Indian Mounds. 350W and 650S.
Buchanan: Moccasin Bluff Site. Three-quarters mile north of town on Main.
Crown Point: Solon Robinson Memorial. Joliet and Court.
Demotte: LaSalle Expedition. Rt. 231 at the Kankakee.
Dyer: Continental Watershed. Rt. 30.
East Chicago: First blast furnace. 3201 Watting.
Hammond: Monument of l821.
   George Hammond Meat Packing Plant site. Hohman Avenue.
Hebron: Indian Village. Rt. 2.
Indiana Dunes State Park: Revolutionary War Battle. Rt. 49 (926-4520).

Kouts: Baum's Bridge. Baun's Bridge Road and the Kankakee.

Dunn's Bridge. 500E and the Kankakee.

Tassinong Grove. Baum's Bridge Road and 550S.

Lake Station: Potawatomi Trail. Rt. 51.

Lowell: Three Creeks Monument. Library Square.

Merrillville: Potawatomi Trail. Homer Iddings School. 7249 Van Buren.

Michigan City: Battle of Trail Creek. East 8th and Liberty Trail.

Camp Anderson. 1702 Michigan.

Munster: Brass Tavern. Columbia and Rt. 6.

Niles: Grave of Father Allouez. Bond.

Fort St. Joseph. Bond.

Carey Mission. Phillips and Niles-Buchanan Roads.

Catholic Mission. Clay and Lincoln.

Sauk Trail Crossing. West side of St. Joseph River and Rt. 31.

Porter: Porter Train and Tower Wreck.

South Bend: Highland Cemetery. 2557 Portage.

Pierre Navarre Cabin. Leeper Park, 900 North Michigan (284-9405).

HORSEBACK RIDING (T = Trails only)

Cedar Lake: Willowdale Stables. 12808 Wicker (374-9875).

Crown Point: Carriage Gate Equestrian Training Center. 14516 Reeder (663-2615).

L. Fox Saddle Horses. 4612 East 109th (663-3222).

Deep River: Deep River County Park. County Road 330 (769-9030).T

Dyer: Sladich Tumbleweed Ranch. 9223 Sheffield (365-8003).

Indiana Dunes National Lakeshore: Ly-co-ki-we Trail. Rt. 20 and 275E (926-7561).T

Leroy: Stoney Run County Park. 450S (787-2020, ext.391). T

Michiana Shores: Michiana Riding Academy. 3848 Academy (872-2114).

Niles: Diamond D Ranch. 3232 Dunning (683-5892).

Larry Smith Stables. 2224 Reum (684-0167).

Valparaiso: Timberlake Farm. 3354 South Rt. 2 (464-7796).

St. Joseph: Stockbridge Stable. 1995 Dickinson (429-9892).

HUNTING

Hebron: Grand Kankakee Marsh County Park. Rangeline Road (696-9951).

Kingsbury: Kingsbury State Fish and Wildlife Area. Rt. 35 (393-3612).

Knox: Kankakee State Fish and Wildlife Area. Rt. 8 (792-4125).

LaCrosse: Kankakee State Fish and Wildlife Area. Rt. 8 (754-2237).

Medaryville: Jasper-Pulaski State Fish and Wildlife Area. Rt. 421 (843-3641).

Schneider: LaSalle State Fish and Wildlife Area. Rt. 41 at 150N (992-3019).

LODGINGS

Berrien Springs: Pennellwood Resort. Range Line Road (473-2511).

Duneland Beach: Duneland Beach Inn. 3311 Potawatomi Trail (874-7729).

Lakeside: Pebble House. 15197 Lake Shore (499-1416).

Merrillville: La Quinta Motor Inn. 8210 Louisiana (736-2879).

Michigan City: Creekwood Inn. 600W (872-8357).

Niles: Lilac Hill. 1720 Killarney Lane (683-2188).

South Bend: Bed and Breakfast (233-7791).

Morris Inn. On Notre Dame campus (234-0141).

Union Pier: Gordon Beach Inn. 1642 Lakeshore (469-3344).

MILLS

Coloma: Indian Summer Inc. Cider Mill. West Street (468-3101).

Deep River: John Wood's Grist Mill. County Road 330 (769-9030).

LaPorte: Garwood Cider Mill. North of Rt. 2 (362-4385).

Michigan City: Arndt Cider Mill. Wozniak Road (872-0122).

New Troy: New Troy Grist Mill (426-3422).

Valparaiso: Tratebas Mill. Tratebas Road. (Not in operation).

MOVIES

Benton Harbor: Fairplain Cinemas I-V. Napier and M-139 (927-4862).

Crown Point: Crown. 19 North Court (663-1616).

Gary: Ridge Plaza I and II. 5900 West Ridge (923-9100).

Griffith: Griffith Park Cinema I and II. 236 West Ridge (923-4300).

Hammond: Hammond Outdoor Theater. Borman and Indianapolis (844-0219).

Kennedy Theater. 6735 Kennedy (844-9769).

Highland: Town. 8618 Kennedy (838-1222).

Hobart: Art. 230 Main (942-1670).

LaPorte: LaPorte Cinema Quad. 608 Colfax (362-7569).

LaPorte Deluxe Drive-In. Rt. 2 East (362-4013).

Lowell: Polo Theater. 133 Mill (696-8246 or 696-7244).

Merrillville: Crossroads Cinema I and II. 6180 Broadway (980-0558).

Southlake Mall Cinema I-IV. 2479 Southlake Mall (730-2652).

Y & W Twin I and II. 6600 South Broadway (769-2203).

Michigan City: Dunes Plaza Cinema I-VI. 100 Dunes Plaza (874-4281).

Marquette Theatre I-IV. Marquette Mall (872-9101).

212 Outdoor Theatre. Rt. 212 (872-1472).

Miller: Dunes Cinema I and II. 8090 East Rt. 20 (938-0700).

Mishawaka: Town and Country. 2340 Hickory (259-9090).

University Park Cinema. University Park Mall. 6501 Grape (277-2223).

South Bend: Forum Cinema. 52709 Rt. 31 North (277-1522).

River Park Theater. 2929 Mishawaka (288-8488).

Scottsdale Theater. 1153 Scottsdale Mall (291-4583).

St. Joseph: St. Joseph Auto Drive-in Theater. 4023 Red Arrow Highway (429-3926).

Southtown Twin Theaters. 815 St. Joseph Street (983-3233).

Valparaiso: County Seat Cinema I-VI. Rt. 49 (462-1999).

MUSEUMS AND LIBRARY COLLECTIONS

Benton Harbor: The Josephine Morton Memorial House. 501 Territorial (925-7201).

Berrien Springs: Berrien County Historical Association. Rt. 31 and Union (471-1202).

Chesterton: Historical Collection. Westchester Public Library. 200 West Indiana (926-7697).

Crown Point: Old Lake County Courthouse. Courthouse Square.

Gary: Indiana Room, Gary Public Library. 220 West Fifth (886-2484).

Calumet Regional Archives. Indiana University-Northwest. 3400 Broadway (980-6628).

Griffith: Grand Trunk Depot Museum. 201 South Broad (924-2155).

Hammond: Calumet Room, Hammond Public Library. 506 State (931-5100).

Purdue University Calumet Archives. Purdue University Calumet. 2233 171st (844-0520).

Hebron: The Stagecoach Inn. Main (996-2700).

Hesston: LaPorte County Steam Society. 1000N (778-2783).

Hobart: Hobart Historical Museum. 4th and Earl (942-5536).

Knox: Archbishop Andrew Sheptytsky Museum. 700E.

Starke County Historical Museum. 401 South Main (772-5393).

LaPorte: LaPorte County Historical Museum. Courthouse Annex (362-7061).

Merrillville: Lake County Reference Library. Rt. 30 (769-3540).

Michigan City: Lighthouse Museum. Harbor (872-6133).

Indiana Room, Michigan City Public Library. 4th and Franklin (879-4561).

Mishawaka: Mishawaka Children's Museum. 410 Lincolnway East (259-3475).

Niles: Fort St. Joseph Historical Museum. 508 East Main (683-4702).

South Bend: Discovery Hall Museum. 120 South St. Joseph (284-9714).

Old Courthouse Museum. 112 South Lafayette (284-9664).

Studebaker Exhibit. 520 South Lafayette (284-9108).

St. Joseph: Fort Miami Heritage Society. 116 State (983-1191 or 983-1375).

Valparaiso: Porter County Historical Museum. 153 Franklin (464-8661).

Wilbur H. Cummings Museum of Electronics. Valparaiso Technical Institute. West Chestnut (462-2191).

MUSIC (J = Jazz)

Cedar Lake: After Four Supper Club. 13109 Wicker (374-7636). J

Torrey Auditorium, Cedar Lake Bible Center. 13701 Lauerman (374-5771). Sacred music concerts.

Gary: Blue Room Lounge. 1654 West 11th (no phone). J

Mona's Lounge. 1537 Broadway (882-6550). J

Griffith: Rick's Cafe. 520 East Main (924-9669). J

Harbert: Blue Chip Lounge. 13982 Red Arrow Highway (469-5199).

Michigan City: International Friendship Gardens. Liberty Trail (874-3664).

Mirage Lounge. 5820 South Franklin (879-0311).

Sloan's. 4122 South Franklin (874-7203).

Mishawaka: Bethel College, Goodman Auditorium. 1001 McKinley (259-8511).

Band Organ. 211 East Day (255-6777).

Porter: The Spa. Mineral Springs Road((926-1654 or 762-8765). J

South Bend: Saint Mary's College (284-4176).
South Bend Symphony. 211 North Michigan (232-6343).

NATURE CENTERS, PRESERVES

Benton Harbor: Sarett Nature Center. Benton Center Road (927-4832).
Berrien Springs: Love Creek Nature Center. Huckleberry (471-2617).
Buchanan: Dayton Prairie. Off Dayton Road southwest of Buchanan.
Deep River: Deep River County Park. County Road 330 (769-9030).
Griffith: Hoosier Prairie State Nature Preserve.
Hammond: Gibson Woods Nature Preserve. 6201 Parrish (769-9030).
Indiana Dunes National Lakeshore: Cowles Bog. Mineral Springs Road (926-7561).
Pinhook Bog. Wozniak (926-7561).
Indiana Dunes State Park: Easterly two-thirds of the park. Rt. 49 (926-4520).
Lakeside: Robinson Preserve. East Road.
Lake Station: Deep River Nature Center. 3100 Liverpool (962-3579).
Lowell: German Methodist Cemetery Prairie Nature Preserve (988-7547).
Medaryville: Teft Savanna Nature Preserve. In Jasper-Pulaski Fish and Wildlife Area. Rt. 143 (843-4841).
Michigan City: Barker Woods Nature Preserve (879-3227).
Mishawaka: South Bend Audubon Society Nature Sanctury. Clover Road off Dragoon Trail (291-2830).
Niles: Fernwood. 1720 Range Line (695-6688).
Schneider: Beaver Lake Nature Preserve. In LaSalle State Fish and Wildlife Area. Rt. 41 (992-3019).
South Bend: Spicer Lake Nature Preserve. County Line Road (277-4828).
Swamp Rose Nature Preserve. 25601 Rt. 4 (656-8186).
Stevensville: Grand Mere Nature Preserve. I-94 exit 22 off Thornton (927-4832).

Lincoln Township Nature Center. Notre Dame Road (465-6235).

Three Oaks: Warren Woods. Warren Woods Road (426-4013).

Valparaiso: Moraine Nature Preserve. 750N (464-4941).

PARKS

Benton Harbor: Riverfront Park. Riverview Drive.

Bridgman: Warren Dunes State Park. Red Arrow Highway (426-4013).

Cedar Lake: Lemon Lake County Park. 6322 West 133rd (663-7627).

Crown Point: Fancher Lake Park. South Court and West Greenwood.

Deep River: Deep River County Park. County Road 330 (769-9030).

East Chicago: Jeorse Park. Aldis at Lake Michigan (392-8320).

Washington Park. 141st and Grand (392-8320).

Gary: Gateway Park. 4th and Broadway.

Lake Etta County Park. 3100 Clark (769-PARK).

North Gleason Park. 3200 Jefferson.

South Gleason Park. 3400 Jefferson.

Griffith Oak Ridge Prairie County Park. 301 South Colfax (769-PARK).

Hammond: Dowling Park. Kennedy and Borman.

Lakefront Park. Calumet at Lake Michigan (853-6379).

Riverside Park. Calumet and Borman.

Wolf Lake-Forsythe Park. 121st and Calumet.

Hebron: Grand Kankakee Marsh County Park. Rangeline off Rt. 2 (696-9951).

Highland: Wicker Park. Rt. 6 at Rt. 41 (932-2350).

Hobart: John Robinson Park. 53rd at Liverpool (942-9321).

Fred Rose Park. 8th off Wisconsin (942-9431).

Kingsbury: White Oak County Park. Pin Oak and Hupp.

Lake Station: Riverview Park. Rt. 51.

LaPorte: Kesling Park. 18th off Kingsbury (326-9600).

Fox Park. Truesdale and Pine Lake Avenue (326-9600).

Soldiers' Memorial Park. Waverly (326-9600).

Leroy: Stoney Run County Park. 450S (787-20220, ext. 391).

Lowell: Buckley Homestead County Park. 3606 Bellshaw (769-PARK).

Merrillville: Hidden Lake Park. 63rd and Broadway.

Michigan City: Washington Park. Franklin (879-8393).

Miller: Marquette Park. Marquette and Grand (844-9404).

Mishawaka: Battell Park. Mishawaka Avenue (255-6610).

Merrifield Park and Recreation Complex. East Mishawaka Avenue (255-6610).

New Carlisle: Bendix Woods County Park. Rt. 2 (641-3155).

Munster: Bieker Woods. Ridge and Columbia.

Portage: Woodland Park. 2100 Willowcreek (762-1675).

South Bend: Potato Creek State Recreation Area. 25601 Rt. 4 (656-8186).

Potawatomi Park. 2105 Mishawaka (284-9401).

Rum Village Park. 1304 West Ewing (284-9455).

St. Patrick's County Park. 50650 Laurel (277-4828).

St. Joseph: Lake Bluff Park. Lakebluff between Park and State.

Margaret Upton Arboretum. State.

Riverview Park. Niles Avenue.

Valparaiso: Sunset Hill Farm. Meridian and Rt. 6. To open fall, 1985.

Rogers-Lakewood Park. Campbell east of Rt. 49 (464-5144).

Whiting: Whihala Beach County Park. 117th and Park at Lake Michigan (769-PARK).

Whiting Park. 117th off Indianapolis (659-0860).

RELIGIOUS SITES

Cedar Lake: Cedar Lake Bible Center. 13701 Lauerman (374-5941).

Franciscan Retreat. Parrish (374-5741).

Crown Point: Hyles-Anderson College. 8400 Burr (769-4901).

Munster: Carmelite Hall. 1628 Ridge (838-9257).

South Bend: Lourdes Grotto. Notre Dame (239-5000).
Valparaiso: Seven Dolors Shrine. 700N (759-2521).

RESTAURANTS

Baroda: Bill's Tap. 8906 First (422-1141).
  Tabor Hill Restaurant. Mt. Tabor Road (422-1165).
Benton Harbor: Captain's Table. 655 Riverview (927-2421).
  Bill Knapp's. Rt. 139 at I-94 (925-3212).
Beverly Shores: Red Lantern Inn. Lake Front Drive (874-6201).

Cedar Lake: Dick's Tap. Rts. 8 & 41 (365-5041).
  Heritage. 13242 Wicker (374-6200).
  Tobe's Steak House. 7301 West 138th (374-9805).
Chesterton: Wingfield's. 526 Indian Oak Mall (926-5152).
Crown Point: Bon Appetit. 302 South Main (663-6363).
  Lighthouse South. 101 South Courthouse Square (663-7141).
  S.O.B.'s Speakeasy. 211 South East (763-SOBS).
Demotte: Forest River Lodge. Off Rt. 231 at the Kankakee (996-4472).
East Chicago: Casa Blanca. 4616 Indianapolis (397-4151).
  El Tapatio. 4020 Main (398-6992).
  Jockey Club. 4624 Magoun (398-2353).
  Kay and Danny's Greenhouse. 1208 Carroll (398-1010).
  Puntillo. 4905 Indianapolis (397-4952).
  The Cotton Lounge. 502 West 151st (397-8411).
Gary: Calvary Institutional Church. 230 Virginia (883-4422).
  Davis Seafood. 3405 West 15th (944-8555).
  Miller's Restaurant. In The Boy's Club. 225 West 5th (882-3303).
Griffith: Herman and Mary's Steak House. 216 South Broad (924-9685).
  Magma Restaurant. 101 North Broad (924-6454).
  Pagoda Inn. 1207 East Ridge (923-7170).
  San Remo. 112 East Ridge (838-6000).
  Sherlock's Holme. 921 West 45th (924-2200).
Hammond: Cam-Lan. 132 Sibley (931-5115).

Cataldi. 576 State (931-0200).

El Taco Real. 935 Hoffman (932-8333).

Purdue University Calumet. 2233 171st (844-0520).

Phil Smidt. 1205 North Calumet (659-0025).

Harbert: Blue Chip Lounge. 13982 Red Arrow Highway (469-5199).

Hebron: Country Kitchen. 20 North Main (996-9221).

Old Heritage Inn. Main (996-9010).

Hesston: Heston Bar. Fail at 1000N (778-2938).

Highland: Miner-Dunn. 8490 Indianapolis (923-3313).

Town Club. 2904 45th (924-5227).

Hobart: Country Lounge. 3700 Montgomery (942-2623).

Indian Ridge Supper Club. 6363 Grand (342-0666).

Knox: Courthouse View Lounge. 60 East Washington (772-5535).

Kouts: Baum's Bridge Inn. Baum's Bridge Road (766-9925).

John's Corner Tap. Main (766-9933).

LaPorte: Ole's Meat, Fish & Liquor Company. 502 State (362-8270).

Tangerine. Michigan (326-8000).

The Timbers. In LaPorte Holiday Inn. 444 Pine Lake Avenue (362-8040).

Tom's Landing. 304 Detroit (362-2916).

Merrillville: Angelo's Sicilian Cart. 1515 East 82nd (769-2429).

Bon Femme Cafe. 6 West 79th (no phone).

El-Mar's. 7404 Broadway (769-5000).

Michigan City: Maxine and Heine's. 521 Franklin (879-9068).

Panda. 3801 Franklin (872-7566).

The Pub. 723 Franklin Square (872-8631).

Miller: Beach Cafe. 903 North Shelby (886-9090).

Golden Coin. Rt. 20 and Clay (989-8357).

Mishawaka: Band Organ. 211 East Day (259-0050).

Doc Pierce's. 120 North Main (255-7737).

New Yorktowne Deli. 106 North Main (259-6600).

Papa Joe's Casa de Pasta. 1209 South Union (255-0890).

Munster: Bombay Bicycle Club. 9201 Calumet (836-9114).

Giovanni's Restaurant. 603 Ridge (836-6220).

Gold Rush. 1745 45th (974-6630).

Schoop's Hamburger. 215 Ridge (836-6233).

Star Delicatessen. 229 Ridge (836-9224).

The Charley Horse. 8317 Calumet (836-6100).

New Carlisle: Miller's Home Cafe. 110 East Michigan (654-3431).

New Buffalo: Lighthouse. 144 North Whittaker (469-5489).

Little Bohemia. 115 South Whittaker (469-1440).

Redamak's. 616 East Buffalo (469-4522).

Skip's Other Place. Red Arrow Highway between New Buffalo and Union Pier (469-3330).

Theo's Lanes. Rt. 12 (469-0400).

Niles: Franky's. 1033 Lake (683-7474).

Happy House. 3121 South 11th (684-0484).

Porter: The Spa. Mineral Springs Road (926-1654 or 762-8765).

St. Joseph: Holly's Landing. 105 North Main (983-2334).

Schererville: Teibel's. Rt. 30 at Rt. 41 (865-2000).

South Bend: Captain Alexander's Moonraker. 320 East Colfax (234-4477).

East Bank Emporium. 121 South Niles (234-9000).

Eddie's. 1345 North Ironwood (232-5861).

Lee's Grill and Barbecue. 1132 South Bend (237-9167).

Morris Inn. Notre Dame campus (234-0141).

Senor Kelly's. 119 North Michigan (234-5389).

Tippecanoe Place. 620 West Washington (234-9077).

Stevensville: Grande Mere Inn. 5800 Red Arrow Highway (429-3591).

Win Schuler. 5000 Red Arrow Highway (429-3273).

Tosi's. 4337 Ridge (429-3689).

Three Oaks: Carpenter's. West Rt. 12 (756-6821).

Village Pump. 13 South Elm (756-9132).

Valparaiso: China House. 120 East Lincolnway (462-5788).

Court. 69 Franklin (462-2141).

Golden Dragon. 1706 LaPorte (462-3003).

Old Style Inn. 5 Lincolnway (462-5600).

Strongbow Turkey Inn. Rt. 30 (462-3311).

Vale of Paradise Delicatessen. 64 West Lincolnway (462-7242).

The White House. 303 Jefferson (464-9515).
Whiting: Condes. 1440 Indianapolis (659-6300).
  Granny's Tearoom. 1950 Indianapolis.
  Vogel's. 1250 Indianapolis (659-1250).

SHOOTING RANGES (I = Indoor O = Outdoor)

Highland: Hansen's Sports. 3750 Ridge (838-7495). I
Kingsbury: Kingsbury State Fish and Wildlife Area. Rt. 39 (393-3612). O
Medaryville: Jasper-Pulaski State Fish and Wildlife Area. Rt. 421 (843-3641). O
Whiting: Whiting Park. 117th off Indianapolis (659-0868). Skeet shooting. O

SHOPS—Craftsmen

Beverly Shores: Save the Dunes Council Shop. Rt. 12 west of Broadway (879-3937).
Chesterton: Freight Station. 123 North 4th (926-6030).
  Jeweled Gazebo. 132 South Calumet (926-2555).
  Sleepy Hollow Leather. 145 Indian Boundary (926-1071).
  Yellow Brick Road. 762 Calumet (926-7048).
Lakeside: Arts and Crafts of Lakeside. 14876 Red Arrow Highway (469-2771).
LaPorte: Elwyn Ames. 400N off Fail (325-8368). Blacksmith.
Porter: Jean Segal (926-1919)). Lapidary.
South Bend: South Bend Cut Glass Company. 225 South Michigan (288-0347).
Union Mills: Ed Klein's Saddle Shop. Rt. 39 (767-2640).

SHOPS—Discount and Outlets

Bridgman: Little Red Shoe House. 4236 Lake (465-6825).
Gary: Joyce Sportswear. 2100 East 15th (883-9681).
Merrillville: Century Plaza Mall. Broadway and Rt. 30.
  Great Western Boot Outlet. Rt. 30 west of I-65.
  Quality Discount Apparel. 6136 Broadway (980-3980).
Michigan City: Burnham Glove. 1608 Tennessee (874-5206).

Jaymar-Ruby. 209 West Michigan (879-6336).

The Mart. 650 East Rt. 20 (874-6236).

Munster: Big Red Sports. 921-A Ridge (836-8088).

Niles: Fa$hion Outlet Center. 219 East Main (684-4443).

Jay Arrels Sample Outlet. 1400 Niles Road (684-4104).

Schererville: Preferred Stock. Rts. 30 and 41. (865-2593).

Three Oaks: Gerber's Children's Wear Outlet. West Rt. 12 (756-7311).

Valparaiso: Fetla's. 1475 South Rt. 2 (462-5221).

SHOPS—Flea Markets and Salvage

Benton Harbor: Community Expo Flea Market. Rt. 139 and Napier.

Cedar Lake: The Barn & Field Flea Market. 9600 West 151st (696-7368).

Chesterton: Second Time Around Shop. 200E one block north of Rt. 20 (926-5555).

Coloma: Farmer's Flea Market. Red Arrow Highway east of town.

Hammond: International Bazaar. Sibley and Hohman.

Knox. Toto's. Toto Road (772-4533).

Michigan City: Anxious Al's. East Rt. 20 (874-4130).

Wildwood Park Flea Market. 4938 Rt. 20 (879-5660).

The Pines: The Junk Shop. 3026 2nd Place (872-7485).

SHOPS—Flowers and Seeds

Buchanan: Herman's Haven. Elm Valley Road (695-6736).

Chesterton: Chesterton Feed and Garden Center. 400 Locust (926-2790).

Mrs. Walter Erickson. 450 Burdick (926-6866).

Hammond: Indiana Botanic Gardens. 626 177th (931-2480).

Solan's Greenhouse. 6804 Columbia (932-8257).

Highland: Mary Ann Garden Center. 3405 Ridge (838-0015).

LaPorte: Bernacchi Greenhouse. 1010 Fox (362-6202).

Medaryville: Jasper-Pulaski Tree Nursery. Rt. 421 (843-4827).

Michigan City: Bortz. 519 Chicago (874-4188).

Stevensville: Emlong Nursery. Red Arrow Highway (429-3431).
Valparaiso: McMahan Seed Company. 6 North Michigan (462-1411).

SHOPS—Foods

Baroda: Tabor Hill Vineyard and Winecellar. Mt. Tabor Road (422-1161).
Berrien Springs: Apple Valley Markets. Andrews University., Rt. 31 471-7771).
Bridgman: Tabor Hill Champagne Cellars. Exit 16 off I-94 (465-6566).
Buchanan: Marz Sweet Shop. 205 Front (695-9110).
East Chicago: Supermercado del Puebla. 4610 Indianapolis.
   Supermercados Mexico. 4022 Main (398-6900).
Hammond: Import Food Market. 120 Sibley (932-7711).
   Queen Ann Chocolates. 604 Hoffman (932-2400).
Harbert: Harbert Bakery. 13746 Red Arrow Highway (469-1777).
   Lakeside Vineyard and Winery. 13581 Red Arrow Highway (469-0700).
LaPorte: Boulder Hill Vineyard. 3366 West 400N (326-7341).
   Sages Ice Cream. 204 2nd (362-2252).
Michigan City: Furness Fisheries. 2nd at Trail Creek Bridge (874-4761).
   Parco. 502 West Rt. 20 (879-4431). Cookies at discount.
Miller: Wilco. 6300 Miller (938-6631). Greek bakery.
Munster: Munster Sausage Company. 615 Ridge (836-9050).
Niles: Paris Candy Company. 220 East Main (683-9792).
Sawyer: Schlipp's Pharmacy (426-3487).
South Bend: Farmer's Market. 760 South Eddy (282-1259).
Stevensville: A Bit of Swiss Bakery. 4337 Ridge (429-1661).
Three Oaks: Drier's. 23 South Elm (756-3101).
Valparaiso: Coffee and Tea Market. 108 East Lincolnway (462-7265).

Whiting: Kitchens of Sara Lee. 1749 Indianapolis (659-5108).

SHOPS—Miscellaneous

Buchanan: Proud's V & S General Store. 120 East Front (695-2250).

Timberlou. 105 East Front (695-5374). Gifts.

Cedar Lake: Artists Den. 200 Jefferson (462-3883). Gifts.

Crown Point: Lake County Court House Shops. Courthouse Square. 21 emporiums.

Dyer: Holly Wreath. 1562 Joliet (322-2500). Gifts.

Furnessville: The Schoolhouse Shop. Furnessville Road (926-1875). Gifts.

Hammond: Army and Navy Store. 5145 Hohman (932-9010).

Highland: Brumm's Bloomin' Barn. 2540 45th (924-1000). Gifts.

Cranberry Cove. 2933 Highway (923-8529). Imported merchandise.

Michigan City: Anko. 731 Franklin Square (874-5555). Women's high fashion designs.

Mishawaka: 100 Center. 700 Lincolnway West (259-7861). Many shops of all sorts.

Watson's Part II. Lower level 100 Center (259-2105).

Munster: Barton Imports. 419 Ridge (836-2115). Gifts.

Bruna Christopher. 417 Ridge (836-2015). Jewelry and gifts.

Joe Hirsch. 8250 Hohman (836-8888). Clothing for men and women.

The Fabric Shop. 427 Ridge (836-8080).

New Buffalo: Decors. Red Arrow Highway (469-2745). Objets d'art.

New Carlisle: Watson's. 135 East Michigan (654-3511). Plates.

Pines: Vernier China Co. 3986 West Rt. 20 (872-6605).

Porter: Saylor's Basket Place. 1300 West Rt. 20 (926-6740).

Sawyer: The Book Rack. Red Arrow Highway (426-4120).

Haaląg's, Red Arrow Highway (426-4233). Swedish imports.

Valparaiso: The Artist's Den, 203 Jefferson (462-3883).

Hans and Fritz Antique Clocks, 9 North Washington (464-2010).

Marrell's Gift Shop, 1004 Calumet (464-3585).

Whiting: Anne's Linens, 1419 119th (659-1628).

SKIING (C=Cross Country   D=Downhill)

Baroda: Tabor Hill Winery, Mt. Tabor Road (462-1161). C

Berrien Springs: Love Creek Nature Center. Huckleberry (471-2617). C

Buchanan: Royal Valley Ski Resort. Main State Road (695-3847). D

Coloma: Pine Ridge Ski Shop and Trails. 46th (468-8415). C

Cedar Lake: Lemon Lake County Park. 6322 West 133rd (663-7627). C

Deep River: Deep River County Park. County Road 330 (769-9030). C

Griffith: Oak Ridge Prairie County Park. 301 South Colfax (769-PARK). C

Hebron: Grand Kankakee Marsh County Park. Rangeline off Rt. 2 (696-9951). C

Indiana Dunes National Lakeshore: Calumet Trail. Mineral Springs and Rt. 12 to Michigan City (926-7561).

Inland Marsh Trail. Rt. 12 at Ogden Dunes (926-7561). C

Ly-co-ki-we-Trail. Rt. 20 and 275E (926-7561). C

Marquette Trail. Lake-Porter County Road to the Lake (926-7561). C

Indiana Dunes State Park: Trails 2, 8 and 9 (926-4520). C

Lakeside: Harbor Country Cross Country Ski Club. (469-2181). C

LaPorte: Ski Valley. Forrester (362-1212). D

New Carlisle: Bendix Woods County Park. Rt. 2 (641-3155). CD

Niles: Madeline Bertrand Park. Laurel east of Stateline Road.

Three Oaks: Warren Woods. Warren Woods Road (426-4013). C

Bob-A-Ron Campgrounds. Warren Woods Road (469-3894). C

Valparaiso: The Pines. 674 North Meridian (462-4179). D

SKI RENTAL (C = Cross Country D = Downhill)

Cedar Lake: Lemon Lake County Park. 6322 West 133rd (663-7627). C

Coloma: Pine Ridge Ski Shop and Trails. 46th (468-8415).

Indiana Dunes National Lakeshore: Ly-co-ki-we trailhead. Rt. 20 (926-7561). C

Indiana Dunes State Park: (926-4520). C

LaPorte: Ski Valley. Forrester (362-1212). D

Deep River: Deep River County Park. County Road 330 (769-9030). C

Merrillville: Brown's Sporting Goods. 2278 Southlake Mall (769-9075). D

Camp-Land. Rt. 30 and Madison (769-8496). D

SLEDDING, SNOWMOBILING AND TOBOGGANING

(S = Sledding Sn = Snowmobiling T = Tobogganing)

Cedar Lake: Lemon Lake County Par. 6322 West 133rd (663-7627). S

Deep River: Deep River County Park. County Road 330. (769-9030). Sn

Griffith: Oak Ridge Prairie County Park. 301 Colfax (769-PARK). S

New Carlisle: Bendix Woods Count Park. Rt. 2 (641-3155). S T

SPECIAL EVENTS

Very subject to change, check carefully.

Baroda: Annual Blessing of the Harvest. Tabor Hill Winery. Mt. Tabor Road (422-1161).Weekend after Labor Day.

Benton Harbor: Blossomtime. 151 East Napier (926-7397). First week in May.

Western Amateur Golf Tournament. Point O'Woods Country Club. 1516 Roslin (944-1433). August.

Berrien Springs: Berrien County Youth Fair. Fairgrounds (473-4251).

Beverly Shores: Fireman's Ball. Fire Station, Broadway. Saturday night closest to the 4th of July.

Chesterton: Chesterton Art Fair. 640 North Calumet. First weekend in August.
Duneland Folk Festival. Westchester Public Library. 200 West Indiana (926-7696). July.
Festival of the Dunes. Downtown. Last Week in July.

Coloma: Coloma Gladiolus Festival (468-3285). First week-end in August.

Crown Point: Lake County Fair. South Court and West Greenwood (663-0428). Third week in August.
Festival Days. First week in July.

Demotte: Art and Crafts Fair. Halleck Street. Second Saturday in August.

Deep River: Wood's Mill Faire (769-PARK). Second weekend in September.

East Chicago: Mexican Independence Day (398-1600). Early September.
Puerto Rican Constitution Celebration Day (397-5607).

Gary: Steel City Fest (885-5437).

Hammond: A Taste of Yesterday. Hessville Park, 7205 Kennedy (844-7627). Last Saturday before July 4th.

Hobart: July 4th Celebration (942-5774). July 4th weekend.

Indiana Dunes National Lakeshore: Duneland Folk Festival. Bailly Homestead grounds (926-7561). July.
Maple Sugar Time. Chellberg Farm (926-7561). March.

Knox: Bass Lake Festival (772-3909). Third and fourth week-ends in July.

Kouts: Arts and Crafts Festival (766-3766). Third Saturday in September.

LaPorte: July 4th Parade (362-3718).
LaPorte County Fair. Rt. 2 at 150N (362-2647). Second week in August.

Leroy: Bluegrass Festival. Stoney Run County Park (769-PARK).

Lowell: Buckley Homestead Days. 3606 Belshaw (769-PARK). Second weekend in October.
Old Fashioned Day (696-0231). Second Saturday in June.
Oktoberfest (696-0231). Last weekend in September.

Merrillville: Italian Festival. Michael Angelo picnic grounds 6220 Broadway (980-9410). Last Wednesday-Sunday in June.

Grecian Festival. 8000 Madison (769-8421). Second weekend in July.

Serbfest. 8700 Taft (769-2122). Third weekend in June.

Michigan City: In-Water Boat Show. Port Authority Basin (872-5355). Last week in August.

Lakefront Music Festival. Bicentennial Amphitheatre, Washington Park (879-6440). Last weekend in June.

Lighthouse Treasurama. Lighthouse Museum grounds, Washington Park (872-6311).

Miss Indiana Pageant finals. Rogers High School (872-5055). Last Thursday-Saturday in June.

Oktoberfest. Washington Park (872-5055). Labor Day weekend.

Summer Festival (872-2162). Second week in July.

Miller: Art Fair. Miller School grounds, Lake Street (938-1308). First weekend in June.

Mishawaka: Arts and Crafts Fair. 100 Center, Rt. 33 (256-9626). July.

New Carlisle: Historical Days. Michigan Street. Last week in July.

Maple Syrup Program and Pancake Breakfast. Bendix Woods County Park (654-3155). Spring.

Winter Festival. Bendix Woods County Park (654-3155). Winter.

Niles: Fort St. Joseph Days. Riverfront Park. June.

Four Flags Area Apple Festival. 67th and Lake Street (683-8913). Autumn.

Portage: Annual $10,000 Big Fish Contest (762-3300). July.

Annual Grand Prix Jamboree (762-3300). June.

St. Joseph: Art Fair. Lake Bluff Park, Lakebluff Avenue. July.

St. Joseph River Venetian Festival. St. Joseph-Benton Harbor on the St. Joseph River (983-7917). Midsummer.

Tri-State Regatta. Lake Michigan. Labor Day weekend.

South Bend: Firefly Festival. St. Patrick's County Park. 50651 Laurel (277-4828). First three weeks in July.

Gem, Mineral and Jewelry Festival. Athletic and Convocation Center, University of Notre Dame. September.
North Liberty Potato Creek Festival. Downtown City Park. Mid-August.
South Bend Ethnic Festival. River Bend Plaza (284-9328).
St. Joseph County 4-H Fair. Jackson and Lakewood (291-4870).
Zoofest. Potawatomi Park. 2105 Mishawaka Avenue (288-8133). June.
Three Oaks: Cross country skiing and snowmobile weekends. Bob-A-Ron Campgrounds. Warren Woods Road (469-3894). January and February.
Maple Syrup Festival. Bob-A-Ron Campgrounds. Warren Woods Road (469-3894). March.
Valparaiso: The Art Event. Courthouse Plaza (464-4080). First weekend in June.
Popcorn Festival (462-1105). September.
Porter County Fair. 1948-Old Porter County Fair Grounds, Evans and Indiana. 1985-Porter County Exposition Center. 215 East Division (464-8661).
Wanatah: Summer Festival. Third weekend in July.
Whiting: Lakefront Festival (659-0292). First week in July.

SWIMMING (I=indoor)

(* = admission fee ** = parking fee)

Check YMCA's and high schools in communities for hours and fees for public swimming.

Benton Harbor: Rocky Gap Beach. Rocky Gap Road and Lake Michigan.
Berrien Springs: Lake Chapin. Near the village.
Oronoko Lakes Recreation Area. Snow Road four miles west of town.
Bridgman: Warren Dunes State Park*. Red Arrow Highway (426-4013).
Weko Beach. Lake Street (465-5407).
Cedar Lake: Pinecrest Marina. 14415 Lauerman (374-5771).
Coloma: Hagar Shore and Roadside Parks. Northwest of town off the Blue Star Memorial Highway.

West Paw Paw Lake. Off Paw Paw Lake Road.

Crown Point: Fancher Lake. South Court and West Greenwood.

East Chicago: Jeorse Park. Aldis at Lake Michigan.

Gary: Borman Park. 7th and Madison.

Washington Park. 13th at Pennsylvania.

Hatcher Park. 21st and Missouri.

Fisher Park. 43rd and Fillmore.

Roosevelt Park. 2nd and Burr.

Tolleston Park. 15th and Rutledge.

Hammond: Wolf Lake. 121st and Calumet.

Harbert: Cherry Beach. Red Arrow Highway between Harbert and Lakeside.

Highland: Wicker Park. Rts. 41 and 6 (839-9809).

Hobart: John Robinson Park*. 53rd at Liverpool (942-5498).

Indiana Dunes National Lakeshore: West Beach. Lake-Porter County Road**.

State Park Road, Beverly Shores.

Central Avenue, Beverly Shores.

Mount Baldy Beach, Rice Avenue just east of Beverly Shores.

Indiana Dunes State Park: Rt. 49.***.

Knox: Bass Lake State Beach (772-2351).

Kankakee State Fish and Wildlife Area. Rt. 8 (792-4125).

LaPorte: North and South Pine Lakes. Waverly (326-9600).

Stone Lake. Soldiers' Memorial Park, Rt. 35 (326-9600).

Upper Fish Lake*. Rt. 4 (325-8385).

Merrillville: Hidden Lake Park. 63rd and Broadway.

Michigan City: Washington Park**.

Miller: Lake Street**.

Marquette Park**.

Mishawaka: Merrifield Park and Recreation Complex. East Mishawaka Avenue (255-6610).

New Buffalo: Public beaches on Lake Michigan. Riviera Road.

Niles: Kugler's Beach on Barron Lake. Northeast of town.

Rolling Prairie: Saugany Lake*. Rt. 2 (778-2926).

St. Joseph: Lion's Beach. End of Pine.

Silver Beach. Broad below Lake Boulevard.

Tiscornia Beach. Park Road off Ridgeway.
South Bend: Potato Creek State Recreation Area*. 25601 Rt. 4. (656-8186).

Potawatomi Park. 2105 Mishawaka (284-9401).

St. Patrick's County Park*. 50650 Laurel (277-4828).
Valparaiso: Lake Eliza*. Rt. 30 (462-1935).

Loomis Lake*. Two and a half miles north on Burlington Beach Road off Rt. 49 (462-5144).
Westville: Clear Lake*. LaPorte-Porter County Line Road (872-9363).
Whiting: Memorial Community Center. 1938 Clark (659-0860). I

Whihala Beach**. 117th and Park at Lake Michigan (769-PARK).

THEATERS

Buchanan: Buchanan Fine Arts Council cinema and stage series. P.O. Box 3.
Gary: Theater-Northwest. Indiana University-Northwest. 3400 Broadway (980-6808).

The Company Playhouse. Broadway, north of Ridge (no phone).
LaPorte: LaPorte Little Theater Company. Old St. John Lutheran Church. 218 A (362-5113).
Michiana Shores: Dunes Summer Theater. Oakdale (879-8782).
Michigan City: Footlight Players. Johnson Road (874-4035).

Festival Players. Canterbury Theatre. 907 Franklin (874-4269).
Munster: Gallery Players. Northwest Indiana Art Association. 8317 Calumet (836-1839).
South Bend: Broadway Theater League. 211 North Michigan (234-4044).

Century Productions. 120 South St. Joseph (284-9111).
Stevensville: Lakeshore Community Theater (429-6131).

Twin City Players. 600 West Glenlord (429-0400).
Valparaiso: Community Theater Guild. Memorial Opera House, Indiana and Franklin (464-1636).
Whiting: Marion Theater Guild. 1844 Lincoln (659-2118).

TOURS

Benton Harbor: Heath Company. Hilltop Road (982-3200).
Whirlpool Company. Upton (926-5000).
Burns Harbor: Bethlehem Steel Company. Rt. 12 (787-2120).
Crown Point: Old Homestead. 220 South Court (663-0456).
Hammond: Joseph Hess School House. 7205 Kennedy (845-4155).
Kouts: Cargill Fertilizer. Rt. 8 (766-2234).
Heinhold Hog Yards. Off Rt. 49 (766-2221).
Cargill Grain. Off Rt. 49 (766-2234).
Merrillville: SS Constantine and Helen Greek Orthodox Cathedral. 8000 Madison (769-2481).
Michigan City: Barker Mansion. 631 Washington (872-0150).
Mishawaka: 100 Center. 700 Lincolnway West (259-7861).
Lowell: Buckley Homestead. 3606 Belshaw (769-Park).
St. Joseph: Nye's Apple Barn. 4716 Hollywood (983-6602).

WILDLIFE AREAS

Kingsbury: Kingsbury State Fish and Wildlife Area. Rt. 39 (393-3612).
Knox: Kankakee State Fish and Wildlife Area. Rt. 8 (792-4125).
Medaryville: Jasper-Pulaski State Wildlife Area. Rts. 421 and 143 (843-4891).
Schneider: LaSalle State Fish and Wildlife Area. Rt. 41 and 150N (992-3019).

ZOOS

Michigan City: Michigan City Zoo. Washington Park. Lakefront (872-8628).
South Bend: Potawatomi Park. 2000 Wall (288-8133).

Farewell

In farewell, we invite you to send in your corrections, comments and suggestions. Changes occur so quickly, that your help can make the next edition of this book even more accurate. Please use the form below to hasten the processing of your valuable additions. Thanks in advance for your help.

County _____ Town _____

Category (Shop, Restaurant) _____

Change or Comment _____

_____

_____

_____

_____

Name _____

Address _____

Telephone Number _____

Please send to:
Dunes Enterprises
Box 371
Beverly Shores, IN 46301